THE BUYING AND SELLING OF

America's Newspapers

THE BUYING AND SELLING OF

America's Newspapers

Edited by
Loren Ghiglione

R. J. Berg & Company   Indianapolis, Indiana 46220

To Nancy

CONTENTS

Acknowledgments

Versions of three of this book's chapters were published first in *The Bulletin* of the American Society of Newspaper Editors. I owe a great debt to the society, to its board of directors, to Executive Director Gene Giancarlo, and to Tom Winship, Mike O'Neill, John Quinn, and Creed Black, recent presidents past and present.

Helen Rhodes, my ever-efficient assistant, typed and retyped the manuscript and, despite my procrastination, kept the book moving toward publication. As to publication, Ray Berg deserves special thanks (as does Judy Clabes who put me in touch with him).

At sometime or another, I've lusted in my heart (my pocketbook hasn't permitted a more active form of lust) for three of the newspapers discussed here. My ardor hasn't affected the content of this book. But, in the spirit of full disclosure, I feel I should mention my past interest in buying those papers.

Finally, the greatest debt, as always, is to my family—my daughters, Jessica and Laura, and especially my wife, Nancy—without whose sacrifice this book would not exist.

Introduction

The daily newspapers of the United States are being put in chains, newspaper chains.

Of thirty-five dailies sold in 1982, thirty-two were absorbed by newspaper groups. More than 88 percent of the 354 dailies sold since 1976 were purchased by groups, reports *Editor & Publisher*, the trade magazine.

At the current rate, there will be no single, family-owned dailies by the year 2000. And, as groups buy groups, the American press of tomorrow may begin to look like the Canadian press of today—two groups, Thomson and Southam, control about half the nation's circulation, and ten groups control 80 percent.

The situation in the United States recalls a prediction four generations ago by Frank Munsey, that famous publisher-executioner of newspapers, who prophesied the day when "the publishing business in this country will be done by a few concerns—three or four at most."

What does the change in ownership mean to the quality of the American press? Do the groups restrict the papers' editorial freedom? Do the chains ruin—or improve—the news product? Are groups' owners journalistically more timid than their independent-owner predecessors?

To find the answers, the book's authors examined ten family-owned papers sold in recent years to major American chains. The authors sought geographical diversity, with papers representing every part of the country from Alaska to Mississippi, from California to Massachusetts. But they also sought, in terms of circulation, typicality.

The typical American daily is smaller than most people think. The average circulation touches 38,000, the median circulation 12,000. The papers discussed here range from the *Atchison* (Kansas) *Daily Globe*, circulation 5,909, to the *Anchorage* (Alaska) *Daily News*, circulation 47,000.

Each is someone's hometown daily, a paper relied upon for news of that person's life—his birth, his death, his marriage (and often his divorce)—as well as for news of the world. That person probably thinks of the local paper in personal terms (he may call it "my paper"), although increasingly it is likely to be owned by a billion-dollar conglomerate headquartered in New York or Miami or some other metropolis.

This book examines papers purchased by the nation's most acquisitive groups—Ingersoll, Gannett, Scripps League, Thomson, and others. In fact, the country's five largest groups measured by number of weekday papers are represented here: Gannett (eighty-nine papers), which purchased the *New Mexican*, Santa Fe, New Mexico, in 1976; Thomson (eighty-one papers), which bought the *Atchison* (Kansas) *Daily Globe* in 1979; Donrey (forty-three papers), which acquired the *Redlands* (California) *Daily Facts* in 1981; Knight-Ridder (thirty-one papers), which purchased the *Centre Daily Times,* State College, Pennsylvania, in 1979; and Freedom (twenty-seven papers), which acquired the *Delta Democrat-Times,* Greenville, Mississippi, in 1980.

It's virtually impossible to generalize—good guys or bad?—about the groups' impact. If you believe the chains are destroying American journalism, read how McClatchy Newspapers brought back from death's door (and lost $2 million a year while doing it) the *Anchorage Daily News.* And review the impact of Knight-Ridder on the *Centre Daily Times*: tighter writing, better layouts, more training, and tougher editorials, including political endorsements where before there were none.

But another more common pattern presents itself too. First, many groups set high profit goals for their papers—as much as 40 percent before taxes—and these goals, in turn, push the companies to operate tightly budgeted, often miserly, news operations.

Second, the people running the papers reflect the bottom-line mentality of the ownership. Some groups replace the old-fashioned editor-owners, who often wrote their own columns and editorials, with business-side people—in some cases, M.B.A.s who worry only about M.B.O.s.

Third, while virtually every group (except perhaps Freedom) leaves the editorial-page policies to the local management, more than one de-emphasizes the importance of a paper's voice by chopping the editorial-page budget and staff. The editor responsible for editorial writing at the *Transcript*, North Adams, Massachusetts, was fired (and not replaced) within two weeks of Ingersoll's purchase.

Fourth, the paper's relationship to the community, as one might expect of absentee ownership, is more distant. This isn't necessarily all bad (one person familiar with the *Centre Daily Times* said that, prior to purchase by Knight-Ridder, it "had sort of become slaves of community organizations"). But some group-owned papers participate less actively in the life of their communities and make less effort financially to support local projects.

The distance between newspaper owner and community may turn out to be very important. Judging from a study of subscribers' attitudes, Americans—concerned about increased absentee chain ownership of their local papers—may welcome increased government regulation of the press. Already, as a Public Agenda Foundation survey shows, a majority of Americans, when faced with a choice between continuing to permit press freedom and legislating fairness, vote for the government to regulate newspapers.

Regardless of the groups' impact, the "distortions in the tax law" (to use the language of a 1982 study by James Dertouzos and Kenneth Thorpe) and the high selling prices for dailies guarantee that the chains will own a larger and larger share—if not all—of America's daily press. For that reason alone, the topic of this book deserves America's concern.

Loren Ghiglione

Southbridge, Massachusetts
July 1, 1983

Anchorage Daily News

Suzan Nightingale

It was in the early morning hours of April 2, 1979, that the presses rolled and the champagne flowed for the "bright, bold, and brand new" *Anchorage Daily News.*

California-based McClatchy Newspapers had purchased 80 percent of the dying *News*; moved it from its shabby storefront office to new, expanded facilities; coordinated installation of a Goss Community Press and computer system; redesigned the entire paper; and expanded the staff from 11 to 110—all in seventy-three days. Time was so short, McClatchy actually bought the new building before the contract to purchase the *News* was signed.

The source of the crunch was the out-of-court termination of the *News*'s joint operating agreement with the dominant *Anchorage Times*. With six months and a $750,000 settlement standing between it and the cold Alaskan winter, the *News* had no press, no computers, no composing room, no advertising or circulation departments, and no general manager. Under the terms of the agreement, it had until April 1, 1979, to find them. In C. K. McClatchy, it did.

And so on April 2 the staff and community supporters gathered to watch the shiny, new, baby-blue press run off the first "new" *Daily News*. Unlike its skeletal sixteen-page predecessor the Monday before, this *News* was forty pages long and four sections thick. A cheer went up, and local television cameras zoomed in to capture *News* employees hugging one another. One reporter, buoyed by equal parts champagne and giddy exhaustion, sought out C. K. McClatchy, president and chief executive officer of McClatchy Newspapers, in the crowd.

"Mr. McClatchy," she said, "I don't know if this means anything to you, but we're all glad [publisher] Kay Fanning sold the paper to someone we respect. We would have rather seen the paper die than go to someone we couldn't work for."

"Well, don't attribute too many charitable motives to me," McClatchy smiled back. "I didn't buy this paper to lose money."

Three years later, the *Anchorage Daily News*—which had never turned a profit in its thirty-six-year history—was still losing money, more than $2 million in 1981. Losses for the previous two years had been even higher. But when McClatchy said, "The momentum is clearly in our direction," there appeared to be reason to believe him.

 • Circulation, a sickly 11,547 when McClatchy acquired 80 percent of the *News,* topped 37,000, according to the *News*'s Audit Bureau of Circulations 1981 third-quarter publisher's statement. The competing *Times,* meanwhile, had dropped from 45,615 in 1979 to 43,478 by June 1981.
 • Circulation gains so outstripped the ten-unit Goss Community Press purchased just three years earlier that McClatchy had to replace it with a $2.5 million Goss Urbanite with double the old press's capacity. The Community Press was retained for job-shop work, printing local weeklies and monthlies.
 • The new plant, a 15,000-square-foot cavern three years earlier, also was outgrown. McClatchy bought an adjoining 6,800-square-foot structure in 1980 and leased a third building of 6,700 square feet in 1981 to house the new press.
 • The *Daily News*'s percentage of the print ad market went from less than 25 percent to more than 40 percent. (Revenues did not mirror those percentages; the *News*'s rates were still lower than the *Times*'s.)
 • And the editorial staff, totaling five reporters and four editors when McClatchy entered the scene, jumped to forty-six full-time employees. The entire payroll mushroomed from 11 (including Fanning) to 260.

The figures astounded even McClatchy executives.

"Hell," said Erwin Potts, vice-president and director of business operations of McClatchy Newspapers, as he held up a freshly typed *Anchorage Daily News* Five-Year Plan, "we must have gone through ten of these damn things."

No one, it seems, thought the *Daily News* would go so far, so fast.

Daily News Executive Editor Stan Abbott remembers with a sheepish grin the first lunch he ever had with C. K. McClatchy, who was then considering acquiring the *News.*

"Well, Stan," McClatchy asked, "what would you need in the newsroom?"

"Well," a nervous Abbott replied, "I'd say one more person."

Doing more with less had indeed been the standard practice at the *Daily News* since Norman C. Brown, a job printer and former journalist, started it as a weekly in 1946. The resulting thirty-six-year saga is one the *Washington Post* called "rags-to-riches-to-rags—and maybe now to riches again."

Brown and his wife, Blanche, started the *News* "as a small voice," according to Mrs. Brown, now retired with her husband in Sun City, Arizona. The Browns, like the *Times*'s conservative Robert Atwood, are Republicans, but they liked the idea of an alternative forum. Although the *News* was never a moneymaker—the Brown's printing operation subsidized it—it expanded into a daily, and the Sunday after the Good Friday earthquake in 1964, the Browns made good their promise to go to mornings.

"That was quite an experience," Blanche Brown recalls of that first Sunday morning delivery, "because some of the houses were there, and some weren't."

When Abbott arrived as a general assignment reporter in 1965, the Browns were already talking about retiring. Two months after Abbott signed on, the paper hired a newly arrived divorcee to act as librarian. Katherine Field, former wife of Marshall Field IV of the Chicago newspaper and department store empire, was paid two dollars an hour. She was looking for "a new life, a new place to live, and a little adventure." On her own time, the Smith College English literature graduate wrote an enterprise story on a reported new cancer cure. Brown liked her work and moved her to a cityside desk in front of Abbott's. "Stan was very shy and I was very insecure, and I don't think we spoke for the first month," Katherine Field Fanning, age fifty-four, laughs now. Shortly thereafter, Abbott left for a one-year tour with the National Guard. When he returned, the shy reporter who had sat in front of him owned half the *Anchorage Daily News.*

Field had married respected newsman Larry Fanning, the former editor of the *Chicago Daily News,* and they had bought the *Daily News* from the Browns. "Larry was going to get me back to civilization and sell the house, and we were going to buy a little newspaper somewhere," Fanning says. "But he fell in love with Alaska—as I knew he would—so we bought the *Daily News.*"

In a front-page editorial on September 6, 1967, Larry Fanning noted that Anchorage, with a population of about forty-five thousand, was the smallest city in the country supporting two separately owned, separately printed dailies. (Its current population is two hundred thousand.) "Our purpose is to serve the interests of all the people and to provide a forum for dissent as well as consensus," he promised.

And so they did. The Fannings' brand of journalism was something new for Anchorage. In a state where it is not unusual to take a gun on a camping trip for protection, the *Daily News* editorialized in favor of gun control. And when the city was just beginning to realize the economic benefit that could come from North Slope petrodollars, the *Daily News* took a long (thirty-two-part), critical look at the effects of the trans-Alaska pipeline—a sharp contrast to Atwood's enthusiastic prodevelopment policy. Another in-depth series in 1969 looked at the quality (or lack of it) in the bush justice system. It was quite a jolt for readers used to the Browns' more conservative editorial policy, and it was not the sort of copy designed to engender warmth in the hearts of advertisers.

"We got," Kay Fanning says today, "a rude awakening very quickly. I think Larry was convinced, and so was I, that all it took was good people to put out a good product and put it over the top. We thought we'd hire very good reporters and have a lot of good news and everybody would want to buy it. The old mousetrap. It was probably naive. We took editorial positions which were not compatible with the general Alaskan viewpoint. Advocating gun control is a suicidal impulse in Alaska. Guns are a symbol of people's freedom and independence here."

If the advertising dollars did not come their way, several national reporting awards did. Both the bush justice series and the "Oil on Ice" series won national honors, the former an American Bar Association Gavel Award, and the latter an Edward J. Meeman Award, a Thomas L. Stokes Award, and a National Headliners Club Award. But despite Larry Fanning's renown as an innovative editor—he encouraged a new columnist named Ann Landers while executive editor of the *Chicago Sun-Times* before becoming editor of the *Chicago Daily News,* where he encouraged another young columnist, Mike Royko—he was not an experienced businessman.

Under Brown, the *Daily News* had been subsidized by job printing; when the Fannings bought the paper, Brown retained the job printing equipment, and the Fannings received a 1901 press. The paper continued to lose money.

"A series of disastrous business managers, some no more than just accountants," followed. The seventy-year-old press was replaced by another letterpress, this one thirty-five years old, "probably not a brilliant buy at the time," Mrs. Fanning acknowledges in retrospect. But Fanning, whose charisma (a word he would have snorted at) and enthusiasm were contagious, was convinced that, with time, the paper would be a success. Unfortunately, time was the one thing Larry Fanning did not have.

The new press from Bellevue, Washington, had just been installed when Larry Fanning, trademark bow tie untied and shirt sleeves rolled up, suffered a fatal heart attack at his desk in February 1971. He was fifty-six.

Abbott, who by then was managing editor, was joined by Juneau Bureau Chief Tom Brown as associate editor, and working in tandem the two oversaw the shattered staff and put out the paper.

Already dealt the blow of Fanning's death, the paper—subsidized by Kay Fanning's son's (Frederick "Ted" Field) trust—continued to lose money. Although Fanning says she "never considered anything but keeping the paper going," former reporter Elaine Warren remembers "an impending sense of doom" heavy over the newsroom after Larry Fanning's death.

The following fall, Morton Frank, publisher of *Family Weekly* and a mutual friend, approached *Anchorage Times* publisher Atwood, seventy-four, to sound him out on a possible joint operating agreement with the *Daily News.* Gradually, talks commenced. "It was a closely guarded secret,"

Fanning recalls. "I used to meet Atwood in parking lots so people wouldn't see us together. Our advertising and circulation was tenuous enough without raising fears."

An agreement was finally reached, and Fanning and Atwood approached the Justice Department. Under federal guidelines, the *Daily News* had to qualify as a failing newspaper, "which we had no trouble doing," Fanning recalls dryly. "There was no hearing." When official approval came, the *Anchorage Daily News* and the *Anchorage Times* entered into the first Joint Operating Agreement since passage of the Newspaper Preservation Act legalizing such partnerships.

On August 1, 1974, the Joint Operating Agreement (JOA) was publicly announced, to take effect the following December. Spirits high, the *Daily News* moved from its sardine-can-like offices (appropriately located by the Port of Anchorage) to a breezy office with a view of Mount McKinley across the alley from the *Anchorage Times*. Under the agreement, the *Times* would handle circulation, advertising, and printing; the *Times*-owned *News* office was exclusively a newsroom. In nailing down the bargain, Fanning had signed away the Sunday morning paper to the *Times*. It had been responsible for 40 percent of the *News*'s ad revenue. It was the only card Fanning had left to play.

"I had mixed feelings about it," Fanning says about the JOA today. "It meant everyone at the *Daily News* lost their jobs except the editorial department. But there was simply no alternative." Unlike many other joint operating agreements, where an independent, third corporation is formed to administer the agreement, the Anchorage JOA was to be administered by the Anchorage Times Corporation. "I wanted it to work, but in my heart I knew it wasn't a very good JOA," claims Fanning. "It lacked an essential element, which was profit pooling. They weren't really accountable to us in any way. We had no control over our own business affairs, but if there was a loss, we had to pay up."

(Atwood refused to grant an interview for this chapter, questioning the ability of a former *News* reporter to write it objectively, but over the years he has repeatedly taken offense at Fanning's comments about the JOA, saying if he had wanted to sabotage the *News*, he simply would not have entered such an agreement.)

By June 1975, Fanning was "deeply concerned. Circulation was going down and there was no sense of mutuality about the project." The *News* was losing "an increasing amount every year." Atwood meanwhile contended the *News*, which lacked the *Times*'s emphasis on community news and had scared off some advertisers with its proconsumer orientation, was "unsalable."

But, determined to carry on the investigative tradition Larry Fanning had started, Fanning freed three reporters to work full time on an in-depth look at the increasingly powerful Teamsters Local 959. In December 1975, their findings were published in a weeklong series, "Empire," which outlined the scope and power of the Teamsters, and how the organization was using its sizable trust fund. Five months later, in May 1976, "Empire" won the Pulitzer Prize for Public Service. The *Times* printed a congratulatory editorial, and a beaming Atwood presented Fanning with a huge engraved loving cup at a subsequent Chamber of Commerce luncheon. The happiness was short-lived.

Within months, Fanning's son, Ted, decided to stop subsidizing the *Anchorage Daily News*. He had injected $5 million of his inheritance in the *News* since 1968. When, at twenty-five, he decided to pursue other interests, trustees of the Marshall Field IV Trust agreed.

So, in October 1976, five months after receiving journalism's highest honor, the *Daily News* laid off five staffers leaving it with five reporters to cover Alaska's four time zones. The belt-tightening started in earnest.

In a front-page editorial entitled "A Message to Our Readers," the *News* said it was facing "a severe financial crisis. We need substantial community support to continue."

A "Committee for Two Newspapers," consisting of community supporters, was formed to encourage subscriptions and advertising. Although committee members represented a spectrum of political ideology, many were liberals who expressed concern about balanced coverage of such issues as the pending Alaska Lands Bill and continued oil development if the *Daily News* faded from the scene. Committee members visited local advertisers, talked on local shows, and even set up circulation booths in local shopping centers.

Small circulation gains followed, but the financial picture continued to worsen. In the two years since the JOA took effect, home delivery of the *News* dropped from 11,600 to 7,580 copies, according to *News* figures.

On February 9, 1977, deciding "there literally was no other recourse," the *Anchorage Daily News* filed a $16.5 million lawsuit against the *Anchorage Times* claiming breach of contract and unfair competition. The two newspapers' cases might best be capsulized by their page-one headlines announcing the suit. The *News* read: "*Daily News* Sues the *Times*—Breach of Agreement Cited." The *Times* read: "*News* Suit Follows Ultimatum."

The *News,* claiming the *Times* had not lived up to obligations assumed in the joint operating agreement, said the *Times* had violated both the Clayton and the Sherman Antitrust acts by attempting to "monopolize, control, and dominate" Anchorage's newspaper market. The *News* alleged that the *Times* influenced potential subscribers to buy the *Times* and employed joint advertising rates that discriminated against the *News*. Potential *News* advertisers, phoning the number listed for advertising, were greeted with the salutation, *"Anchorage Times,"* and *News* ads were offered as an "add-on" buy to the *Times* ads, the suit charged. The *Times* flatly denied it had violated the contract, calling the lawsuit the result of a *Daily News* ultimatum.

Atwood said Fanning had demanded he must either relinquish control of the Times Corporation or be replaced by an independent manager who would report to a committee, whose members could not be a majority of *Times* representatives. The other demand, according to Atwood, was for the *Times* to give the *News* a share of *Times* profits.

Atwood maintained that nothing in the JOA guaranteed the financial solvency of the *News*—which he said consistently failed to pay the *Times* monies owed—and pointed out that if he had wanted the *Daily News* to fail, he would not have entered a joint operating agreement in the first place. "We wouldn't have even talked about a joint operation if it hadn't been for our friendship with the Fannings," he told the *New York Times*.

Not surprisingly, relations became less cordial. Much of the town literally chose sides. At least one member of the Committee for Two Newspapers resigned. Even social events felt the tension, with hostesses carefully telling Fanning when the Atwoods were expected to arrive so she could make her appearance at another time.

Eight months later, Atwood announced his intention to terminate the JOA, saying the *News* owed the *Times* $300,000. But a U.S. District Court judge ruled the *Times* could not unilaterally block the agreement without submitting the debts to arbitration.

As the battle heated up, the *Times* cited nonpayment of debts and evicted the *News*. On moving day the *Daily News* staff left one thing standing in the center of the *Times*-owned office—the loving cup Atwood had presented a year earlier.

In June 1978 a panel of arbitrators found that Atwood had "directed his employees to do their best to make the joint operation successful and to fairly allocate the revenues and the expenses of the joint operation." But the panel said Atwood had erred in the allocation of some costs under the joint operating agreement, inappropriately charging some items to the *Daily News*. The *News*, according to the arbitrators, did not owe the *Times* money, but it had violated part of its portion of the agreement by failing to purchase computerized newsroom equipment compatible with the *Times*'s equipment. Both sides claimed victory and prepared for the sure-to-be-costly court fight ahead.

The following September, though, after months of negotiations—and the certainty of even costlier litigation in the future—both papers announced an out-of-court settlement. Under the terms of the settlement, the *Times* paid the *News* $750,000 and agreed to print it at no cost until March 31, 1979, when the joint operating agreement would terminate. Again, both sides claimed victory. (Atwood called it "good business practices to pay the *News* $750,000 instead of spending that much or more . . . for lawyers, accountants, and the other expenses of court trials and appeals.")

The divisive fight was finally over. The *News,* now lacking both young Field's subsidy and the Sunday paper, was even weaker than when it entered the JOA three years earlier.

Meanwhile, Fanning, who had kept the paper afloat by acquiring donations from East Coast liberals concerned about environmental coverage and loans from such diverse sources as Alaska's Bristol Bay Native Corporation and Tish Hewitt, the Illinois heiress to the John Deere farm equipment fortune, was faced with a familiar dilemma: money. Armed with $750,000, she had six months to purchase a press and production equipment, assemble a composing room, and organize advertising and circulation departments. "It quickly became apparent that three-quarters of a million dollars wasn't going to go very far," she says today.

But Fanning was also armed with an unwavering Christian Science faith that repudiates the possibility of failure. ("Christian Science has saved this paper before," she once told a staffer over lunch, "and it will save it again.")

Refusing to entertain the possibility of folding (at least in front of staff members), Fanning ordered the press and composing room equipment. But blending pragmatism with her optimism, Fanning also started looking hard for an investor. A multimillionaire in Kansas City expressed interest, "but he didn't know anything about newspapers, and I wanted to deal with someone who knew what they were getting into. And anybody who knew the kind of losses we were sustaining didn't want to come in here because they didn't have the vision McClatchy did."

Newspaper consultant Jim Smith, who had been the business manager for the *Sacramento Bee,* suggested McClatchy Newspapers. Long a political and journalistic force in California—it owned the *Sacramento Bee, Fresno Bee,* and *Modesto Bee* triumvirate—the McClatchy organization was looking to expand its horizons beyond central California. Exhausted by the lengthy fight behind her and mindful of the uphill battle ahead, Fanning made plans to spend Christmas with her mother in Florida. Prompted by Smith's suggestion, she telephoned McClatchy before she left town. Could she make a detour and stop in and see him on the way to Florida? Although the two had never met, they knew of each other. Fanning knew of McClatchy's sound reputation (and profitable newspapers), and he "was vaguely aware they were having problems" in Anchorage. In an afternoon stopover, Fanning presented her case. McClatchy listened politely.

The next week, chasing off the Alaskan chill with the Florida sun, Fanning continued to mull over the possibilities of saving the *News.* She convinced herself McClatchy was exactly what the *News* needed. She telephoned him again. Could she stop in on the way back to Anchorage? This time McClatchy expressed more detailed interest, but said his organization would want to acquire majority interest—"very much an emotional hurdle" for Fanning at the time, "but it compared to oblivion, to the paper folding. What I would have loved was them putting up all the money and me keeping majority interest," she laughs now. "Who wouldn't?" She tentatively accepted the initial terms.

A week later McClatchy, accompanied by Potts and a team of advisers, was in Anchorage, visiting the Chamber of Commerce, shaking hands with the mayor, and talking to advertisers. McClatchy was impressed with the potential for the only morning paper in Alaska and with the spunky fight that had been put up to save it. Over lunch Fanning and McClatchy finalized their agreement and shook hands on it. "I think some people thought we were crazy to do it that way," Fanning recalls, "but there was a basic sense of trust."

On January 17, 1979—less than a month after Fanning's initial phone call—the board of directors of McClatchy Newspapers purchased 80 percent of the *Anchorage Daily News,* Kay Fanning retained 10 percent, and her two daughters, Cathy and Barbara, retained 5 percent each. Neither Fanning nor McClatchy will reveal the purchase price, although $250,000 plus the *News*'s debts remains an oft-repeated figure. Says Fanning, "There wasn't much money that changed hands, but they repaid all the loans with interest." Says McClatchy, "Every year that we lose money, it's like a purchase price." Under the purchase agreement, Kay Fanning would remain as publisher for three years, with an option to renew her contract.

"I think C. K. ought to get either the credit or the blame because he really was more intrigued by it than anyone else," says Potts. "I was intrigued, but wary." McClatchy claims to have trouble putting his finger on the facet of the *Daily News* that intrigued him, but associates suggest it was a combination of forces.

After years of working his way up the company ladder as a reporter and editorial writer, McClatchy, fifty-five, had just become president and chief executive officer, taking the corporate reins from his strong-willed aunt, Eleanor McClatchy. Unlike Eleanor, whose grandfather had purchased the infant *Bee* in 1857, McClatchy did not want to limit his interests to the state capital and the farm-rich San Joaquin Valley to the south. Then too, the *Anchorage Daily News* was a respected liberal paper in a state where environmental concerns were strong. Without its voice, some important stories likely would not get told. Although McClatchy and Fanning had never met, both had long-standing establishment newspaper family ties and knew *of* each other. And finally, there was the bottom line. Alaska, with its oil development, growing population, and long-range prospects, was a young market with a lot of potential. The *Sacramento Bee* had just gone from an afternoon to a morning paper, and McClatchy's people believed strongly in the *News*'s "morning factor."

"We were carried along by our do-goodism, but there were project costs, and it seemed to be a do-able project," says McClatchy.

Back in Anchorage, Fanning triumphantly broke the news to her staff, emphasizing that the McClatchys were not a chain, but a family. The staff had two questions. Were new people going to be brought in? And were they going to call it the *Anchorage Bee?* Yes and no, respectively. What Fanning did not tell the staff that day—and has never told the staff to this day—was that, if McClatchy had not purchased the *News,* she would have folded it in mid-January.

That night four *Daily News* staffers worked their way through four bottles of champagne and proceeded to make a four-way bet about what the *News*'s circulation (then 11,000) would be in a year. The winner, who scribbled the high guess of "over 20,500" on the back of a bank deposit slip, collected just three months later. It was a bet no one minded paying off.

"Everything happened faster than we thought it would," says Potts. "We thought we could establish a holding pattern, keep the ship afloat a while at least, and then we got there and upped the ante." McClatchy remembers his goal as being "to save the paper with the least expense and the least commitment. But the more we looked at it, that didn't seem to be the road to success. It quickly became apparent to us that the initial pro forma we'd made to just keep the thing afloat was unrealistic. We had to add staff, and we had to add the newshole." It was that key decision—McClatchy's February decision to not just save the *Daily News,* but to resurrect it as a totally new, much expanded product—that has apparently made all the difference.

With weeks to go before the *News* started publishing with its own (not yet arrived) press, McClatchy decided the "new" *News* would never have fewer than thirty-two pages, and would, from day one, be marketed as a complete newspaper instead of the add-on buy it had become.

An aggressive general manager, thirty-one-year-old Jerry Grilly, was recruited from his post as Sun Coast Division director of a chain of Florida shoppers and weeklies owned by the Tribune Co. Graphics, circulation and advertising experts from McClatchy's Modesto operation were temporarily reassigned to the *News,* formulating a new layout, new logos, and new features. Taking the offensive, McClatchy even bought up every available news and feature service—many of which were never used—hoping to cut the *Times* off at the pass if it decided to beef up its own operation. Clay Haswell, former *Daily News* managing editor, remembers McClatchy telling him, "I want you to buy everything that will help you and everything that could be of any possible use to the competition."

"They wanted to make sure that everything that was available for money was locked up—wires, syndicated columns, syndicated comics," recalls Haswell, now writing a novel in Vermont. "We bought five wires and sixty-three syndicated columns and forty-four comic strips."

Meanwhile, a new plant had to be found. Deciding that Anchorage's downtown real estate was prohibitively expensive for the amount of space that would be required (a press, plus newsprint storage, in addition to personnel), McClatchy bought an unfinished warehouse in a new industrial park on the southern outskirts of town where most of Anchorage's new growth is centered. Offices and newsroom space were built into the cavernous building; carpet was laid; and an artificial, lower ceiling was installed.

As the staff continued to put out the "old" paper, still printed and delivered by the *Anchorage Times,* the *Daily News* formed new advertising and circulation staffs to prepare for startup.

The last week of March, a skeleton staff, working off card tables and folding chairs in the rapidly evaporating downtown office, continued to put out the last of the old *Daily News,* while colleagues moved into the new plant across town, familiarized themselves with the new agony of composing on computer terminals, lived on cold, delivered pizza, and started stockpiling features for the new, thicker *Daily News.*

But the cold pizza and the long hours were forgotten when, in the early hours of April 2, the staff watched the first press run. Hours later, as the sun rose over Anchorage, a new *Daily News* was on the streets.

To make sure the community saw its new product, the *News* made Anchorage an offer more than twelve thousand families could not refuse: a free one-month subscription. Not only did the new circulation department have to take off from a dead stop, it took off running. "Circulation just exploded," says Grilly. "I remember one day we had one thousand starts. We had starts in areas where we didn't even have carriers. Sometimes a start took two or three weeks."

With the cold, dark Alaskan winter mornings, delivery had always been one of the *Daily News*'s weaknesses. So, in addition to the tried-and-true Disneyland Contest employed by many papers, the *News* implemented a "Carrier Winter Bonus." Under that program, any carrier who stayed on the job for five months with a good record got his choice of a bicycle, a stereo, or a black-and-white television. "The first year, we paid better than two hundred carriers," says Grilly. "It assured good delivery. We were so concerned about delivery, collections were really taking a back seat." It was a back seat that was to return to haunt the *Daily News.*

"The main problem we've had since day one is to be able to prove our circulation and readership," says marketing manager Mark Hamilton. "With Audit Bureau of Circulations (ABC) audits, they're auditing history. It's a disadvantage to a paper on the grow. We've had circulation and not had audits to back it up until recently."

Although "auditing history" has been a concern, woefully inadequate circulation records in those booming months after the transition created their own problems. Thousands of nonpaying subscribers took advantage of the *Daily News*'s one-free-month offer. But when it came time to transfer those free customers to paying status, literally thousands of willing readers fell through the cracks. Although at least half the "free" readers opted to continue their subscriptions, the *Daily News* did not have the paperwork to prove it.

So in June 1979, when the *Daily News* was loudly proclaiming twenty-five thousand circulation, ABC auditors were able to confirm only about twelve thousand—a direct result of poor record keeping in the circulation department. "When the auditors came in, we didn't have a proper audit trail," says Grilly. "We had just taken an adding machine and totaled all the checks up and made a deposit. When he wanted to trace an individual audit to individual subscribers, we couldn't do it."

The ABC auditor gave the *Daily News* a choice: It could either accept his solution—take the three-quarters of that audit year maintained properly by the *Times* under the JOA, divide the total by three, and use it as an average circulation figure—or be suspended. The *Daily News* swallowed hard and accepted the twelve thousand circulation figure. "He said he understood how it had happened because he had never seen a newspaper grow so fast," says Grilly, "but he had no choice but to penalize us."

Not surprisingly, *Times* advertising salespeople pointed out the discrepancy, leaving many advertisers uncertain about the *News*'s circulation claims. "Certainly if I was a competitor, I'd go out there and plant the seed of controversy," says Grilly matter-of-factly. "But we carefully prepared a dialogue and went out and explained what happened to us. For the most part everyone understood. When our [June 1980] audit came out, it verified our third quarter of 1979. So now we could say, 'See, we were telling you all the time.' "

When the circulation discrepancy came to light, the *News*'s inexperienced circulation manager—a twenty-one-year-old who had been in charge of the *News*'s street boxes before he was promoted—was promptly replaced. The new circulation manager was Tim Whiting, a graduate of the *Akron Beacon Journal* circulation training program. Whiting set about organizing the department, and the next time ABC auditors asked for paperwork to substantiate *Daily News* claims, they got it. By September 1979 verifiable circulation had doubled to nearly twenty-five thousand.

"McClatchy has done the only thing we couldn't do under the joint agreement," *Anchorage Times* general manager William Tobin told the *Washington Post*. "He's changed the paper. And he's had some degree of success because of it."

Indeed, change had come so rapidly to the *Daily News,* it made some people suspicious. Although many businesses leaped at the *News's* aggressively discounted ad rates, Anchorage's number one advertiser, J. C. Penney, was one business that still hung back. "I had some very difficult times believing some of their numbers," says Penney's Anchorage marketing manager Doug Rush. "Circulation wasn't based on anything. It was based on giveaways. My feeling was, 'Let's wait and see what the other advertisers do. Once they got off the special programs, were they going to stay with the *News?*' As the retailers went off the special rate program and on the regular rate, they were staying with the *News*—and that's how we made our decision. The *News* may be a viable force in the market, and we should be a part of it."

Rush still reserves the lion's share of advertising for the *Times,* but he admits the *News* has changed the market. When Nordstrom's, a major quality clothing retailer in Anchorage, decided to place 80 percent of its print advertising in the *News,* Penney's realigned its policy to include *News* advertising aimed at that demographic market. Rush also believes "the *News* has made the *Times* more competitive." It is a statement repeated by many business people. And indeed, to talk to an advertiser in Anchorage is to hear detailed breakdowns of readership versus circulation, demographics, and Belden Surveys—clearly aggressive advertising salespeople are alive and well on both staffs.

"There is a great deal of bitterness between the papers," says longtime realtor Brooke Marston. "I've had both *Times* and *News* salesmen tell me the other side is lying about circulation. I accept the fact that they're about equal." Because Marston likes to be the largest classified advertiser in a particular paper, he tends to concentrate his advertising in one paper at a time. That paper is generally the *Times,* which has always dominated the classified market. The *Times* has taken pains to retain that business. "I'd say our advertising rates have been cut in half," Marston says.

Advertising agency owner Rick Mystrom cites "a great deal of loyalty to the establishment at the *Times*" as one reason some advertisers have dragged their feet to the *News,* but predicts, "The day, the hour, the *Daily News* becomes the biggest paper in Anchorage, I think you'll see some major changes in advertising. I think it will happen pretty soon, within the next year."

Former Chamber of Commerce president Bob Penney theorizes the *News's* "antibusiness" stands of the past have kept a few advertisers away. "The *News* continues to be on the left side of the aisle, that's for sure, in its editorial policies," says Penney. "I think sometimes it's detrimental to their attempt to increase its advertising base." But Penney, a mobile-home developer, adds, "The paper is more business-oriented because of

McClatchy. I think part of that has come from their understanding that there's balance in the community, and you can't just attack it. There has to be balance there."

Haswell, the former managing editor, agrees the *News* is more business conscious these days. "There's no question at all in my mind that the paper took a lot less risks after the purchase than they did beforehand," says Haswell. "Let's face it, it's a lot easier to be a liberal paper when you're broke. If nobody's advertising in you anyway, there's no one to really antagonize. Before the purchase, I don't remember a single conversation when we were concerned about antagonizing an advertiser. Boy, I remember just loads of those conversations after."

Haswell cites a business story that was held for days because its subject was a major supermarket chain—a business still refusing to advertise in the *News,* despite ardent wooing. The story outlined how the chain was buying milk from Seattle, causing serious financial hardship on local dairies in Alaska. "The story ended up waiting for at least two days," says Haswell. "The truth of that is Kay Fanning just sat on that story and would not let it go for two days."

In the end, the story—substantially softened—ran, but Fanning openly acknowledges she took special care with it. "In a sense, that's true. But we have, over the years, had certain areas or people that we seem to gravitate toward making goofs on. We seem to have had an absolute genius for the Carr-Gottstein people [owners of the supermarket chain] for getting it wrong. Although I feel that 90 percent of the time we get it right, whoever we're writing about, Barney Gottstein gave us chapter and verse of mistakes we'd made about him. It was a case of, 'For crying out loud, get it right. Let's make sure it's right and it's fair before we get it out.' "

It is, says Fanning, one example of the McClatchy influence. "One of the few directives I ever received from the McClatchy people was that we be perceived as a fair, accurate paper by the community. Rightly or wrongly, we were perceived as antibusiness by the community, so there were, indeed, a number of sessions in which we discussed that, that we didn't want to go out of our way to antagonize the business community."

There *is* more business coverage these days—mug shots of award-winning salespeople, short briefs on career promotions, in addition to hard-hitting business news (such as possible conflicts of interest in legislative support of Alaska's young farming industry), and complete stock listings.

It is indicative of the expansion of the news product as a whole. More news, more features, more sports, more graphics, more business, even a community news tabloid complete with Cub Scouts and Miss Alaska Teen, not likely candidates to appear in the "old" *News.* There's a weekend opinion section now, a television magazine, and a *Daily News*–produced general interest magazine, *We Alaskans*.

Such expansion is a direct result of space and people provided by McClatchy money.

"I think there's a pretty clear understanding that the paper has to serve a variety of interests to make money in order to exist," says Howard Weaver, current managing editor. "When anybody comes to the newspaper and says what happened, I want us to have a home for it. That's a terrible feeling to have to say, 'It may be the most important thing in your life, but we don't care.' "

It is a decidedly different philosophy than the *News* labored under before the McClatchy acquisition. With only five reporters and an extremely limited newshole, the paper opted to leave the baton-twirling photos to the *Times*. "I think we decided we couldn't do everything, so what we chose was politics and enterprise," says Weaver, one of the Pulitzer-winning "Empire" team.

When McClatchy came in, he made the decision to open up pages (including an open Metro page) and fill them with local news, sign on local columnists, and initiate community feedback sessions. Those sessions reaffirmed McClatchy's belief that local news is important to newspaper readers. But, according to Weaver, the *News* tried to go beyond reprinting PTA press releases. "Community news has to have cohesion, a plan. If names were news, we'd just reprint the phone book. We try to profile organizations and seek out things that have a little broader appeal."

The *News* today does have broader appeal. More international and national news (important to Alaskan readers thousands of miles from the Lower Forty-eight), and more local news of all sorts, including breaking news as well as general interest features.

As part of the "new" *Daily News*, McClatchy created a strong weekend package for Saturday. It included comics, the TV log, a weekly magazine, a travel section, and book reviews—all the trimmings of a traditional Sunday paper, twenty-four hours before the *Times*'s Sunday edition comes out.

In November 1980 the *Anchorage Times* responded by taking its Saturday afternoon paper to Saturday morning. As a two-month introductory offer, it reportedly offered Saturday morning advertisers 50 percent off pickup ads that ran any other day of the week. (The *News* had been offering a variety of reduced rates. When *We Alaskans* was launched, advertisers were given a two-for-one offer.)

The *News* responded to the *Times*'s campaign by offering 90 percent off full-page pickups and 75 percent off pickups less than full page. Those *News* rates held until February 1981, when the *News* kicked off its own Sunday paper.

The decision to go Sunday was mandated by the concept that "advertisers didn't accept you as a complete newspaper until you fill the hole," according to McClatchy Newspapers executive editor Frank McCulloch. But the *News* kept its strength in its Saturday package, designing the Sunday product to be "brisk, easy reading, guaranteed to get you away from your breakfast table in fifteen minutes."

"It made no sense to try to tackle Atwood where he was strongest, which is Sunday, and give up what the *News* had that was strongest, which was Saturday," says McCulloch. "Anchorage people have come to expect a big Saturday package from the *News* and a big Sunday package from the *Times*."

Although the McClatchy formula has obviously caught on with readers, some purists look at Sunday's light package and fret that the *News*'s tradition of investigative reporting may be suffering.

Bob Porterfield, one of the *News* reporters who won the Pulitzer in 1976 (now at Long Island's *Newsday*), told students at Yale in 1981 that, "when the McClatchy chain bought into the *Anchorage Daily News*, they made a big infusion of cash. But it intrigues me that a newspaper that was a boat-rocker and a bush-shaker until 1978 and was very committed to investigative journalism is not doing that now. They say they want to build advertising before rocking the boat."

Porterfield says his remarks, printed in *Editor & Publisher*, were part of a speech on investigative reporting and were taken out of context—a key omission being his stated faith in Kay Fanning's pledge to refocus on investigative reporting once the paper has conquered the challenges of expansion.

"It ended up being harder to do [investigative reporting] after they were in than before, because they were making so many other demands [on local coverage]," says Haswell.

"The *News* is more like the *Times* was two years ago if you take away the appearance," charges *Anchorage Times* managing editor Drex Heikes, one of several *Times* staffers who have turned down job offers by the *News*. "They seem to have fallen in this formula of a couple of local stories on page one, a couple on Metro, a business page, a back page, and the rest is *Los Angeles Times, Christian Science Monitor,* and *Washington Post* wire copy. They don't rock the boat. Three years ago, if there had been a series done on cocaine in this town (which the *Times* recently ran), it would have been in the *News*. Five years ago, if someone was going to take on the basketball coach for playing a player illegally (as the *Times* recently did), it would have been the *News*."

News staffers disagree, reciting numerous examples of investigative work in recent years. "With McClatchy, our newspaper has realized more resources for investigative reporting than ever before, and we've pursued more than a dozen projects in the past several years—investigations that any paper would be proud to claim," insists Abbott. Those investigations range from a series on inhumane pit-bull gambling to the state's largest arson-for-hire case.

When the 1981 Alaska Press Club Awards were handed out, the *News* won the top four awards for series (there is no "investigative" category, per se), including a series on the legacy of a state supreme court decision on bush schools; the mixing of politics and business by a prominent state senator (who was not reelected); the power and influence of the state supreme court since statehood; and the long-range development plans for Mount McKinley. When the awards banquet was over, the *Anchorage Daily News* had walked off with thirty-two of the fifty-four awards it qualified for in statewide competition. (The next day the *Times* carried the story, "*Daily News* leads the pack in journalism honors." The *News*'s aggressive advertising department promptly reprinted the *Times* story and headline and circulated it to advertisers.)

"I don't think the paper's more cautious, I think it's more complete," says Grilly, given high marks by reporters for his noninterference in the newsroom. "We haven't won another Pulitzer, but it doesn't mean we're not doing investigative reporting. I haven't heard that complaint internally."

McCulloch also gives short shrift to the theory that investigative reporting is on the wane. "I'm not at all certain what it used to do, but I can do some reasoning, and the reasoning is this: The *News* of the past had very limited resources, people, and newsprint. In *proportion,* it may have had more investigative reporting. You take forty-five reporters times sixty pages, it gets submerged."

Perhaps a defining of terms is called for. In December 1981 the *News* ran a twenty-nine-story series, "The Village People," about the ten-year ramifications of the 1971 Alaska Native Claims Settlement act and what it has done to the politically and economically emerging bush population. Seven reporters were freed full time to work on the project, spending weeks at a time in the Alaska bush. It is the largest project, both in scope and time and money, the *Daily News* has ever undertaken. It is the kind of project that could not have been carried out without McClatchy money.

"It cost us tens of thousands of dollars," McCulloch says of "The Village People." "Anywhere else, it would have cost hundreds of thousands. I think dollar for dollar, it's the best paper McClatchy produces, journalistically. Somehow the staff and its management absorbed the diversion of those hours with no additional expense."

Although *Daily News* staffers would bask in McCulloch's praise, they might resent his "dollar-for-dollar" comparison. If there is any complaint oft-repeated by *Daily News* employees today, it is money. Before the McClatchy acquisition, staffers understood how precarious finances were, and—bound by a fierce personal loyalty to Fanning and the close-knit camaraderie that comes with siege mentality—they were generally satisfied they were being paid the most the paper could afford. They do not appear to share that conviction about the McClatchy organization.

Although the *Daily News* is considered a full-fledged part of the McClatchy organization, its reporters average at least $100 a week less than reporters for the *Bees,* and they work longer hours. Guild minimum in Sacramento is $535 for a 37½-hour week. In Anchorage, a non-Guild town with a considerably higher cost of living, the minimum newsroom salary in late 1981 was $375 for a 40-plus-hour week. The average weekly salary in the newsroom was reportedly $425. The crucial difference is obvious: The *Sacramento Bee* makes money; the *Anchorage Daily News* does not.

But improvements are being made gradually. The newest morale booster is a weekly fifty-dollar bonus to the employee showing outstanding work in headlines, photos, stories, layout, or other contributions. And despite the usual grousing about salaries, reporters are genuinely pleased with the McClatchy affiliation, and not just for the obvious reason of economic survival. Alone or in a group, they profess pride in their product.

"I've never felt we were getting beat, except when we had those people in the bush [for 'The Village People']," says metro editor Rosemary Shinohara. "I really, deep down in my soul, think it will become the dominant paper in Anchorage. I don't think it will take anything from the editorial department; I think it's in the hands of advertising and circulation."

"I think it has a more deliberate editorial policy now," says Weaver, one of four members of the *Daily News* editorial board. "It's not just one person doing it on deadline. We have editorial board meetings and bring people in and get opinions from them."

Equally important to Weaver and Shinohara—both lifelong Alaskans—is the editorial autonomy of the *Daily News.* Unlike the three California *Bees,* the *Daily News* writes all of its editorials locally—and sometimes, they are 180 degrees from the *Bees'* editorial positions. Probably the most important example was in the papers' positions on the Alaska Lands Bill. The *News* endorsed the state's "moderate" bill; the *Bees* backed the more "restrictive" environmental bill. No pressure was ever brought to bear on the *News* to conform—though Fanning tried to change McClatchy's mind about the *Bees'* editorial.

It is part of McClatchy's determination to retain the *News*'s strong local identity, complete with Kay Fanning at the helm and longtime staff members in management positions.

"They've said very explicitly and directly, 'We're not going to try to edit your paper from three thousand miles away,'" says Weaver, who speaks appreciatively of the tactful McClatchy approach, even though he admits,

"I'd rather they're in Sacramento than in Fairbanks."

So what is it about this reincarnation of the *Anchorage Daily News* that appears to be succeeding where others have failed? Well, millions of McClatchy dollars provide one obvious answer. ("The one frightening aspect is that McClatchy has more millions than I do," Atwood told *Newsweek* magazine, "and he's apparently willing to blow them.") But *News* executives say it is more than just dollars.

"It's a rather complete, broad formula," theorizes Grilly. "I think we put out a package that was entirely different from what existed in this community and entirely different from what the *Anchorage Daily News* was. It was complete, packaged for the reader, well-written, extremely well-balanced, objective. And we packaged it so it was easy to read. That's the number one reason. Then you've got to get the paper delivered on time. We promoted it. We told them we were different. Then after we told them, we went out and asked them what they thought. We try to stay in tune with the readers' thoughts and needs, and we tailor our package according to our findings. We have had the guidance of McClatchy. They're certainly not here every day, but when we do strategic planning, they're involved. We've learned from their mistakes, and their expertise. As long as it's smooth sailing, they leave us alone."

To mix metaphors, some of that sailing promises to be uphill. Although the *News* recently hiked its ad rates 20 percent, its cost-per-thousand rate is still lower than the *Times*'s.

And the *Anchorage Times,* using just about anybody's yardstick, has vastly improved.

"They reacted constantly with stories and layout changes," says Shinohara. "At one point, they had a different front page every day. We even had a name for it."

Times reporters credit Fred Dickey, former managing editor, hired after the McClatchy acquisition, with sweeping improvements in the paper as well as lifting staff morale and pride. Dickey left the *Times* in 1981.

Under the twenty-eight-year-old Heikes's direction, "They seem as aggressive as ever," says Shinohara. Indeed, a recent issue of "Samurai Editor," a *Daily News* newsroom communication, noted a single issue of the *Times* carried four page-one stories the *Daily News* had overlooked. "Overworked reporters cannot be blamed for not writing one more story on a long day," the Samurai suggested. "They *can* be blamed for not telling city desk folk about it so someone else can chase it."

"I think the *Times* has responded very effectively, purely in journalistic terms," says McCulloch. "Where the *Times* appears more lethargic is in the business and marketing ends."

McClatchy and his people have a theory about "the new economics," a theory that, with modern technology, a competitive paper in a smaller market can still make money. They think the morning factor, coupled with a quality product and aggressive marketing, can prove them right.

And McClatchy Newspapers is willing to take the multimillion-dollar gamble in Anchorage to prove it.

"Frank McCulloch has a phrase for it," says Stan Abbott. "Frank says, 'If we can make this work, we're all golden.' "

POSTSCRIPT: According to the publisher's statement filed with the Audit Bureau of Circulations for the three months ending September 30, 1983, the *Anchorage Daily News* had a weekday circulation of 49,255. The *Times*'s circulation was 46,694. The *Times*'s Sunday circulation was 54,011, and the Sunday *News* was at 53,375. The *Daily News* claims 52 percent of the October 1983 print ad market at rates that are "slightly lower than the *Times*," says *News* general manager Jerry Grilly.

In June 1983, Katherine Fanning was named editor of the *Christian Science Monitor*. Stan Abbott is now night city editor of the *Columbia* (Missouri) *Columbian*. Grilly and managing editor Howard Weaver now share the helm of the *Daily News*.

Atchison Daily Globe

G. Mark Zieman

O n a quiet day in December 1877, Edgar Watson Howe delivered to the farming and milling folk of Atchison, a town of twelve thousand in the hills of northeastern Kansas, the first edition of his *Globe*.

This one-sheet, two-page newspaper—"A Daily Evening Poster Devoted to Gab and Gossip, and Paid Locale"—was, as Howe described it, "the queerest daily paper ever seen in the United States."

In the traditional salutatory editorial, the twenty-four-year-old Howe wrote:

> The first thought of the average Atchisonian respecting the little *Globe,* if he is so good as to think of it at all, will be that it is very small. We frankly admit it—it is the smallest paper we have ever seen, but may it not occur to you that it will, therefore, have abundant room to grow? . . .
>
> We shall confine ourselves almost exclusively to the small affairs of humanity not ordinarily noticed by newspapers. While, perhaps, only one man in twenty will read an article on the expansion or contraction of the currency, every man, woman, and child, will read of the new baby, or the new preacher, of a party, social event, or other item not confined solely to great men and lunatics.

Thus was born the *Atchison Daily Globe,* in its time edited by one of the most influential newspapermen in the United States. During its 106-year history, the *Globe* has had only four owners, three of them independent: Ed Howe; his son, Gene; and Howe-trained Paul Allingham. In 1979 the *Globe* was purchased by a chain, Thomson Newspapers.

In many ways the newspaper is better today than it was as an independent. There are, for instance, more pictures, more syndicated columnists, better office equipment, a staff pension plan, and a group insurance policy. But the personal style of reporting made famous by Edgar Watson Howe and to a certain extent carried on through the days of his former reporter, Paul Allingham, is no longer a part of the *Globe*.

The *Atchison Daily Globe* has lost its spirit.

Atchison in Ed Howe's time was a promising Missouri River city, rivaling nearby Kansas City in importance. Its rich black soil and grassland prairie were ideal for farming, and grain and flour-milling industries sprang up in the late 1800s.

Howe's Atchison was steeped in history, dating back to at least July 4, 1804, when the Lewis and Clark expedition moved through the area. On July 27, 1854, a town company was formed, and on September 21 of that year David Rice Atchison, U.S. senator from Missouri, gave an address in the town. Although it was the only time he ever visited the area, the town—and the county—were named for him.

The Atchison, Topeka, and Sante Fe Railroad was founded in Atchison at a meeting held on January 2, 1859. Buffalo Bill Cody started his rascally career as a pony express rider there, and Montgomery Ward, of department-store fame, was born in Atchison.

But most importantly, for a young Ed Howe, Atchison was a newspaper town. "There was a press in Atchison before there were schools and churches," writes Calder Pickett, professor of journalism at the University of Kansas and author of *Ed Howe: Country Town Philosopher*.

"Ed Howe had chosen a city where he would have to fight hard to survive," Pickett continues. But Howe did survive, and his "little *Globe*" prospered. This "plain man who lived a plain life among plain people," as he was eulogized by William Allen White, swiftly became the most-quoted smalltown editor in the United States—later to be replaced only by White himself. Howe's most famous novel, *The Story of a Country Town,* an early work of literary realism, was read, enjoyed, and critiqued by such men as William Dean Howells and Mark Twain. Twain told Howe, "You write as a man talks, and very few can reach that height of excellence."

But Ed Howe was more than a good newspaper editor and novelist; he was a leader in personal reporting too, as his salutatory editorial may have hinted. Howe would stride through the Atchison streets every day, notebook in hand, taking down bits of information that he might use later in a series of brief, barbed commentaries, "Globe Sights."

Some examples:

After a woman has been married a few months, she goes around with a look on her face indicating she smells a dead rat.

Unless they are good-looking, young people are apt to be hopelessly uninteresting.

"No woman loves you very much," said a man to a friend today, "or she would squeeze that blackhead out of your face."

A woman ought to be pretty, to console her for being a woman at all.

The less you know about the poetic sort of things, the better off you are.

Too many men honor women, and neglect their wives.

If a man should be suddenly changed to a woman, he couldn't get his clothes off.

An Atchison man went to Topeka yesterday, and says the most wonderful thing he saw was at a house where he was invited to dinner: green jelly. And Topeka is the state capital!

Who ever found good gravy at a hotel?

No wonder people hate Polk Tansil: he is so mean. He said today, "When I see a Salvation Army drum, instead of feeling like throwing a dollar on it, I feel like kicking it in."

Many of these comments may not seem as bright today as they apparently did more than a hundred years ago, yet "Globe Sights" still remain a part of the modern *Globe*'s editorial page. A similar series of comments appears every day in eighteen-point, boldface type underneath the newspaper's nameplate, above the eight columns of news on page one. These commentaries are called "OK lines," as Paul Allingham explains, "Ed Howe named them that because he wrote them, and then he wrote 'OK,' for Charlie O'Keefe, the printing foreman."

Ed Howe retired on the last day of 1910, turning the paper over to his son, Gene Howe. The younger Howe later became publisher of the *Amarillo News-Globe* in Texas but continued to be owner, publisher, and editor of the *Atchison Globe* until 1951, when Allingham purchased control.

Gene Howe remained in Amarillo and became popular through his column, "The Tactless Texan." Not much is written about the *Atchison Globe* under him, and perhaps not much is warranted. The *Globe* appears to have been paralyzed, not relinquishing its role as a smalltown, personal newspaper, and not striving to move ahead. Perhaps this was because of Gene's split loyalties, to the *Amarillo News-Globe* as well as to the *Atchison Globe*.

The end of the direct Howe influence came in two parts: Ed Howe suffered a stroke on July 17, 1937, and died in his sleep on October 3 of that year. Gene Howe committed suicide in 1952.

A year earlier, Paul Allingham had bought the paper. Allingham and his wife, Winney, first worked for the Howes in Amarillo. He was advertising director and assistant publisher of the morning and evening Amarillo papers.

Winney was national advertising manager. Allingham was sent to Atchison by the Howes in 1937 at the age of twenty-four to run the paper, but returned to Amarillo shortly thereafter.

Finally in 1951, Allingham, along with Al Bennett of Atchison, assumed ownership of the *Globe*. Bennett at that time had been editor of the *Globe* for five years. In the ensuing years, Allingham took control of the *Globe*. His goal? "To run it like Ed Howe did," he said strongly, sitting in the living room of his Victorian house overlooking the Missouri River.

(Allingham's house, on the National Register of Historic Places, is probably the oldest large home remaining in Atchison. On July 24, 1897, Amelia Earhart was born in the southwest bedroom on the second floor. The world's foremost woman flyer is remembered by a bronze statue unveiled in 1981 at the downtown mall; members of the Ninety-Nines, the International Organization of Women Pilots of which Earhart was president, come to town each summer for a reunion. Atchison's airport, stadium, and athletic field are named for Earhart.)

"Ed Howe was excellent in the area of getting people involved, which is no longer true with a lot of people," Allingham said. "I was trained to do that."

Indeed he was. Allingham continued two of Ed Howe's most important newspaper techniques: the booster editorial and the practice of sending reporters into the streets for the story.

As Pickett described Howe's technique:

> Globe reporters were all over Atchison. A tour of the local jail brought a Globe cry for improvement of conditions: "The foul odor which continually hovers about the general cell is sufficient to take the flesh off any man who is accustomed to decency and cleanliness. We asked the prisoners how they fared, and they could not find words to express themselves." (October 20, 1884) A tour of the local packing house brought another kind of plea from Howe: "The next time a Globe reporter makes a tour of the packing house, please run him through the scalding tub and scraper before dismissing him. On his return to the office this morning, after visiting your guano and killing departments, our Mr. Rank had the air of a foul sewer about him." (December 22, 1886)

And Ed Howe was no less fervent in his editorials:

> If you want your town to improve, improve it. If you want to make your town lively, make it. Don't go to sleep, but get up and work for it. Push. Advertise it. Talk about it, and talk favorably.

This type of community involvement was the legacy the Howes left Paul Allingham. To his credit, Allingham attempted to carry on that tradition.

Just south of Atchison on a beautiful slope overlooking small Lake Warnock is a site called the International Forest of Friendship. The forest is the brainchild of the city of Atchison and the Ninety-Nines. It is made up of trees from the fifty states and thirty-three countries where there are Ninety-Nines, plus trees from historic sites, such as Mount Vernon. It is not an overwhelming drawing card for the city, yet it is important to the local people. They remember those who helped start it—one of whom was Paul Allingham.

"To a large degree, I think the project got off the ground because of Paul Allingham's backing," said Frank Carpinelli, Atchison city commissioner and head of the department of English at Benedictine College.

"He was very much involved . . . and got committed to it, and consequently that paper [the *Globe*] gave it a tremendous amount of publicity and got it started."

Such a community role was not unusual for the *Globe* under Allingham, Carpenelli said. "He proposed we have a cost-sharing program on sidewalk and curb repair. We now have that." The same with a high school bond issue. "The paper was obviously behind it and helped drum up the support of it," Carpinelli said.

One of the *Globe*'s strongest assets under Allingham was a man named C. V. "Cotton" O'Neill. O'Neill worked as a paperboy for the *Globe* as a child and then became a cub reporter in 1926 after he was graduated from high school. He later became sports editor, wire editor, news editor (for thirty-three years), and in 1961, editor.

Cotton O'Neill wrote a popular out-and-about column called "Gathered On Commercial." (Commercial is one of Atchison's main streets.) Father Angelus Lingenfelger, director of the Atchison County Historical Society, remembers O'Neill: "This Cotton O'Neill, he knew the people in town, and people would come to him with something interesting. He had a white head, and people called him 'Cotton Top.' "

"Cotton O'Neill was a very fine editor, and he kept on me all the time [to write editorials]," Allingham said. "Cotton spent all his life on the newspaper, on the *Globe*. He was one of the best editors I've ever run into. He also was one of the best writers and reporters, too." Allingham, moving forward in his chair, pointed to his chest. "We were not all this man, is what I'm saying."

But Cotton O'Neill and the *Globe*'s editorials are not what Paul Allingham remembers most proudly from his days as publisher of the *Globe*. It is a disaster he recalls, a disaster he will talk about at length—if pressed a bit—and with great passion. A disaster that brought offset printing to the

Globe—the most important change in the newspaper since 1884, when the *Globe* became the *Atchison Daily Globe* and converted to a steam press.

"We had a flood, and the plant was flooded out," Allingham recalled. He estimated that the *Globe* lost forty-five thousand dollars. "There's nothing worse than a basement press full of water. We didn't sit up on the hill and editorialize—hell, we were in it."

So were most of the residents and business people of Atchison. In July 1958 twin flash floods—great walls of water rushing down the hills of the city toward the Missouri River—destroyed downtown Atchison. Efforts to rebuild earned the town two nicknames: "The Miracle City," and because of a series of twenty-five detention dams built along local streams, "The Dammedest City in Kansas."

"It's a tough town," said Pat Walker, executive director of the Atchison Chamber of Commerce. "The people in the community just won't give up."

When the flood waters receded, Atchison built anew. Since that time the town remains much the same: one hospital, thirty-one churches, four public tennis courts, one public pool, three banks, two savings and loans, four motels, one newspaper, one radio station, ten elementary schools, one junior high school, three high schools, one vocational-technical school, Benedictine College, and several large manufacturers.

"It's an old town, heavily industrialized," Walker said. "The recent figures from the Department of Human Resources show 30 percent of its people employed in manufacturing."

Rockwell International, established in 1872, manufactures casting parts for railroad and rapid transit; it is the city's largest employer, with 1,040 people. A Pillsbury Company flour mill, founded in 1904, is the city's third largest, with 224 employees. The odor from a plant making a Pillsbury product—"Wheat Nuts"—mixes with the smell of fermenting alcohol from Midwest Solvents Company, giving the entire town a strong, rich, pecan smell.

At 1015 Main Street, directly across from Pillsbury's two-million-bushel, seven-story silos, Paul Allingham erected the new building for the *Atchison Globe*.

Robert Wellington, publisher of the *Ottawa Herald* in northern Kansas, recalled Allingham's feat: "Paul went out at the edge of the business district and quietly went about putting up a new building. It was all very hush-hush. When the building was done, he brought in the equipment—at night, I think. Then he hired some women and trained them at night on how to run the machines and do paste-up. When everything was ready, he walked into his old plant one morning and told everyone that it was closed—the printers were no longer needed. Just like that."

Allingham's version is slightly different.

The *Globe* publisher contacted a man named Staley McBare from Fort Worth. "He helped me. He showed me how to put out a paper without a linotype. He had the only [offset] press," Allingham said, "and the other [manufacturers of] presses didn't know how to make one yet."

When the newspaper was ready for the switch to offset in 1962, "most of our printers were old enough that they retired," Allingham said. "They couldn't even make the leap into the era."

Other Kansas editors disapproved of the change to the untested, risky, new printing method. Allingham remembers a call from William L. White, son of William Allen White, who had taken over the *Emporia Gazette*.

"He said, 'Paul, have you gone crazy? You're one of the first people in that area, that crazy offset.'"

But, of course, the five-unit, Harris V-5 offset press worked—splendidly.

"The offset printing opened up a whole new vista for certain people," Allingham said with conviction. "To me, that meant something."

Paul Allingham was not the only member of his family to be spending long days and most nights as a pioneer of offset. Winney Allingham pitched in too. "At one time, I knew how to operate all the machines," she said.

Paul nodded. "When we went into offset, she had to help because nobody could help train. There were no people trained in offset."

With offset printing, the Allinghams began a series of major changes in the *Globe*. They brought the first cameras to the paper, taking their own pictures. To pick up advertisers, they changed the Saturday edition to Sunday. "We also developed more women's news and pictures, that sort of thing," Paul Allingham said.

Winney joined in, "We changed the format completely. Everybody screamed their heads off. Any town is hard to change."

"In fact," her husband said, "Winney wrote one of the best-read columns."

She smiled. "For a while I did a picture page—'As You Know'—because everything I wrote, somebody already knew. I also instituted a women's club edition and a cookbook edition."

Thus, the *Atchison Daily Globe* grew and changed. By 1978 the *Globe* had a subscription price of $33.80 per year and a weekday circulation of 7,035. The Sunday circulation was 7,326. Paul Allingham was a popular publisher, and the *Globe* regularly published what many Atchison residents considered to be the newspaper's most important item, an Allingham column called "Goals For Atchison."

On January 21, 1979, for instance, Allingham published five goals: more city government cooperation and assistance with housing developers to encourage construction of much-needed housing, both for rent and for purchase; improved entrances to the city by zone controls at least three miles around the perimeter; street improvements and paving along with city participation in the construction of new sidewalks and curbing; a new industrial park; and a home improvement campaign—"We need a year-round paint-up, clean-up, and beautification program."

But, by 1978, Paul and Winney Allingham, in their sixties, were beginning to feel their age. Cotton O'Neill was also getting along, as was advertising manager Harvey Buckley. In 1966 the Anthony family, close friends of the Allinghams, had sold their nearby newspaper, the *Leavenworth Times,* to Thomson Newspapers. Paul Allingham had closely watched the newspaper under its new ownership, and had liked what he saw—the paper was not changed drastically. The estate taxes on his newspaper were starting to worry him. On March 15, 1979, the lead story in the *Globe* read:

> Sale of the Atchison Daily Globe to Thomson Newspapers Inc., Des Plaines, Illinois, was announced today in a joint statement by Paul Allingham, president of The Globe Publishing Co. and owner-publisher of The Globe, and St. Clair McCabe, president of Thomson Newspapers, and Frank Miles, general manager of Thomson Newspapers.
>
> Both McCabe and Miles in commenting on the purchase of all shares of Globe Publishing Co. by Thomson Newspapers stated, "There will be no change in the newspaper's policy nor its personnel."
>
> "We have a great deal of confidence in Atchison and this area, evidenced by the fact we purchased The Globe," McCabe said. "Each of our newspapers are entirely autonomous, and have the responsibility of serving the community. The editor and publisher shape the paper's policy."
>
> Said Allingham: "For several years we have had interested buyers contacting us about the Globe, but after meeting with several, we chose Thomson Newspapers Inc., because we observed the way they operated the Leavenworth Times nearby on a local basis."
>
> "Winney and I are retiring from active management because we were unable to get anyone in our family to follow us in the business and, after twenty-eight years with the Globe, we want to devote our time to personal affairs and do some traveling."
>
> "We will continue to maintain our home here and want to thank our friends and associates for many good years, and we will serve the new owners as advisors."

The purchase price was not disclosed.

For the first time in 102 years, the *Globe* was not owned by an Atchison resident. Cotton O'Neill, in ill health, retired from the *Globe* two months after Thomson bought the paper. He died a year later. Harvey Buckley left the *Globe* a few months after O'Neill.

Although Paul Allingham had stated that he and Winney wanted to take time off to do some traveling, he fell and injured his back a few months after selling the paper. Then in June 1982, he suffered a stroke, from which he is still recovering. He and Winney now most often stay at home. They seldom receive visitors. He does not like to talk about the current *Atchison Daily Globe.* When asked if he had served as an advisor to Daryl Henning, the new publisher, as he had volunteered to do in the *Globe* news story, Allingham sharply replied, "They haven't asked me."

Allingham said he still subscribed to the *Globe,* but he turned away when asked if he read it. Winney was more eloquent. "I just glance at the headlines, and if there's a local story—which there's not too much of usually—I may read it."

Paul Allingham, who speaks slowly now because of his stroke, talked about his reasons for not discussing the *Globe* under Thomson management. "I walked out of it and sold it completely. After you spend fifty years in the newspaper business, you don't need more of it all the time, despite the fact it was very interesting."

He said he did not get together with staff members of the Thomson *Globe*. "I've tried to stay out of all of this. I like those I know."

Although he will not talk specifically about the *Atchison Globe,* Paul Allingham will critique the trends he sees in modern journalism. "They've gotten away from people and started taking pictures of dogs and things—and they don't subscribe."

He shook his head, searching for words—"If newspapers will stick to what they're supposed to do, which is write about people, who read the paper. . ."—and then he stopped.

If Paul Allingham does not choose to talk about the *Globe* under Thomson ownership, others do.

"This town, going back to Ed Howe, has a history of some pretty popular publishers," said Norman Ellis, chairman of the Atchison County Democratic League. "This one [Daryl Henning] is not that easy to get along with. He has the personality of a bowl of cold mush."

Ellis continued: "I think Paul Allingham carried on much of the tradition of the Howes, and I don't think it's being carried on today. I think it's pretty much of a farce, and most people know it."

One positive aspect that Ellis has seen is the newspaper's political stance, which was staunchly pro-Republican under the Howes and Paul Allingham. In recent elections, the *Globe* has appeared to be independent. It has endorsed some Democratic candidates, including Congressman Jim Slattery

(Democrat, Topeka). "We [Democrats] received extremely fair press here," Ellis said.

Still, Ellis, a former city commission member who also runs a downtown barber and style shop, says he is not satisfied with the *Globe*'s new management. "I see a difference in that they are less responsive than Allingham was," he said. "It's a typical chain operation, and the town perceives it as cold and heartless."

"Cold and heartless" does not seem to accurately describe Daryl Henning, the publisher of the *Globe* under Thomson. Like Cotton O'Neill, Henning delivered the *Globe* as a boy. In June 1968 he worked as an advertising salesman under Paul Allingham.

Henning has a mother, grandmother, and brother-in-law living in the community. When he came to the *Globe* from his position as advertising manager of the *Leavenworth Times,* Allingham showed him the *Globe*'s yellowed staff roster that he kept underneath his glass desk top—with Henning's name still on it.

One would expect Henning, as a local boy, to be more easily accepted by the Atchison residents. But he does not seem to be.

"He's a puppet of the chain," Ellis said. "I would not rate him very well in running a newspaper."

Regardless of opinion, some hard facts are known about the *Atchison Daily Globe* under Thomson ownership. The 1982 *Editor & Publisher International Yearbook* lists the *Atchison Daily Globe* as having a weekday circulation of 5,909—a 1,126 (16 percent) decrease from Allingham's day. Sunday circulation is 6,135—a 1,191 (16 percent) decrease.

The *Globe* offers no explanation for the decline. Daryl Henning, because of what he claims is his own caution, not Thomson policy, refuses to speak on the record about the paper. (In the past, Henning said Thomson officials have provided information that was later used to the group's disadvantage by union leaders.) So it is not clear whether the 16 percent decrease is a result of the economy, higher subscription rates, or newspaper competition.

Since Thomson's purchase of the *Globe,* the *St. Joseph News-Press,* twenty miles to the northeast on the east side of the Missouri River, has increased its Atchison coverage.

"You get pretty near as much local news in the St. Joseph paper as you get in the Atchison paper anymore," complained Father Angelus.

Frank Carpinelli agreed. "They made a very definite attempt to move into this area. We noticed it on the city commission because they sent reporters to cover the meeting—full-time reporters."

Jim Carrithers, circulation manager of the *St. Joseph News-Press,* said, "We feel that Atchison is our community. It's our town. It's only twenty miles away—you can throw a rock that far."

Carrithers said that the Atchison economy has been slipping a bit. Major industries like Rockwell, for instance, are weakening, becoming "kind of spongy." City records show that the unemployment rate in Atchison, a community of about eleven thousand, had risen from 6.2 percent in 1980 to 8.6 percent in 1982.

"I think the pricing of what the people get, as opposed to their economic situation, could be the main factor," Carrithers said. Certainly the decline in the *Globe*'s circulation has not brought a drop in its advertising rates. In 1978 the *Globe*'s rate for classified ads was $2.10 per inch, or $9.00 per inch for six inserts. Today, under Henning, the *Globe*'s classified rate is $9.00 per fifteen words for six days. Fifteen words is about half an inch under the *Globe*'s layout; thus the rate has almost doubled.

The nearby *Lawrence Journal-World* and the *Olathe Daily News,* both with circulations of about fourteen thousand, offer the same number of words and days for $6.90 and $7.20, respectively, about 20 percent less for twice the circulation.

But a higher ad rate may be required in Atchison to meet Thomson's corporate profit goals. Certainly the *Globe* cannot expect to get rich on the quantity of advertising it publishes. While a larger daily might hope to devote at least 50 percent of its space to advertising, the *Globe* has to settle for much less. In a typical week, with the *Globe* publishing from eight to twenty-two pages, the percentage of advertising (not including five fliers inserted in the paper) was: Sunday, 41 percent; Monday, 19 percent; Tuesday, 17 percent; Wednesday, 48 percent; Thursday, 35 percent; and Friday, 24 percent. The average for the entire week was 38 percent.

Although many advertisers contacted said that they believed the ad rate was not overly high, several expressed dissatisfaction with the layout of the advertisements, noting that after Allingham's Harvey Buckley retired, Henning did not choose to fill the ad manager's position.

"I really don't feel that they have a first-class advertising layout person now," Norman Ellis said. "To me they're running a shirt-tail operation."

Several others agree, including past and present *Globe* staff members. They cite a litany of problems: low salaries, a high turnover rate, heavy workloads, a tight budget, and inexperienced editors.

Under Thomson Newspapers, the *Atchison Daily Globe* employs twenty-nine full-time and seven part-time workers, not including carriers and truck drivers. There are six full-timers in the news department: a city reporter and an agriculture reporter (a husband-and-wife team), a society and women's news reporter, a sports reporter, a news editor, and a managing editor. A Benedictine College student acts as a part-time reporter and photographer.

As in many small towns, the reporters frequently are asked to double their beats and go off their beats to cover stories. All of the reporters also act as photographers.

Arne Green began working at the *Globe* after his graduation from the University of Kansas in 1981. He is currently the *Globe*'s sports editor, as well as its sports reporter and photographer.

"There has been quite a turnover," he said. "I've been here the longest of any reporter. To be quite honest, I'm not looking to stay around that much longer myself."

Green covers sporting events at about a dozen area schools and lays out his page. Although he is paid for his mileage, he said, he seldom has time to cover out-of-town events of the Kansas City Royals, Chiefs, Kings, or Comets or of University of Kansas teams.

Green also must cover nonsports stories. He reports frequently on the town's school board, for instance, and often works on special projects, such as an Atchison "Progress Report" published in January 1983.

"I think they're too budget conscious. I just think they could loosen up a little bit," he said. "It's just that I'd like to concentrate on sports."

Green said the publisher was strict about keeping staff members to forty hours a week. Green's nonsports workload means that many times he is unable to cover scheduled sporting events. "There've been occasions when I was told to cover things on my own and not get paid."

Reporters at the *Globe* start out at about $170 a week. "I've had two small raises," Green said. "The only reason, really, that I'm staying is that I planned next summer to take some time off and travel, and I didn't want to take a job for just a few months."

Green said he did not know how financially sound the newspaper was, but that "judging by my financial condition, it's probably not terribly good."

Lori Jabara also took a reporting position on the *Globe* after graduation from the University of Kansas. Six months later she left for a job as press secretary to David Owen, former lieutenant governor of Kansas, who was seeking the Republican nomination for governor.

"Three people left [the *Globe*] during the six months I was there," she said. They left, she thought, "to better their careers." Jabara said she was satisfied with her time at the *Globe*. "The salaries were a little low, but I enjoyed the work." The newsroom management, however, was weak, she said.

The direction provided the paper's forty correspondents—primarily from neighboring small towns—disappointed her. "The paper used to have an area editor who took care of that news."

Jabara, like Green, also felt Jerry Wallace, the *Globe*'s new managing editor, did not lead. "The staff was very disappointed. He had not worked the streets, and the news staff was frustrated with him. As I understand it, Mr.

Henning made the decision to hire him, but he was recommended by the Thomson people," Jabara said.

Green said that Wallace "pretty well does what Daryl Henning says automatically. The only thing he'll ever do is check punctuation."

Wallace, age twenty-five, came to the *Globe* about one and a half years ago from the *Southeast Missourian,* a seventeen-thousand-circulation Thomson paper in Cape Girardeau, Missouri, where he was a sports reporter.

Wallace sees himself as "an organizer and a planner" at the *Globe.* "I make all the story and photo assignments. I have to be a working managing editor, as Daryl likes to say."

Wallace agreed that the *Globe* news staff has a high turnover rate. Since he came to the paper, every member has left except one, Mickey Parman, the news editor.

"Salary is the reason they would cite," he said, for leaving the paper. But he thought that the *Globe* could afford to pay a lower salary than many papers because of the fringe benefits that went with working for a group.

Those benefits, he said, were important to him. When he began working for Thomson in Cape Girardeau, he was "looking for security and advancement."

"I was looking ahead," he said. "I know I'm not dead-ended here. They [Thomson] are always buying new newspapers, and they're apt to move a younger person like myself into something like that."

Despite the benefits, the reporters leave. The steady ebb and flow of *Globe* reporters has discouraged many city officials. "Now, very few of the people that work there know much about Atchison. The trouble is people don't know. They say things about old buildings that aren't even true," explained Father Angelus. "Now Allingham, he used to have his reporters, people who lived here all their life. And they knew better."

Faye Bosse, a modern-day Winney Allingham who worked for the *Globe* but later moved to the *St. Joseph News-Press,* wrote a "chatty sort of thing, in which she went around to try to find out who was having a birthday, who's traveling, something like that," Frank Carpinelli said. "She was specific, and people would buy the *Globe* to read that."

Bosse would travel up and down the streets of Atchison, like Ed Howe, Paul Allingham, and Cotton O'Neill. The new reporter does not do that, according to several store owners and businesspeople. John Meier, co-manager of the Pillsbury flour mill across from the *Globe*'s office, said Bosse would pop in to his offices about twice a week. Since taking over the job a few months ago, "the lady that's doing that now has not called on us," he said.

Such subtle changes are noticed by Atchison residents—and by Kansas editors.

Ray Call, managing editor of the *Emporia Gazette,* said one of the first changes that he noticed Thomson had made at the *Globe* was a reduction in the number of exchange papers. (Kansas editors exchange their papers as a courtesy and to keep up on state news.) Call said that the *Atchison Globe* had been out of view for nearly three years.

Call also said that participation in Kansas journalism activities by *Globe* personnel has diminished. At the annual gathering of the fall Associated Press meeting in Kansas City, former *Globe* Publisher Allingham was an active participant. At recent meetings, the *Globe* has not been represented.

Atchison's residents notice different changes. William Sachs, Jr., is the city manager of Atchison, which is governed by the council-manager plan. Sachs also teaches a course in city government at Benedictine College. "There's a lot of conflict between the paper and members of the city commission, which in my opinion doesn't help the city any," Sachs said. "If I weren't in this particular job, I wouldn't even take the paper.

"In 1981 there was a great controversy in the town over where the city was going. During that time, some arguments came between the local paper and the new commissioners.

"I guess for years there was an old guard here, and they were doing real well off the city. It got to the point where the salaries were one-half the budget. I think the newspaper was happy with the old guard." The old guard is no more.

Now, he said, "We don't have a department head who's been with the city for longer than one and a half years."

Sachs also feels the *Globe* should publish book reviews and offer space for political debates. Other wishes are more basic. "They don't have a standard approach to what's going on in our industry. They don't have a standard approach to what's going on with our retailers. [Only] if somebody calls them, then they'll come out."

Another large omission, he said, is feature writing. "There are no feature articles."

This is an overstatement—but only a slight one. A thorough review of six weeks of *Globe* front pages found three local feature articles. One of them, about a recent graduate of Benedictine College, was written by the college's public relations director.

The second article—which could be categorized as a news story—was written by the *Globe*'s managing editor. It concerned Faith Dame, head of the community's PRIDE program—Programming Resources with Initiative for Development Effectiveness. She was named the *Globe*'s Mo-Kan citizen of the year.

The third feature, written by Mickey Parman, was about "Kansas Kate." The story ran on Ground Hog Day. An excerpt:

The reporter looked closely. "Is that you, Kansas Kate? How'd you get out of your burrow?"

Kate cackled. "Boy, are you dumb? Do you think the creatures that live below the earth have been sitting down there for eons waiting for reporters to come by and dig them out every time it snows? My emergency exit," she pointed behind her, "comes up right under this tree—nice and dry. Which is more," she snickered, "than I can say for you."

It was the max. The fuming reporter, tired of being Kate's yearly punching bag, made like a worm and turned.

With a paper averaging eight to ten pages on weekdays—about 60 percent of that space for news—an editor has a great deal to work with, even after subtracting a third of the newshole for the editorial page, the front page, and sports. The current *Atchison Globe,* however, chooses to fill most of its space with wire copy from the Associated Press. "After awhile, there's not too much on the page that's local, or at least current," City Commissioner Frank Carpinelli said.

Carpinelli also criticized the *Globe*'s current coverage of city affairs. "The main thing that bothers me is that I'm disturbed the news editor is writing a column on the editorial page, . . . an unsigned editorial, and also the local [page-one] column," he said. "Sometimes it's just very apparent to me that there's a conflict. As far as I'm concerned, it's just not good when it spills over to the front page."

Carpinelli said that although the city reporter did a good job covering the beat, Mickey Parman, a sports editor under Allingham and now the *Globe*'s news editor, was uninformed. "She doesn't go to our meetings, she doesn't read our minutes, she doen't read our memos," he said. "Her position was she didn't *have* to go to our meetings and didn't *have* to read our minutes."

Parman disagrees. "They need a watchdog. I don't accuse them of anything the town isn't already talking about. I'm more or less the town's spokesman."

Parman has worked at the *Globe* for eighteen years, the first fifteen as sports editor. "I'm not sure, but I think I was the first full-time woman sports editor on a daily."

She said she believed the *Globe* under Thomson ownership still carried on the community involvement that she saw under Paul Allingham. "I think we definitely attempt to back the community on anything that they start—like the PRIDE campaign just organized last year. We've given it very good backing."

Whatever the extent of community involvement, investigative reporting is not present in today's *Globe*. Nor was it in Allingham's day. And readers also complain that there is a dearth of follow-up stories. One story might mention that a traffic light was installed at an intersection to reduce accidents. But the *Globe,* in the weeks and months to follow, would not tell readers whether the light was making any difference. City commissioners complain that the *Globe* will regularly attack their ideas on city management, yet never follow up to investigate if those ideas were effective.

Much of the *Globe*'s inside pages are strewn with bulletin-board journalism—area news from neighboring correspondents, columns by the Atchison and Doniphan county extension agents, a column from a member of the Kansas City Board of Trade, school menus, honor rolls, and "Notes From College." Most local stories take the form of meeting articles, chamber-of-commerce updates, city budget figures, and deadline stories, such as filing dates for social security benefits.

One bright spot in the *Globe*'s added use of wire are stories from "The Globe Washington Bureau"—a Thomson feature. These are stories with a Kansas interest done by a staff of Thomson reporters headquartered in Washington, D.C.

Thomson ownership, unfortunately, has not led to many changes in the *Globe*'s appearance. Cramping the front page underneath the thirty-six-point *Atchison Daily Globe* flag (and underneath the eighteen-point boldface "OK lines") are eight 9½-pica columns, each packed with six-point news type.

"It turns the reader off," said Charles Wanninger, Gannett professional-in-residence at the University of Kansas. "The *Globe* certainly makes no use of modern newspaper layout techniques."

Wanninger, former editor and publisher of the *Bellingham Herald* in Washington and a veteran newsman, is considered by the university journalism school's students and faculty to be the resident expert on newspaper layout and production. He does not like the look of the *Globe.*

"Almost every newspaper in the country has switched over to some kind of a six-column layout," Wanninger said. But with the *Globe,* "there is no modular effect, no effort to make it horizontal at all.

"I suppose from . . . a news editor's standpoint, it's easier to lay out a page this way, rather than modular or horizontal. And when you get to the backshop, it's definitely easier to lay out," he said. But he added, "I have a tendency to think they haven't changed it because they don't know better."

Not only does the narrow column width make the newspaper harder to read, it also must frustrate the *Globe*'s editors, who, as Wanninger remarked, "use an incredible number of verb heads"—omitting subjects—and split heads.

A recent edition of the *Globe* offered these front-page headlines over two or three columns:

| Denies Carlin Favors | Urges Freeze On |
| Gasoline Tax Increase | Natural Gas Cost |

Question EPA's	Push For 10 Weeks
'Sloppy' Books	Jobless Benefits

The one-column headlines are no better, sometimes appearing to be orders to the reader:

Arrest Soviet Spy	Offer $25,000 Reward
Plan Bake Sale	Register To Vote

Seek	Seek To	Cutback
Tax Law	Open Ford	On Fed
Change	Dealership	Program

The short space also makes for some awkward abbreviations, such as "bens" for benefits and "Russ" for Russians.

The typefaces, chosen when the paper went to offset printing in 1962, look old-fashioned. In two-deck headlines that rarely are wider than three columns, the Bodini Extrabold and Bodini Extrabold Italic typefaces appear squat, almost ugly.

The *Globe* does not have a separate layout editor, which may explain why its make-up borders on sloppy. One example is the presence of "naked wraps," columns of type that have no headline, cutline, picture, or graphic above them. Rarely, a newspaper will run a naked wrap on an inside page, when an ad, for instance, leaves an awkward two-inch hole. Wanninger, pointing to the *Globe*'s front page, remarked, "I can tell you that never in my entire life have I seen a naked wrap on page one." Until he saw the *Globe,* that is.

But the *Globe* under Thomson ownership does group news more effectively. For example, the Howes and Allingham had a habit of scattering obituaries, as a way of taking the reader though ad-filled interior pages. Today, all of the obituaries are placed together under a standing head on page two. Readers appreciate the change. "To me, that's very appealing," said Father Angelus Lingenfelser.

Under Allingham, there also was an almost total lack of consistency throughout the paper. Page two might be the "Area News" page. Or the page for articles continued from page one. Or the editorial page.

The editorial page used to contain not only editorials, local columns, a cartoon, and a Jack Anderson column, but also television listings, a health column, Associated Press news stories, "Your Horoscope," a crossword puzzle, and a few odd fillers or news brights, such as, "Vincent Van Gogh treated his insomnia with a large dose of camphor on his pillow and mattress."

The Thomson chain has done away with many of these inconsistencies. Page two, for instance, usually holds hospital news, obituaries, stock market and futures reports, and occasionally court and police reports. Associated Press and local news stories fill out the page.

Area news and state and national news briefs are now placed on page three. Tidbits from the wire and feature services—"Polly's Pointers," "Dear Abby," "Stitchin' Time," "Health," "Business Mirror," "Religion in the News," "Tomorrow's Horoscope," "Bridge," and a few unusual items with such names as "Medicalodge," "Filmeter," and "Stepparents"—are scattered toward the back of the paper.

Perhaps the most consistent page in the *Globe* is the comics page. On one side of the page are ten comic strips, and on the other side are the *Globe*'s television listings, expanded from Allingham's day. The comics are distributed mainly by Newspaper Enterprise Association (NEA), a low-cost feature service. Except on Sunday, the comics section does not include such favorites as "Garfield" or "Peanuts," but the more tired (and often less expensive) "Priscilla's Pop," "Bugs Bunny," "Captain Easy," and "The Born Loser." Henning did replace two old serial strips—"Steve Canyon" and "Joe Palooka" with NEA's "Snake" and "Eek and Meek."

But even though Henning and his staff may have found a place for every news and feature item, the packaging of those items remains woefully inconsistent.

The boxed news briefs on page one may contain local items, such as the showing of a film on sexual abuse or the dispensing by the Salvation Army of free government surplus butter. Or the briefs may be off the Associated Press Kansas wire—legislative stories, for instance. Or they may be national or international stories from the wire service—a trucker's strike or an attack on multinational peacekeeping forces in Beirut.

This by itself is not surprising, yet the *Globe* irregularly runs two other columns of news briefs inside, one labeled "Kansas News Briefs" and the other, again, "News Briefs." These are not boxed, and many times contain stories of the same kind, and seemingly of the same importance, as the page-one news briefs.

There are other inconsistencies. The standing headlines—such as "Area News," "Briefly Speaking," "Polly's Pointers," "Opinion," "Stock Markets. . . ," and "Tiger Tales," written by a high school correspondent—are presented in a motley variety of headline typefaces, from serif boldface to script to sans-serif light. Perhaps the most glaring example of this is the sports head which, as Wanninger said, "looks like it climbed out of a 1948 clip file."

Rounding out the *Globe*'s design are the photographs—all usually routine, stand-them-up-against-the-wall-and-shoot affairs. Such poses are standard in smalltown newspapers, yet an effort could be made to increase the quality. Unfortunately, the reporters must take their own pictures.

The newspaper does not have—and never has had—an Associated Press wire photo machine for state, national, and international pictures. But even without the machine, and with few reporters—and therefore photographers—the *Globe* under Thomson ownership has run more photos, which are usually better than the ones published under Allingham.

No matter what one writes about the *Atchison Daily Globe*'s news pages, the quality of the editorial page has to be of special concern. It was the editorials of Ed Howe that propelled "the little *Globe*" into newspaper history. Colleges and universities still teach students about Ed Howe and his "Globe Sights" in journalism history classes. A picture of the "Sage of Potato Hill," as he was called, graces Daryl Henning's office at the *Globe*. That picture, unfortunately, is about the only part of Ed Howe left in today's *Atchison Globe*.

Under Allingham, the editorial page of the *Atchison Globe* routinely ran at least one local editorial a day, many times two or more. Cotton O'Neill, too, wrote his popular "Gathered On Commercial," column. All of that is gone.

A check of four weeks reveals that of the twenty-four days surveyed, the Thomson-owned *Globe* ran fourteen canned lead editorials, most reprinted from other newspapers, such as the *Sacramento Bee*. Of the ten lead editorials that were apparently written by *Globe* staff members, only two dealt directly with Atchison. "This is an excellent example of that particular chain of newspapers," said City Manager Sachs. "They just don't get involved. More often than not, they don't write editorials. This really bugs me."

Sachs shook his head. "Paul Allingham used to carry a column all the time—the goals of Atchison—and he kept them in front of the people. Now they don't have any editorials that have any suggestions as to what the city should be doing and where it should be going."

Today's *Globe* does run more syndicated columnists than Allingham's. Columns by Jack Anderson, James Kilpatrick, William Rusher, Robert Wagman, Robert Walters, and several NEA contributors are frequent.

The rest of the editorial page includes such standard fare as "Berry's World" (an NEA cartoon), "Today in History," "How Time Flies" (from the *Globe*'s files), and a Bible digest. Mickey Parman, *Globe* news editor, occasionally writes a semi-informative column called "It's My World, Too." And, as the only link to the paper's great past, there are reprints of Ed Howe's "Globe Sights."

Daryl Henning, sitting underneath the picture of a stern Ed Howe, will not talk about the mechanics of the *Atchison Daily Globe*. But he will talk about himself, and how an Atchison boy, working for a chain of newspapers, tries to win over friends, relatives, and neighbors who wonder whether his interests lie in Atchison or Des Plaines, Illinois, Thomson's United States headquarters.

"I know there will be some who will say, "I've known him since he was a little boy, and he doesn't know a goddamn thing about running a newspaper," Henning said. But he laughed. "I'd never go to a doctor I went to school with. I wouldn't trust him.

"I think it puts a little bit more pressure on you when you're from the community," Henning remarked. "There's a strong desire to succeed in your own town."

Looking out his office door at the business he supervises, Henning, age forty-three, remembered his days as a *Globe* delivery boy. "I would have never thought that I would someday run this newspaper," he said. "And without this being chain-owned, I never would have had the opportunity."

Although Henning will not talk for the record, other employees reveal that Thomson has not been as heartless as some suspect. Since the group took over the *Globe,* new drapes, office furniture, office equipment, and a new heating and cooling unit have been purchased. The inside of the building and some of the desks, once painted pink, were repainted; and the outside of the building, also pink, is scheduled to be repainted later in 1983.

More importantly, the chain has given employees a new group insurance plan and a pension plan—the latter the only one in the *Globe*'s history. Employees may also earn up to three weeks vacation, one week more than was possible under Allingham. And work weeks have been changed from six 6½-hour days under Allingham to five 8-hour days under Thomson.

The *Globe* has not changed in a lot of ways—the paper still waits for the late market report from local industries before going to press at 2:00 P.M. But the Howe tradition, if not gone already, is fading.

Seated in his office at the University of Kansas, Calder Pickett spoke of the man he had come to know through the laborious process of writing his biography—Ed Howe.

"That man was a giant," Pickett said strongly. He shook his head. "Giants must be doing something else now—I don't know what—but they're not doing much as Kansas editors."

Centre Daily Times

John N. Rippey

Presidents of organizations that could always count on check-passing photos, publicity chairpersons who seldom found it difficult to get their homemade news releases in the paper almost verbatim, and political partisans who had never before been stunned by an adverse editorial endorsement—those people are probably the only readers who would not agree that Pennsylvania's *Centre Daily Times* has improved at least superficially since it was bought by Knight-Ridder Newspapers on August 30, 1979.

The news staff had welcomed the purchase. One veteran reporter described it as "liberation." The staff had high hopes for increases in salaries. Everybody but the former owners agree pay was proportionately worse than even other small dailies in Pennsylvania. The staff also had high hopes for news and editorial improvements in a twenty-one-thousand-circulation paper that had its share of unprofessionalism.

A number of significant changes were, in fact, made on both the business side and the news-editorial side, though not all of the changes could be attributed solely to Knight-Ridder ownership.

• Pay on the news side was increased, in some cases dramatically, and a scale was instituted to raise all salaries gradually. A commission system was also added to improved base salaries for advertising salespeople.

• Efforts were made to give the news staff more helpful editorial direction, to make assignments more effectively, and to improve professional competence through in-house meetings.

• An attempt was made to improve editing and processing of news copy through establishment of a more formal copy desk.

• Local hard news photos were used more than before; grip-and-grins had to show a lot more action; and Amish buggies disappearing into sunsets appeared less frequently on page one.

• Editorials, which had seldom taken stands on anything except freedom of the press, now did take stands, even in favor of abortion in the Bible Belt of Pennsylvania.

• Serious coverage of local business was pursued, and a business page was started.

• Cosmetically, the paper was divided into more sections, the "product" packaged and departmentalized, the family reunions reduced to agate, and the use of color greatly increased.

• The Saturday edition was changed to morning, and a local television tab was added.

• Advertising salespeople were told to sell advertising, not merely pick up ad copy.

• Big dollars were spent on VDTs and other hardware designed to improve the efficiency of both news and business sides of the paper.

Although not blind to leftover problems, top management people at the *Times* seemed genuinely pleased with changes since Knight-Ridder's purchase and genuinely enthusiastic over improvements they foresaw as the paper moved through the transition period.

Acknowledging certain improvements, news staffers interviewed were, on the other hand, disappointed, and a few were even disillusioned with Knight-Ridder.

Although their opinions were disputed by management to a large extent, the perceptions of many on the reporting staff two years after the purchase seemed to be:

• that pay had not increased as much as expected and that ad salespeople were getting a bigger share of the pie.

• that the news and sports staff had shrunk somewhat (a fact not disputed by management) and that the ad staff was being beefed up.

• that the workload of staffers had, if anything, increased, making improvement in depth and breadth of news coverage and an increase in feature stories next to impossible.

• that the copy desk—more of an ad hoc operation before Knight-Ridder—continued to be a serious problem, despite innovations and reorganizations, essentially because of limited talent.

• that the team of top editors, the same as established by the old regime, provided weak professional leadership for the news staff. Some staffers expressed disappointment that more highly qualified professionals had not been imported by Knight-Ridder.

Although the management team praised the news staff, it expressed guarded reservations about the professionalism of some staffers.

After more than two years of transition, then, things were definitely not the same at the *Centre Daily Times*. Employees felt pride, disillusionment, and hope; and some things Knight-Ridder had not done seemed as important to employees as the things it had done.

Published at State College, the newspaper became a daily in 1934. In 1937 Jerome Weinstein and Eugene J. Reilly, freshly minted across the street at what is now the main campus of Pennsylvania State University, joined the four-person staff. Although duties were blurred, Weinstein, starting at eighteen dollars a week, went the news-editorial direction; and Reilly, although he also did some editing, went the advertising-business route. Over the next forty-three years, the paper took on the Weinstein-Reilly personality. And as the area grew and prospered, Reilly, Weinstein, and the *Centre Daily Times* prospered.

In its early days as a daily, the paper's largest circulation was not in State College, Reilly said in an interview, but in Bellefonte, the blue-collar county seat a dozen miles away. In 1934 there were only several thousand students at Penn State; by World War II there were some 5,000 students plus another 5,000 support people living in State College—"professors and bartenders, whatever," Reilly said. When the paper was sold to Knight-Ridder, however, about 33,000 students were enrolled at the campus in State College; the borough itself had 36,000 residents; the county's population had reached 112,000; and 30 percent of the workers in the State College–Bellefonte labor market were employed by Penn State in one way or another.

From the beginning, the *Times* had contrasting audiences to reach and satisfy. Besides the college-oriented audience and the blue-collar residents of Bellefonte, its circulation area included strip miners in the lumpy north of the county and farmers in the broad valleys between the Appalachian ridges. Reilly says that by the time of the sale at least 60 percent of the circulation was in State College and the surrounding townships, with the balance in Bellefonte and the rural areas. The contrast in readers and its own changes over the years have given the paper a split personality in what it covers and how it should cover things. This problem still bothers some editors and reporters.

In addition to a slowly growing full-time staff, the paper acquired as many as forty county correspondents—stringers who sent in personals and other items. Weinstein stressed that the *Times* readers were not and had never been predominantly Penn State faculty members. Even among those connected with the university, readers were more likely to be secretaries or janitors—people who had less formal education. "Not all of the subscribers of the *Times* 'read or carry' the *New York Times*, the *Wall Street Journal* or the *Washington Post*," Weinstein said. The *Centre Daily Times* tried to give them as much local news as possible.

"I think we gave it all," Weinstein said, "all that there was. . . . We tried to reach everyone. That's not saying we tried to be everything to everyone. We tried to write in such a manner that the Ph.D. in English wouldn't laugh at the way we wrote, and at the same time so that the coal miner with an eighth-grade education in Philipsburg would be able to understand what we were saying. It was not an easy job. But I think we succeeded, if for no other reason than we grew through the forty-three years that I was there."

As circulation grew, ad revenue grew, even though advertising was not pursued as aggressively as Knight-Ridder later would. From the late 1960s until the mid-1970s, the *Times* had a burst of competition from a morning tabloid, the *Pennsylvania Mirror*. But the *Mirror*'s competitiveness for the advertising dollar weakened steadily until its demise. Two local radio stations were strong competitors, and the Penn State student daily and two distant television stations in Altoona and Johnstown also took pieces of the action. But there was only one local daily serving all of Centre County for most of those years.

Revenue figures for the *Times* could not be obtained from Reilly, Knight-Ridder, or the latter's 10-K form for 1979 filed with the Securities and Exchange Commission. But Reilly said that over the last ten years of pre–Knight-Ridder ownership the paper's earnings before income taxes were 22 or 23 percent. He said that in its circulation class it was among the most profitable, in at least the top 10 percent.

Toward the end of the 1970s, Weinstein and Reilly neared the retirement age of sixty-five. The paper had been eyed by outside parties for a number of years. It was a good time to sell—better than they thought, as it turned out, because the paper may not have fetched as high a price after the economy went sour again in 1980. Frank Gappa, Knight-Ridder's first publisher at the *Centre Daily Times*, said a proposal at that time for a new shopping mall with four department stores just outside State College "had a lot to do with the price the paper finally sold at." The mall plan was later aborted.

Weinstein and Reilly were at this time part owners in the parent company, Nittany Printing and Publishing Co. After World War II they had been given stock by the late owner and publisher, Claude G. Aikens, who was president of one of the largest banks in State College. His son, Charles Thomas Aikens II, had become the publisher. At the time of the sale, Reilly said, about 82 percent of the stock was held by Tom Aikens and his sister, Mary Ann. The balance was held by Reilly, Weinstein, the two Weinstein children, and the three Reilly children.

Weinstein said the sale price was $15.5 million. But he said there were "buy-backs," certain items that Knight-Ridder did not want that were bought back by Aikens, including the small Skimont ski area outside of State College, an airplane (Aikens is a pilot), and a sports car. The Knight-Ridder annual report for 1979 lists the paper's price simply as $14.5 million.

Reilly said there were other reasons for selling to Knight-Ridder besides the price, which he said was more than $1 million higher than a Gannett bid and far more than offers by three other parties: the Mead family interests, which run dailies in Erie and Warren, Pennsylvania; Richard M. Scaife, the Pennsylvania newspaper publisher and conservative activist; and Richard H. Mayer, publisher of the Johnstown daily and owner of a Johnstown television station. Reilly said Harte-Hanks and the owners of Pennsylvania's *Easton Express* also made nibbles, but far too late in the game. Reilly said that he and Weinstein—Aikens was an "inactive" publisher and generally went along with whatever the two suggested—felt that Knight-Ridder was "better for our area." Weinstein also said the paper had won many prizes in the past, and he and Reilly wanted to ensure its future under owners who were news people.

Weinstein said he declined an offer to stay on as editor beyond the end of January 1980, when he and Reilly retired. That was also the time Knight-Ridder installed Frank Gappa as publisher. Weinstein and Reilly protected their proteges on the *Times*, however. William L. Welch, Jr., for a number of years the managing editor, succeeded Weinstein as executive editor, and Steve Braver moved from classified ad manager to business manager. He became general manager when Reilly left.

One of the first things Knight-Ridder did was to spend money on the *Centre Daily Times*. Robert E. Orkand, who became publisher when Gappa resigned in November 1981, said more than $400,000 was spent for a front-end news and advertising VDT system, more than $100,000 for quarterfolding equipment to make possible a new television tab, and $120,000 for a computerized accounting and circulation information system. Whether the previous owners would have underwritten those investments, Orkand said, is hypothetical. "But the thing is, Knight-Ridder was willing to undertake it as an exercise in improving the product."

Orkand also noted that the *Times* had long had a press excellent for color. But the paper had used color sparingly. One of the annual entertainments for *Times* watchers was its big spreads of autumn foliage in black and white. Orkand said Knight-Ridder brought experts up from the *Miami Herald* to train *Times* personnel. The paper has used color extensively since.

Of keener interest to employees was Knight-Ridder's investment in the paper's human resources. Significant salary increases were made, especially to correct perceived inequities, and yet the salary situation was still the most galling problem to news staffers two years later. Management, for its part, made the point that when Knight-Ridder took over, salaries had a long way to go.

Weinstein is sensitive on this point. Ultimately, he said, the newspaper's yearly budget was Reilly's. "I used to scratch and fight for every nickel. . . . I usually got what I wanted." In fact, Weinstein said, the business side resented that Weinstein's news staff was paid better than ad representatives. Weinstein said the *Times*'s news salaries were higher than on comparable Pennsylvania papers, except Newspaper Guild papers. For small papers in Pennsylvania, Reilly said, "We weren't all that low. . . . We were in the ballpark." *Times* staffers thought in terms of Philadelphia, Harrisburg, and Pittsburgh salaries rather than comparable papers, he said. "We weren't as low as they thought."

Told that the staff had regarded him and Weinstein as tightfisted, Reilly replied: "Well, I think I was tightfisted, much more than Jerry was. Jerry would have been delighted to raise the salaries but. . . and then, I would have, too, but it was just like anything else, you look at the whole. . . . You have to be successful before you can publish a good newspaper. There has never been a record of a money-losing newspaper that was good and survived for any length of time. It just isn't in the books. . . . So you have to somehow have the wherewithal to do the things that you want to do. You've got your choices."

Weinstein said he always tried to increase salaries, but added, "Reilly was of a school—pay them as little as we can." The former editor said he did have a five-year plan to increase new salaries, but President Nixon's freeze on wage increases in the early 1970s "killed us," and salaries never caught up. Even after the freeze, he said, Reilly worked up a plan to increase salaries that were inordinately low. It helped, but it was too late by then, Weinstein said.

Just before the purchase by Knight-Ridder, Weinstein said, "very few" reporters and other editorial employees were making less than $10,000 a year (about $194 a week), and two or three of the news staff were in the $14,000 to $15,000 ($269 to $288 a week) range. The paper had no real copy desk—copy was processed mostly by the news editor and managing editor—so there were no copy editors with a higher differential than reporters. Weinstein said that despite his wishes the paper never paid overtime, but instead gave compensatory time off, which, he added, was preferred by some on the staff, particularly the married women with children.

"My feelings on salaries are contradictory," Weinstein said. "I was proud that they were higher than most, but I also was ashamed of them. I think that newspaper employees—I'm only interested in the news and editorial side—were when I was still there, and perhaps still are, in the same position that school teachers were ten or fifteen years ago or nurses twenty years ago or policemen ten years ago . . . I just think they are not paid enough money to reflect that responsibility. . . . I think it goes back to the bad old days when we started at eighteen dollars a week in the thirties, and we worked up from there." (Weinstein said he left the *Times* for a brief period before World War II for more money with the Associated Press.)

When Gappa, who had been editor of the Knight-Ridder paper in Boulder, Colorado, for many years and briefly part of management at the group's Duluth paper, came to State College, the *Times* had thirty-one or thirty-two news-editorial employees, of whom ten were reporters, four sports writers, three photographers, and three editors. (It was down to twenty-eight full-time equivalents at the end of 1981.) Gappa and Orkand, his successor as publisher, both said Knight-Ridder considers that number a strong commitment to staff size for a paper of the *Times*'s circulation. But Gappa said, "I was really shocked at the salary schedule." He and Welch restructured the salary schedule and made selective increases for certain people. "Salaries were very low," Gappa said, "and not comparable to other small newspapers even in Pennsylvania, as far as I was concerned. It was a real problem."

Welch said he doubted the salary increases made would have occurred if the paper had remained under the same ownership, "certainly not" under Reilly. "He just wouldn't have gone for it. So that is a Knight-Ridder benefit. You've got to remember that under the old regime we didn't do budgets. We had no looking ahead in any organized fashion."

But Welch said the increase over the first two years of Knight-Ridder ownership had not reached the point at which he thought salaries should be. "Fifteen percent of nothing," he said, "is still nothing." Publisher Orkand said a quantum jump in pay for everyone would have been ruinous for operating profit. Where the paper wanted to motivate certain staff members to perform better, he said, "we are moving at a more measured pace."

The perceptions of many news staffers about the salary situation is reflected in the comments of Jane C. Musala, a highly regarded young reporter whose beat, including State College borough hall, is probably the most important.

"One of the things that we were very excited about when Knight-Ridder took over was that we felt they had a commitment to the quality of the paper and that they had a commitment to their employees," she said. "In the editorial end, I don't think you'll find very many people who will say that anymore." The staff was not satisfied with the slowed pace of the salary catch-up, she said. "To make matters worse, under the Reilly system we felt that *everybody* was getting screwed. We felt that if anything we had somewhat of an advocate in Jerome [Weinstein], not much but somewhat; but now there is becoming a class structure. Knight-Ridder is putting money into the money-making end of the paper—the advertising end, the circulation end, the accounting end."

Musala said she could understand why the paper would try to more aggressively pursue the advertising dollar. "But at the same time we are seeing the advertising people get richer, we feel that we're getting poorer." Besides salaries, she mentioned the loss of a key reporter whose position was not filled for months, the unwillingness of the paper to pay overtime to news staffers except for exceptional circumstances (while routinely paying overtime to a circulation district manager), and earlier deadlines that "wreak havoc" with the reporters but benefit other departments. "We are being expected to bite the bullet . . . when it seems, at least, that money is being spent willingly in those other departments." Problems in other departments should be solved in those departments, Musala said, "not by coming to where labor is cheaper, because we don't get paid overtime, and asking us to reconstruct our schedules." (Since this writing, Musala has left the *Times* to work for another paper.)

Terry Dalton, an enterprising reporter who has covered county government and politics since starting with the *Times* in the early 1970s, also said he expected the staff would have seen more money with the advent of Knight-Ridder. "If they really wanted to keep reporters who were good, one would think they would pay them more. That hasn't happened to any great extent. One of the more disappointing things about Knight-Ridder is that they have not shown much of a commitment to improving and expanding the staff. We still have a tendency to not replace someone at all." He cited the failure to replace two and a half staff positions after the first Knight-Ridder "contingency" cutback was ordered, though he acknowledged these were not all the most productive people. "So that commitment to staff, not only in terms of money, but in terms of not just letting people go but replacing them with better people" is inadequate.

Nobody at the *Times* denies that advertising salespeople are making more money than news staffers with comparable time on the job. The difference is that the paper started paying commissions under Knight-Ridder as incentive for salespeople to more aggressively pursue advertising. While the ad staff also was increased in number, General Manager Braver said the most important difference has been in the caliber of persons hired.

"We used to pay our salesmen a flat salary, which is the antithesis of sales effort, and it was a lousy salary. You would come in, and you were paid to show up, and if you brought in a million inches you got paid the same as if you brought in fifty inches. So we instituted a commission system where the sky is the limit. . . . If they produce, they get paid."

Under local ownership, he said, the salary to start was $550 to $600 a month, and the highest paid salesperson was making about $1,200 a month. A raise might be $50 a month for the year, which "didn't lead anybody to aspire, to achieve," Braver said. Under Knight-Ridder, the base salary for a beginner would be from $10,000 to $11,000 and, Braver said, a really good salesperson could double that salary in commissions. Realistically, he said, the salesperson should make $4,000 to $5,000 in commissions in the first year on the job. He said an experienced salesperson would be hired at a base salary of $13,000 to $14,000 and should make an extra $7,000 to $8,000 in commissions. Any salesperson who wants "the good things in life" can now get it, Braver said, by going out and selling ad linage.

Braver said the starting salaries for reporters and ad salespeople are "fairly close" (the news people are starting at "ten something"). The difference, he said, is in the commissions. The young general manager, who said he regards Reilly and Weinstein as "uncle figures," seemed more exhilarated over the change in ownership than anyone interviewed. The most exciting change, he said, has been the opportunity for individuals to improve themselves.

"One of the liabilities of a small, family-owned newspaper," he said, "is nobody is exactly bending over backwards to bring their people to a level of excellence. You kind of get in the trap of—from the owners' point of view—'we're making good money, we're doing the job, people are buying our paper, therefore we must be doing a good job.' You get in almost to, 'we're doing good enough.'"

There was a very limited ability for people at the *Times* to mix with others in the industry, Braver said. In fifteen years before the sale, he was sent to one ad managers' conference, at Erie, and he did not think it was very good. "I didn't know what the state of the art was." Knight-Ridder has sent him to conferences and to a dozen other papers, and he has exchanged ideas with many other executives. "Our thrust [under the old ownership] was 'If we keep costs down, we can control that, we can control costs. We're not sure about revenue . . . therefore, if we keep our costs to a minimum, we'll do as well as we can.' There wasn't much in the way of 'what can we do to maximize our revenue?' as much as 'what can we do to minimize our costs?'—and that is kind of a stifling way to operate." In the old days, he said, employees literally had to sign out pencils.

Others besides Braver are now sent to take courses. Authorities are also brought in to State College for training sessions.

Under the new ownership, there is pressure to come in at a certain profit level, but how the executives at the paper do it is up to them, Braver said. "In fact, the gauge of who are the bright, rising managers is, 'Are they creative enough to do it?'" In the past, he said, the *Times* hired salespeople who would not get sick and would simply go out and collect the ads. People he hired since Knight-Ridder have been ones who can aggressively sell ads, Braver said. (Commenting on this strategy, Reilly said, "A small town is not a place for a hard sell." He cited mom-and-pop stores as an example.)

After Gappa joined the *Times* as the first Knight-Ridder publisher, ad rates were increased more sharply than usual—an average of 9 percent in 1980 and 12 percent in 1981; the page width was cut from thirty inches to twenty-nine inches, and in 1982, to twenty-eight inches (in effect, a rate increase by another name). In addition, the number of inches required per month to get a long-term reduced rate was doubled to thirty. But Gappa said he believed *Times* rates had been lower than those of comparable papers and that the *Times* could get the higher rates.

Asked whether Knight-Ridder gave the local papers guidelines for ad rates and overall profits, Gappa replied: "They pretty well give you guidelines. The 18 to 22 percent is a standard in the industry for operating profit relating to revenue for papers of this size. . . . We firm those up at the local level and say, 'Yes, we can stick with the guidelines or even do better,' or 'No, we can't make that because of the local economic situation or the loss of an advertiser or a department store closing.'"

Advertisers did not like the increases, Gappa said, but he added, "Where could they go?" As for the smaller businesses in State College, he said with a laugh, "I felt that if a small advertiser can't afford seventy-five dollars a month to advertise their business down on College Avenue, they shouldn't be in business."

On the other hand, the *Times* staff began to offer an artist's services to spruce up ads and to give better advice on how to make ads more effective. The more sophisticated advertisers, ones with some education in marketing, were understanding about the rate increases, Braver said, and although they did not like the increases, they simply demanded that the paper deliver the goods. The serious complainers, he added, were advertisers to whom ads are an overhead cost, not a tool.

Some merchants still grumble about the 9 and 12 percent display ad rate increases in 1980 and 1981, said Ted Connolly, president of the Downtown Business Association in State College. He is manager and a part owner of the Student Book Store, a large establishment across the street from the Penn State campus, which sells collegiate gimcrackery as well as books and supplies. Personally, he said, he did not advertise much in the *Times*, but might if asked. He said his store had yet to see Braver's aggressive pursuit of advertising. Connolly said, however, that the downtown merchants, many of whom are small operators, feel the *Times* "is not giving us breaks to keep us advertising—kind of take it or leave it."

One of the largest advertisers in the paper is Danks, a small department store chain with stores in downtown State College, a perimeter mall, and Bellefonte. The general manager for those stores, George A. Morgan, said Danks had "no problem" with the rate increases and that, given the *Times*'s circulation, its rates were not too high. Morgan also noted that advertising involved more than rates. He said market studies showed that the changes at the *Times* were "going in the right direction in terms of using advertising dollars more effectively." He praised the paper's change to Saturday morning publication, the sectioning of the paper that permits Danks to break its weekend advertising in a more timely manner, the increased use of color, and the long-range plan to publish a Sunday edition. The paper's advertising department, Morgan said, showed more interest and was "receptive to ideas."

The first two years of Knight-Ridder ownership were poor ones for the economy, however, and classified linage was down, although display linage grew. Overall revenue grew slightly, Braver said, but costs of newsprint, ink, film, and benefits soared. For instance, he said, the first-year cost of a revised pension plan was 89 percent higher than it was the year before (though unionized backshop employees were reportedly charging that the plan did not offer the improvements claimed by management). In addition, the paper had not yet been able to make efficient use of new computerized data processing equipment because of inadequate manpower and expertise, Braver said. The paper was, in fact, criticized for that by headquarters after an audit of operations in the summer of 1981. Asked whether Knight-Ridder had been forgiving, Braver replied that it was "understanding."

But the most important change at the *Times* was the opening of new horizons, he reiterated. "I really like this company [Knight-Ridder]. It's not important whether they really mean that they have the individual's best interests at heart. They have to do that because they constantly have people retire and die, and they have to have new phalanxes of people rising up through the ranks to take their places, because this industry is being bitten at the heels by cable, by shoppers, by mailers. . . . If you're good, they have to move you because it is in their own interest." (Braver has, in fact, recently moved upward in the ranks of Knight-Ridder himself.)

Braver said circulation increased about one thousand (about 5 percent) in the first year under Knight-Ridder, but went down a couple of hundred in 1981 as the result of an audit by the Audit Bureau of Circulations, to which the *Times* had not belonged before Knight-Ridder. "We have a lot of ghost subscribers. We'd give papers out the door, and the carrier would get ten extra for his route, and he'd throw them in the garbage. There was no way to check. We had a manual system, twelve to thirteen thousand little three-by-five cards that have the names on them. Some of them would be outmoded for ten years. It was expensive to audit—you had to pay salaries to do it, so we didn't do it that often." The paper is now computerizing its circulation lists. In the number of "real people" who now get the paper delivered to them, the *Times*'s circulation may actually be up eighteen hundred since the purchase, Braver estimated.

But readers do not judge newspapers by ad linage and operating profit. Do readers believe that the *Times* has changed for the better in its news and editorial functions? Since no systematic readership surveys were taken before and after, it is difficult to describe the public's judgment. Reactions in letters to the editor and in comments received by people who work for the *Times* have been mixed. By and large, however, the reaction apparently has been positive. Cosmetic improvements in departmentalizing, sectioning, and packaging improved accessibility and appearance, readers have said. But there certainly have been dissenters. In the eyes of some, for instance, the *Times* has remained amazingly deficient in bona fide local hard-news photos.

Two important officials who saw the *Times*'s new policy of shortening government stories as a disservice to the public are Councilwoman Mary Ann

Haas, a former president of the State College Borough Council, and Borough Manager Carl B. Fairbanks, the borough's chief executive. They said the policy limited not only details, but adequate explanations of the broader issues. Fairbanks also said the council and borough hall were usually covered by young reporters relatively inexperienced in local government affairs. One result, he said, was that news stories about borough government also included instances of editorial commentary; editors at the *Times,* he added, were not reading the copy closely. Haas and Fairbanks also said they regretted the loss of other local news coverage—not "personals" but news of nongovernmental organizations. Haas said she would rather see more of that than the "frivolous" human interest wire and syndicated material that had, in part, been substituted. Fairbanks said that for Centre County some of the "local folksy stuff" was appropriate, but if the *Times* wanted to eliminate it, the substituted material should be stories of substance, such as those offered by the New York Times News Service. Arnold Addison, the part-time mayor of State College, said he is satisfied with the detail and fairness of *Times* government coverage. But he said he regrets elimination of publicity photos, such as proclamation signings, not because he needs the publicity but because the cancer fund and other charity drives no longer benefit from that exposure.

Those who work at the *Times* were sometimes ambivalent in describing the changes. Many said the *Times* was and is a good paper compared to others its size. Moments later they would describe serious flaws.

Editor Welch said lack of packaging was the paper's biggest problem. But he was optimistic about the changes.

"We had sort of become slaves to the community organizations," Welch said. "While we were pruning what we did for them every year, they still very much dominated our coverage. And I'm not sure prior to the Knight-Ridder ownership that any of us here really perceived that as an evil, necessarily." But Gappa brought the message that the *Times* should be a well-rounded newspaper, not just a local one. Welch said the paper still tried to cover the local organizations, but had freed up more space for other news by reducing check-passing photos and the length of the organization stories. The paper is now consciously laid out. Before Knight-Ridder, the only news page that was made up was the front page. The rest was thrown together by the backshop.

In the past, Welch said, the old regime feared to do things with the paper that might "produce explosions." Referring to news-editorial material itself, Welch commented: "I had become increasingly uncomfortable with the sort of negative stance that we had fallen into. We spent more time in keeping things out of the paper, in some senses, than we did putting them in—and I don't mean we were censoring them or anything of the sort." Not endorsing political candidates was an example, he said. "I wanted to open it up. I would rather be criticized for something I ran than for something I didn't run."

Another example, he said, was business-related news, which after Gappa arrived, was covered much more thoroughly and packaged on one page. The paper's newshole remained about the same, with 55 to 60 percent ads.

But, partly at Gappa's insistence, stories were tightened. "I still believe that a paper like this has to be a paper of record, but not every little detail," he said. By the end of 1981, reporters were not allowed to write longer than fifteen inches, except with permission. Gappa said the *Times* made strong progress toward improving both writing and coverage. "But there is still a long way to go for this newspaper. If I could put it on a scale of one to ten, we might be at six right now with four to go. . . . We still need some stronger staffers, quality staffers."

In late 1981 Brian Weakland, a reporter who had resigned that summer to attend law school, described this scene in the *Times* newsroom, the details of which were only slightly different in the testimony of other staffers:

> Under the Aikens regime, the news coverage amounted to whatever four or five reporters felt like writing and to whatever news releases came in the mail. There was little, if any, cohesion between the news desk and the reporting staff. Because the desk was overworked processing whatever drivel seeped through the mail slot, the reporters were for the most part left alone. These were the best of times for reporters, but probably the worst of times for readers who relied on the *Times* for total news coverage. Because the desk job was sheer drudgery and the reporting job total freedom, the senior members on the staff tended to be reporters while the rookies were copy editors. This created a lack-of-authority problem, which exists to this day. Commands from the news desk are rebuffed, and reporters rely on each other for direction and criticism. . . . News coverage changes under Knight-Ridder are more form than substance. More innovative layout, the use of color, and better packaging on display pages have attracted and captured the attention of more readers to stories that in earlier years would have been camouflaged by stalagmitelike ad holes.

Managing Editor Bill Blair, who generally gets good grades from both management and staffers, said the big change when Knight-Ridder took over was that the news department was able to do what it wanted to put out what it thought was a quality paper. "They took the lid off," he said, though the deteriorating economy forced the group to back off somewhat. He said he would like a third photographer, two or three more reporters, and possibly some good stringers. He described the changes in use of color and packaging as remarkable. He contrasted Knight-Ridder's commitment to editorial excellence with his experience working as an editor in the Thomson chain at Pennsylvania's *Connellsville Daily Courier*. "There was no editorial commitment there at all, no editorial focus, no instructions, no nothing. It was just lousy. Compared to Knight-Ridder, Thomson is the pits to work for. Knight-Ridder stresses editorial quality."

At the same time, he said, Knight-Ridder executives would not advise him on what editorial decisions he should make, but instead provided him with resources or resource people to help him make decisions. He said both Weinstein and Welch had tried to get certain commitments for more space, for more use of color, and for packaging, but had been unable to get them before Knight-Ridder.

Gappa and Blair stressed the commitment the new management had made to setting up a full-time copy desk. Before, Blair said, "It was a one-person copy pusher. It resembled nothing of a newspaper." Karen Lobeck, who had held an editing position on a small midwestern paper, was hired as city editor, and copy editor positions were filled by members of the staff. At the end of 1981, the desk was still a problem and was still being restructured, but a start had been made toward improving editorial direction.

Knight-Ridder also had influenced the paper by *not* doing certain things. Specifically, the editorial leadership of the *Times* still bore the stamp of Jerry Weinstein. This had an important effect—in a passive way—on how *Times* stories were written. Except for a brief stint with the Associated Press in Philadelphia and Harrisburg, Weinstein never worked under any bosses except those at the *Times*. Weinstein hired Bill Welch, an English major at Penn State in the 1960s, after Welch caught his eye as an intern. Welch essentially never worked for any editor except Weinstein. In 1974 Blair also impressed Weinstein as an English department intern from Penn State. When the internship was finished, Blair wrote a "beautiful" column about how the *Times* was "put out with love" by the staff, Weinstein said. He kept an eye on Blair when he went to Pittsburgh to work on a chain of suburban weeklies and then when Blair became an editor at Connellsville. Weinstein hired Blair during the interim between the sale in 1979 and his retirement at the end of January 1980.

Although Blair and Welch did some realigning of the staff to make better use of talents, neither they nor staffers said the coverage changed significantly with respect to accuracy, which they gave high marks, or depth (the paper rarely indulged in classic investigative reporting). The staff was urged to do more "people" stories and more features about local government activities. To a limited extent this was done. But the staff had, if anything, shrunk slightly so that staffers complained they did not have time to write enough "people" and feature stories and adequately cover various governmental bodies, too.

Blair was seen as a plus by the staff in bringing some order to the coverage and in sometimes assisting and directing the staff. One staffer wished Blair had more influence. The same staffer said the prevailing view among the reporters was that neither Weinstein nor Welch was an effective editor, that they did not "know news," and that they tried to please everyone and so pleased no one. Blair, the staffer said, was a newsman who got excited over stories, understood what news was, and gave guidance on how to cover it. He knew the paper had problems and discussed them with the staff, something the staff had not seen before. "It was active, not passive" editorial guidance.

Blair, the staffer said, also encouraged the staff to write in "our style" and to featurize the news. Because copy had been touched so little, the *Times,* at least in the 1970s, had always had reporters who wrote with distinctive styles. Some of the reporters' styles were dry and tedious, and the paper missed legitimate opportunities to sharpen leads and include color. At the other extreme, some reporters produced sophomoric leads that left the reader laughing at the reporter instead of "relating" to the story. After Knight-Ridder, the questionable feature leads markedly increased (though the change was really due, at least in part, to Knight-Ridder's tinkering so little with the Weinstein editorial team). Such leads included:

> Last night's State College Area School Board meeting was a lot like Grange Fair's wheel of fortune—around and around and around it goes, where it stops—nobody knows.
>
> Nobody, except for board president Duane J. Doty, who should be named to the parliamentary procedure hall of fame for keeping up with whose motion was on whose amendment—or was it the other way around?

and:

> Faces reflecting skepticism, impatience, and frustration abounded in a University classroom yesterday, but this was no drama course and no one guaranteed a happy ending.

In the latter instance, after giving four more fat paragraphs of background, the reporter spotted and described in the sixth paragraph the "principal concern expressed repeatedly" during the meeting. Summarized, this concern could have grabbed the reader in the lead.

While some *Times* reporters were pleased at the encouragement to get beneath the surface of the news and to write in what they considered a lively style, not all of the reporters agreed the results were effective—even though the "our style" leads were the ones the editors usually pinned on the newsroom bulletin board. One staffer, whose leads had been criticized by Blair as not catchy enough, said, "I'd rather be dry and correct than flashy and wrong." Another reporter noted that feature leads can be effective, especially on second-day stories. At other times "you often fall flat on your face."

There seems to be a presumption among some *Times* editors and reporters that hard *news* is inherently dull rather than *news*worthy. Far too many leads are written as if they were *all* second-day stories when the pitiful news competition of two radio stations hardly justifies it. The short lead that goes crisply to the heart of the story—followed by a couple of "bang-bang" paragraphs of relevant facts or sharp quotes that support the lead—seems little appreciated at the *Times*. The forced feature leads too often ignore the drama inherent in hard news.

The result of the *Times*'s attempts is too often a rocking-chair journalism. In the first few paragraphs, the reporter ruminates *about* the news instead of saying what the news *is*. But how much "people-ization" of the news can the impatient reader stand? How much triviality?

Blair agreed there was an attempt to liven *Times* copy and to put feature leads on hard news. "There is once in a while where maybe it doesn't come off, but I'd rather run the risk in that sense. I'd rather make sure the reader gets a crack at a story. You have to use your common sense, obviously." He said he had not seen a paper in which feature leads always worked on all stories. "I don't think I've seen any newspaper that has done that so thoroughly that you can't quibble every once in a while with their leads."

The matter of featurizing news copy goes deeper, however, than mere quibbling over leads. When the reporter thinks the object of livening up the copy means being clever in the lead, he usually ends by interpreting what happened. By its nature, interpretation usually involves opinion. Few reporters, especially inexperienced ones, are capable of consistently writing interpretive leads that are not arguable at best, or at worst, dead wrong.

R. Thomas Berner, a youthful former city editor under Weinstein and Welch, is a close observer. He left the *Times* in 1975 to teach reporting and editing courses at Penn State and has since published a book called *Language Skills for Journalists*. While acknowledging the cosmetic changes in the paper, he said the *Times* was not really packaging or laying out the paper effectively and was not making proper use of its new high-speed wire—playing stories on page one without update even when they had broken on television the night before; not summarizing world and national news enough on the second page; and not playing enough local stories on page one. Aside from the editorials, he said, there had been no great changes in substance. Follow-ups and depth stories were not done because beat reporters did not have the time, he said, and the *Times* still never upset advertisers or established figures in the community. From Penn State, the dominant factor in the community, the *Times* only wanted features, not coverage in a "hard" sense, Berner said.

Asked about the editorial leadership of the paper, Berner replied: "I'm in a quandary, because personally I like Bill Welch. . . . It has been 'proven' that a company, organization, is a reflection of its leadership. The *Times* is the kind of paper that Bill Welch wants it to be. . . . There are chances the paper could get better. One of Bill's shortcomings is that he hasn't worked for any other newspaper in his entire life, and I think until recently he had very limited contact with other journalists or other journalistic issues. . . . I don't think he reads the trade publications that closely. I'm sure he has great disdain for journalism education. . . . I think he's more interested in running a birthday column that has the correct birthdays in it than whether or not his reporters are doing outstanding reporting on their beats. . . . He's learned a great deal—or he hasn't learned a great deal, as the case may be—from Jerry [Weinstein] and that's his limited vision."

Berner described as "pretty much horrible" the way news was written in the *Times*. "I don't think the *Times* is a very well-edited newspaper, and therefore it cannot be a well-written newspaper." There are very few writers in daily journalism who produce outstanding prose day in and day out, Berner said. "The better writers in journalism, however, produce some fairly decent prose. And then I happen to believe the copy desk improves that—and that's what I don't see at the *Times*. I don't see editors protecting the reporters from their vices or their excesses. . . . I don't think any of the reporters at the *Times* have any clear idea of what's expected of them, and that falls to the editing process."

Some staffers said they were disappointed Knight-Ridder did not bring in experienced, better qualified professionals to run the paper. Publisher Orkand, a career army officer who joined the business side of Knight-Ridder in 1974 but had edited a magazine and a book while at the Pentagon, said he was very happy with the news-editorial team at the *Times*. According to Orkand: "Why bring in someone who does not know the area? Better to give these people their head, but make available to them all the resources of a big company like Knight-Ridder. . . . The assumption would be that given the resources, given their prior experience and training, given their knowledge of the community, and bringing in as the oversight a man like Frank Gappa, . . . let that management team function . . . and I think the paper came a long way." He cited the reorganization of the copy desk and the specific assignment of tasks to the top editors.

But Orkand said the *Times* cannot afford to attract the skilled professionals that a large paper could. "We don't have big dollars to spend for a copy editor . . . so the best way to do that is to develop an ingrown talent through training, through management, through leadership, and through a progressive system of promotions." He said the paper had a comparable talent situation on the business side, though he noted that the paper "did have to go outside to attract an advertising manager," who was first brought in as a retail manager because there had been none and was subsequently promoted to the top advertising position. "But it is just so frightfully expensive to bring people in, because Knight-Ridder pays for moving and transportation costs and that sort of thing, that you really can't afford to be as professional as you would like." He added that staffers with roots in the community can write knowledgeably about it.

Although some staffers are bothered by what they perceive as Welch's limited news qualifications, he presided over an almost universally praised change on the editorial page: The paper began to take definite and sometimes strong stands on issues, local and national. Weinstein said he had received a bum rap from readers who believe he took no stands. Merely to pick a subject and write an editorial about it is to take a stand, he stated. Furthermore, the paper did have some editorial campaigns over the years, but by and large editorial writers cannot get away with telling people what to think today, he said. In a move that produced more criticism than any other change since the sale, the *Times* began endorsing candidates in the 1981 primary. Weinstein, although noting that the paper had on occasion endorsed candidates in the past, said he did not know whether it was a good idea. He noted there has been disagreement in the profession over whether papers should endorse.

Staffers said the stronger editorial voice had little to do with Knight-Ridder but was simply a consequence of Welch taking over. One of his moves was to ask Carol Herrmann, the competent reporter who was developing the new business beat, to also share editorial writing duties with him. They have written with distinction in a tradition of moderation. "A newspaper has a leadership responsibility in terms of trying to let readers know its views on happenings in the community," Herrmann said, "because theoretically the newspaper should be closer to what's going on than the average person in the community." She said Welch believed an editorial should give an opinion and wanted the editorial page to be a place where issues were debated. (Herrmann has since left the *Times* to take a non-journalism position at Penn State.)

One staffer, expressing respect for Welch, said that he has "a moral center that makes me very comfortable"—that even though Welch feels an editor should not tell reporters what to do and believes in giving them a lot of freedom, "I'm not so interested in being directed by Bill as I am in having an editor who I think is fair and moral and committed to truth and openness, and I think he is."

Would the changes during the Knight-Ridder transition, particularly the cosmetic ones such as packaging, have been made anyway without new ownership? As one staffer commented: "Who would have made the changes? . . . There is nothing I ever saw before Knight-Ridder came that would have suggested to me those changes would have been made." The changes were made at a price for the community, when grip-and-grin photo requests were denied, and at a price for the staff, which had to work harder to put out a more professional paper. Changes, if any, would have been made much more slowly. "I sensed a lot of insistence from Knight-Ridder. . . . The motivation to get rid of all that 'crap' came from Knight-Ridder. . . . The packaging of the paper was an area that they were willing to exert their influence and say 'this is how it should be done.' In terms of 'cover this meeting' or 'don't cover this meeting' or 'we want to see this philosophy or that philosophy,' so far as I know they've kept hands off."

Active or not, the Knight-Ridder influence had resulted in improvements. Perhaps the most important question for readers was how much more progress the *Times* staff would make in its ability to recognize what is quality newspapering and what is not.

By mid-1983 readers had been systematically polled by the *Centre Daily Times* and some additional changes had been made. The Saturday morning edition had been killed and a Sunday edition born. Then the Saturday morning edition was reborn, ostensibly in response to persistent reader complaints, and into it was shoveled, in a nicely laid-out way, puff pieces of local organizations and individuals. That material was still limited in other editions. The Sunday paper was crammed with ads and both canned and local fluff, although the new space was helpful in giving news staffers an occasional opportunity to do extra features and analyses. The Sunday and daily editions excelled, however, in wire coverage of Hollywood and television show-business personalities and media freaks in general.

But there had been no real progress in further improving the quality of local news coverage, news writing or editing, despite continued infusions from the nearby Penn State School of Journalism of some good raw talent to replace defectors. The quality of the editorials declined somewhat and, perhaps coincidentally, there seemed to be an outbreak of pious self-adulation in the editorial column that was reminiscent of the old regime. The newsroom people still complained of overwork and poor pay. Stretched further by the needs of the new Sunday edition and the reborn Saturday edition, there was little time to improve reporting and writing, and too little time for the hard-working editing staff to do the best job even if the *Times* had had the best editors.

By mid-1983 it appeared that the strength of the new *Times*—except for coverage of the entertainment industry—was not in journalism, but in merchandising.

Delta Democrat-Times

Lloyd Gray and Tony Tharp

P eople in Greenville, Mississippi—a Mississippi River community of forty thousand—have always prided themselves on being a little different, which is saying something in a state where the different historically have been viewed with suspicion, if not outright hostility.

The late Hodding Carter, who won a Pulitzer Prize largely because he was different, and eloquently so, knew about it firsthand. He called Greenville an "oasis." He wrote about "the kindliness and a rare toleration, a respect for the dissenter and the dissimilar, which are the spiritual hallmarks of my town."

The fertile flatlands from which the town springs were the birthplace of the blues. Before Carter even laid eyes on Greenville, it had endured plagues of yellow fever, purged itself of the Ku Klux Klan, and spent three months under six feet of water in the worst flood of the twentieth century. It was to nourish the talents of a half dozen writers and poets of rank, including the novelist Walker Percy.

But it was Carter's newspaper that would put Greenville on the map.

When his two sons and widow and longtime business partner sold the *Delta Democrat-Times* to the California-based Freedom Newspapers group in 1980, the final chapter was written in one of the most colorful stories in the history of American journalism. The saga had begun more than four decades earlier and had been marked by an abundance of courage, commitment, and love.

The bold, Pulitzer Prize–winning editorials penned by "Big Hodding" earned for the smalltown newspaper a reputation that extended far beyond its home in a region known as the Mississippi Delta. With a voice that decried injustice, Carter plowed straight across the segregationist orthodoxy of his adopted state. "One half of Mississippi's population," wrote Carter, in a withering denouncement of the South's plantation mentality, "receives in general less consideration than a smart planter gives to a mule."

Such talk was heresy in the 1940s, of course. Big Hodding's writing swathed the *Delta Democrat-Times* in a missionary aura that would remain with it through the 1970s. It was not so much the sale of the paper, then, that stunned both friends and foes of the Carters, but rather to whom it was sold. It would be hard to imagine a more unlikely successor to the Carter legacy than Freedom Newspapers, a group of thirty-one daily newspapers in sixteen states with a circulation of nearly eight hundred thousand. Freedom, which also owns two nondailies and two television stations, had been founded seventy-five years before in Ohio by R. C. Hoiles, whose family members still own the stock in the closely held corporation. The group's primary characteristics are a thoroughly libertarian, antigovernment editorial position and a penchant for running financially successful, if journalistically undistinguished, newspapers. In short, it seemed to many that the Carters had sold out in more ways than one. The price, though undisclosed by the principals, is reported by insiders to have been $18 million, which at more than $1,000 per subscriber would be a record for an American newspaper. (Although the publisher's sworn statement for October 3, 1979, put daily circulation at 17,905, Freedom says the circulation was really 15,600 at the time of the sale.)

Carter loyalists were disappointed. As one said, however, "I can say I wouldn't have done it, but then nobody ever offered me $18 million for something of mine." Others trying to uphold their image of the Carters took comfort in the widely circulated story that John Gibson, the tight-fisted business manager who had helped keep the paper afloat during sporadic boycotts over the years, had wanted to unload his 25 percent of ownership and had engineered the sale to Freedom. It is a matter of revered lore among old staffers at the *Democrat-Times* that reporters were not given new pencils without first turning in their well-worn stubs to Gibson. And the story now is that Gibson's maneuvers to unload his shares put the Carter family in the position of being unable to refuse an offer that unexpectedly met their asking price.

The sale came a half century after Carter began his sojourn through the distinctive world of Southern newspapers. From the swampy bottomlands of south Louisiana, a terse telegram sent by the twenty-three-year-old writer to his sweetheart, Betty Werlien, marks the start of the journey. "Get measured for wedding gown. Sold short story to *American Magazine* for $300." The young couple hoped to use the money from "Brothers Under the Skin" to finance a year in Mexico, freeing Carter from a thirty-dollar-a-week newspaper job and giving him a chance to write. But that was not to be. Instead, the story helped catapult him to a fifty-dollar-a-week job with the Associated Press. When Carter was fired a few weeks later—for "insubordination," he would later write—the newlyweds took their savings of about four hundred dollars to Hammond, Louisiana, and founded a daily newspaper.

In Hammond the Carters were to undergo a journalistic baptism by fire in encounters with the forces of Huey P. Long, governor and then United States senator who ruled Louisiana politics. The little daily they had started and kept alive was one of the few voices raised in protest against the dictatorial "Kingfish." Carter's writing soon attracted the attention of Walker Percy's cousin and adopted father, William Alexander Percy, the author of six volumes of lyric poetry and the autobiography, *Lanterns on the Levee*. A genteel lawyer-planter and an enterprising civic leader, Percy loathed Greenville's listless *Daily Democrat-Times*. Along with a few friends, Percy enticed the Carters to sell the *Hammond Daily Courier* and come to Greenville to start a new paper that would compete with the *Democrat-Times*.

With the first edition of the *Delta Star* on November 19, 1936, Carter made it clear in a front-page editorial that he would not straddle the tough issues. "Our editorial columns are our own," he wrote, "and when the occasions present themselves, the editor of the *Star* will write with both legs on the same side of the fence." Within two years the upstart newspaper had swallowed up the rival *Daily Democrat-Times*. On September 1, 1938, Greenville saw the first edition of the *Delta Democrat-Times*. The newspaper would build a reputation as one of the liveliest and gutsiest little papers in the country while standing virtually alone in Mississippi as a voice of reason during a time when raw emotion prevailed.

There was a period, long since past, when the *Democrat-Times* stood apart from other newspapers in Mississippi and much of the South, not only for its courageous editorial stance against racial injustice, but also for its aggressive and all-inclusive pursuit of the news as well.

Carter became a legendary figure as his battles against the established political and social order elicited cries of denunciation from well beyond the outer reaches of his paper's circulation area. Much of his writing was unequivocally opposed to the mainstream of Southern thought. "For seventy-five years," wrote Carter in a typical editorial, "we sent the Negro kids to school in hovels and pig pens, and even now we kid ourselves when we say we are approaching equality." The Mississippi House of Representatives in 1955 even passed a resolution condemning him for deviation from the officially sanctioned segregationist orthodoxy. The hot-headed editor stormed into his office from a fishing trip when he learned of the legislators' action, and in typical form told them on the front page of his newspaper to "go to Hell, collectively or singly, and wait there until I back down." Big Hodding waged a long-running battle with Mississippi's Senator Theodore G. Bilbo, an unabashed bigot who rode roughshod over the state for twenty years. After Carter won the Pulitzer Prize, Bilbo journeyed to nearby Leland to harangue the editor on his home turf. "No red-blooded Southerner worthy of the name would accept a 'Poolitzer Prize' given by a bunch of nigger-loving Yankeefied communists for advocating the mongrelization of the race," the senator decreed. For his part, Carter applauded Bilbo's remark as a "Grade-A vote-getting technique in Mississippi."

With the harangues, of course, came plaudits, if most of them from afar. Carter's reputation drew eager young journalists from across the country to hone their skills for a year or two on the *Democrat-Times,* and not incidentally, to feel as if they were doing a little missionary work in the process. As more and more people of talent were attracted to work for Carter, the *Democrat-Times* became a crackerjack smalltown newspaper, significantly better than it was when Carter first caught the nation's attention in the 1940s with his editorials against racial injustice. As the paper became more than just Big Hodding's editorial forum, its value to the community increased.

World War II had ended before the Carters secured complete financial control of the paper. In the 1950s the family built on the southern outskirts of Greenville a mansion called Feliciana, which soon became a stopping-off place for a retinue of journalists, diplomats, and assorted intellectuals, many of whom were treated to excursions on the Mississippi River aboard the Carter's yacht, the *Mistuh Charlie.*

But as Big Hodding's reputation spread, he began spending more and more time away from the daily tasks of putting out an afternoon newspaper. Increasingly, Carter wrote for a wide range of publications, including *Colliers, Readers' Digest, New York Times Magazine,* the *Saturday Evening Post, Look, Nation's Business,* and even the *Ladies Home Journal.* Eventually, the elder Carter accepted a position as writer-in-residence at Tulane University in New Orleans.

He died in 1972, nearly ten years after having turned over the day-to-day management of the six-day afternoon paper to his oldest son, Hodding III. The younger Carter, inevitably known as "Little Hodding," was to remain at the paper for nearly seventeen years. Pic Firmin, managing editor during much of that time, recalls the years as difficult ones for the newspaper.

"Big Hodding was the type of guy who would bite a buzz saw," Firmin recently told a writer for *Memphis Magazine.* "He was breaking new territory of thought about how things ought to be in the South and the nation. By God, things were black and white, and I don't mean racially; this was wrong, and that was right. And he handled it well—to do what he did took guts, and nobody can take that away from him."

But Firmin, who now works for a paper on the Mississippi Gulf Coast, maintained that the world had become more complex by the time Little Hodding became editor. "The right and wrong were still there, but we were getting into an era of application. It's one thing to say, 'this is wrong, and this is how we ought to do it.' But when Little Hodding came along, we had to work out how to do it, and we had to work it out not just on paper but in real life. Things were more difficult to deal with when he was the editor."

But deal with them he did. There is no disagreement among journalists familiar with the *Democrat-Times* that it became a better newspaper under Little Hodding's guidance. John Emmerich, a second-generation Mississippi journalist who edits and publishes the *Greenwood Commonwealth* and has been a member of the Pulitzer Prize selection committee, believes the paper reached its peak during the 1960s and 1970s, in no small part because its reputation enabled it to attract gifted young reporters who were anxious to advance their careers with a stint on the *Delta Democrat-Times*.

But the younger Carter eventually entered the political arena, which had become his consuming passion. He was one of Jimmy Carter's (no relation to the Greenville Carters) earliest supporters; after the 1976 election, he went to work for Cyrus Vance at the State Department where he became something of a national celebrity as an administration spokesman during the Iranian hostage crisis. With his departure from Greenville, the torch at the family newspaper passed to his younger brother, Philip, a proven journalist whose career had taken him from the *New York Herald Tribune,* to a position with *Time* magazine. He was publishing a weekly called the *Vieux Carre Courier* in New Orleans when his brother moved to Washington, D.C. Philip, as he himself has acknowledged, was little more than an overseer at the *Democrat-Times* until the family could make up its mind about the paper's future. He never really had his heart in Greenville. The elder Mrs. Carter, still active but with a multitude of other interests, could not run the newspaper by herself. So by the time the paper was finally sold, rumors had been circulating for two years that the Carters were looking for a buyer.

While they have not publicly given out details of the transaction, the Carters have defended their decision to sell the paper to Freedom. They have pointed to the changes in Mississippi that had made the old *Democrat-Times*'s editorial mission less significant. Responding to an editor friend who had written in dismay at news of the sale, Hodding wrote: "I cherish every minute of the great fights in which we were engaged, not least because we ultimately emerged victorious from so many of them. But I have to say to you that our, and my, final responsibility is not to others' image of what we should do but what each of us who were participants in those wars now feel is the best thing for us to do. I for one expect to be engaged in the enterprise of advancing human values for the rest of my life. That I no longer choose to do it in Greenville cannot be fairly used to call into question that commitment."

Of course, there are those who believe such an answer does not address the real issue of the paper being sold to a chain whose editorial stand represents virtually an about-face from that of the Carters. A Greenville businessman who worked for several years at the *Democrat-Times* and is closely associated with the Carter family insists that the *New York Times* and a few other companies or individuals wanted to buy the paper but were outbid by Freedom. "I'm one of those who believe that the Carters not only sold the paper, but sold out as well," he said.

Yet Philip Carter suggested that his father would have admired the business triumph that the sale represented. "I think Dad ultimately would have been enormously proud that a small business he helped create in a far different Mississippi had survived and thrived to the point that it could be sold for a price absolutely unheard of in the history of American newspapers," he told the *New York Times*. "Every newspaper publisher is a businessman. What made my father extraordinary in his time was that he was a businessman with an intense social conscience. I think he would feel that much, if not all, of the social mission of the *Delta Democrat-Times* had been fulfilled."

While the Carters were explaining the reasons for the sale, the new management was quickly putting its stamp on the newspaper and the community. Charlie Fischer, a New Mexican who had been vice-president of Freedom's New York properties, was sent in as the new publisher. He was at Betty Carter's home the night she had the editorial staff over to break the news of the sale, and he was in the office the next day. Bill Williams, from a Freedom paper in Florida, became the *Democrat-Times*'s new business manager. And Eric Grunder, from Freedom's daily in Marysville, California, arrived a few weeks after the sale to take over as editor. All three were in their early thirties.

There was no massive personnel shake-up in the early months of Freedom's management. Sallie Ann Gresham, who was hired by the Carters in 1966 to write women's news and features and worked her way through the ranks to become managing editor in 1975, survived an initial trial period and remained with the paper as it headed into its third year under Freedom. But Gresham's name and title were dropped from the *Democrat-Times* masthead shortly after Freedom took over, one of the earliest indications that the new owners would reorganize the editorial staff. A few months after Grunder arrived from California, carpenters were in the newsroom walling off an office for him; Little Hodding had occupied a similar office when he was managing editor at the *Democrat-Times*'s old downtown location. From his office with its plate glass windows overlooking the newsroom, Grunder soon assumed many of the tasks that had fallen to Sallie Gresham during Philip Carter's absentee rule.

When one of two editors on the news desk was removed, Gresham was forced, largely by default, to help lay out the daily paper. Increasingly her time was spent proofreading local stories, sorting through the wire for accounts the paper might run, and writing headlines. Mitch Ariff, the sports editor at the *Democrat-Times* who had started working for the Carters as a carrier when he was still in grade school and had finished high school as a classmate of Little Hodding's, stayed on and was selected Mississippi Sports

Writer of the Year for 1982. Lynn LaFoe, women's editor, and her assistant, Doris Maggio, a woman with a thirty-year association with the Carter family, both left the paper before Freedom's third year.

Maggio retired. She almost certainly would have done so regardless of who the new owners might have been. But LaFoe was one of several reporters who made virtually no effort to conceal their contempt for the new owner. These reporters left the paper under less-than-amicable conditions during the early months of Freedom's management.

Despite some staff continuity, the change in the character of the paper came quickly and noticeably. The editorial position shifted 180 degrees, and a new set of syndicated columnists appeared. The reporters, who under the Carters had fanned out over six surrounding counties, including one across the Mississippi River in Arkansas, were reined in. On-the-spot news coverage was limited to Greenville and Washington County. A long-established bureau in Cleveland, a university town of fourteen thousand some thirty-five miles to the north, was temporarily shut down; and the part-time correspondent who covered the Mississippi legislature in Jackson for the *Democrat-Times* and several other papers was told her services were no longer needed.

"We went back and checked, and we had used no story from her in several months," Fischer explained. "We just weren't using that much in the paper that she was writing, and we were paying her every week." At one point during the first few months of Freedom's takeover, the full-time reporting staff fell to four, two short of what it had been during the Carter years. The new owners blame the staff shortages on the vagaries of the newspaper business. "We have increased staff from the very beginning," insisted Fischer. "We have no more or less attrition than any other newspaper."

In November 1978 the Carters' *Democrat-Times* had six full-time reporters covering news, five in Greenville and one in the bureau at Cleveland. Freedom had the same number in its news department in February 1983, having restored the Cleveland bureau after leaving it unstaffed for almost a year. Yet it is generally believed by followers of the newspaper, including townsfolk and other journalists, that the news coverage in Greenville and Washington County has not improved or even held steady under Freedom. There are also doubts that the paper's new commitment to an expanded coverage area will ever match, in output or quality, that of the Carters.

Such claims are not easy to analyze. But it can be pointed out that five of the six news reporters with the paper in 1978 were college journalism majors; most had prior newspaper experience before coming to Greenville. Except for one, who went to work in a university public relations office, all of those reporters have gone on to larger newspapers. Only one of the news reporters on the *Democrat-Times* staff in early 1983 was a journalism major, and she joined the paper with no prior experience after finishing school.

But does this suggest in any way that the quality of reporting, and thus the quality of the newspaper itself, has declined? Charlie Fischer is adamant that it has not. "We are always looking for a better quality person, just as all newspapers are. We're not out beating the bushes, but when a spot opens up, we try to get the best person we can."

The Carters had a reputation for paying their reporters skimpy salaries. In fact, the head of one of the state's largest labor unions has said that the family's predilection for liberal causes never extended to their employees or interfered with their penchant for making a buck. The same things are now being said of Freedom Newspapers, although Fischer said salaries are probably higher now than they were under the Carters. Both Freedom's publisher and its editor say they are awarding merit raises, but reporters claim those raises have been infrequent.

Fischer says that salaries for reporters start at $225 per week, "if they are any good." One need go no further than the *Democrat-Times* newsroom, however, to find reporters who will guffaw at the publisher's claim. "Well, now I know what to shoot for when I ask for a raise," said one reporter who has been at the paper two years.

There are newsroom cynics who believe that the company's attitude toward its editorial department is to staff it as cheaply as possible and get as much out of employees as it can. Susie James, the only holdover from the Carter days, displayed a check stub showing that her base pay for a forty-hour week under Freedom is $168. James has more than ten years of daily newspaper experience and since late 1982 has been almost solely responsible for the *Democrat-Times* women's section, a job handled by two people under the Carters.

In fairness, it should be pointed out that James earned an additional $50 in overtime, bringing her pay that week up to about $218. But that's still short of the $225 that Fischer said new reporters are getting. Of course, the overtime pay James earned would not have been possible under the Carters. In those days, overtime was figured on what staffers jokingly called a "Chinese work week" because it was all but impossible to understand. Reporters were paid overtime on a sliding scale—earning less money for each additional hour they worked. Freedom junked that policy shortly after taking over the paper, paying overtime on a time-and-a-half basis. At the same time, the new owners actually rolled back the base pay of several reporters, a step that bruised egos, raised hackles, and added to the already common dread that the Freedom chain was fueled not by any concern for quality journalism but by a devotion to the bottom line.

"Everybody assured me the paper wasn't going to be as bad as I thought," said Larry Looper, a *Democrat-Times* photographer several years ago.

"Well, it wasn't as bad as I thought. It was worse."

Such comments are not hard to find among former staffers who have watched the paper evolve under Freedom. A number of them were demoralized by the California group's takeover of a paper they saw as the embodiment of America's free-spirited and independent newspaper heritage.

"I wanted to give them a chance, even though I'd heard a lot of bad things about the chain," said David Saltz, who had been with the *Democrat-Times* for two and a half years at the time of the sale. "I didn't want to act rashly or precipitously and quit before seeing firsthand what it would be like working for them."

Saltz, who was covering law enforcement and courts at the same time, had disagreements with Grunder over the kind of news he was to cover. Under the Carters, the paper had always reported felony assault cases, but not misdemeanors. But Grunder said he wanted the misdemeanor cases in the paper because people wanted to read about them; Saltz took that as evidence of a tendency on the part of the new management to favor boosting circulation by using the news columns for items of questionable news value. Saltz also balked at Grunder's instructions to collect and run the list of everyone in the county who had filed for divorce, as opposed to divorces that actually had been granted.

Another change that rankled the sensibilities of some reporters was Grunder's instruction that any homicide in the paper's circulation area be played on the front page, period. Reporters were urged to pad their stories with as much detail as they could muster. Along with this, the new management ordered photographers to get art of every shooting and mishap they could. When they could not, news editors were instructed to use disaster photos supplied by the wire service. The result, some reporters felt, was a kind of twisted sensationalism.

This policy still holds as the paper enters its third year under Freedom. Readers of the *Democrat-Times* are assured, therefore, that virtually any fender-bender that can be reached by the paper's photographer will earn front-page space. Furthermore, if the mishap results in injuries, the photo is almost certain to be played as the day's leading art, above the fold on page one. Under the Carters, judgments of the news value of homicides and accidents were made on an individual basis. As often as not, slayings were reported on an inside page in a standing brief box.

The holdover reporters became convinced that the new management's commitment to sound journalistic principles was limited. They were disappointed when Bill Williams, the business manager before he left the paper in 1982, was permitted to read over a story about a shooting involving an acquaintance of his before it went into the paper. They were devastated when Publisher Fischer, over the protests of the managing editor and others in the newsroom, came into the editorial department just before deadline one day and ordered that a canned feature about a local jewelry store's anniversary celebration be run in the paper the same day the business had purchased a full-page ad. Fischer himself looks back on the incident as an unfortunate one and blames it on a staffer having promised the store that the feature would run alongside the ad. "When I found out we had been committed to that fact, I felt like we were obligated to run it," the publisher explained. "We were going to run the story anyway, and I didn't think one day made any difference."

But at the time, no explanation was offered. It is, of course, doubtful that Fischer's explanation would have satisfied reporters anyway. "The mood around the place was so strange," one recalled, "and we were all so shell-shocked that people felt defensive about just being there."

It is easy to make too much of such incidents, however. There are occasional vicissitudes at most newspapers. When Philip Carter was at the *Democrat-Times*'s helm, a reporter uncovered evidence that a Greenville attorney had been arrested in a neighboring county on a marijuana charge. What made the story interesting, the reporter thought, was that the attorney had jockeyed successfully to have the record of the arrest kept off the jail docket where anyone scrutinizing the public document could have come across it. Furthermore, the attorney was with another *Democrat-Times* reporter the night he was stopped by law enforcement authorities. A story was written and turned in to the news desk. It was never published, Carter explained, because the story dealt with a misdemeanor. As a matter of unwritten policy, the *Democrat-Times* did not consider misdemeanors newsworthy. Predictably, some of the reporters objected to the editor's decision.

Perhaps, when all is said and done, there are only philosophical objections to Freedom's takeover of the Greenville newspaper. After all, as late as September 1976, *Time* magazine could write, "The South has long been a land of first-rate newspaper editors and second-rate newspapers. . . . Hodding Carter of the *Delta Democrat-Times* and other Southern editors became more distinguished for the strength of their convictions than the quality of their coverage." But even such a left-handed compliment acknowledges that the utter audacity of Big Hodding's writing helped the newspaper mature.

Under Freedom, newsroom morale was deflated by Grunder's decision to eliminate the by-lines of reporters except for stories deemed exceptional. "When I came in, they were putting by-lines on any story more than three paragraphs long, and I thought that was rather silly," said Grunder. The restrictive by-line policy was designed to encourage enterprising reporting and good writing, but instead it discouraged reporters who no longer got credit for their day-to-day, bread-and-butter work. Furthermore, the standards by which a story was to be deemed worthy of a by-line were never enumerated. "It really just amounts to a judgment call on the part of whoever's editing the story," Grunder acknowledged. The by-line policy caused so much dissension within the staff that it was abandoned long before Grunder had finished his third year in Greenville.

Fears on the part of some reporters that the rigid Freedom editorial stance would affect the new management's expectations on how the news should be written proved unfounded. There have been no known incidents of reporters being told to slant a story to conform to the Freedom philosophy or to write about something because of its relevance to libertarianism. Reporters occasionally were invited to write editorials on subjects they covered and were told what conclusions to reach. But they were not pressured to write the editorials. They understood that if they submitted editorials inconsistent with Freedom's libertarian position the editorials would not be published.

Reporters during the Carter years were also asked to write editorials on occasion, but the Carters allowed the reporters to use their judgment and the knowledge they had gained covering issues to formulate opinions. If the Carter in charge disagreed with the conclusion a reporter reached, the editorial would not be run or would be substantially rewritten.

Aside from editorial requests, Grunder said that Freedom has never required its employees to agree with the group's libertarian outlook. "I don't care what a reporter's philosophy is as long as he can turn out copy that's readable and accurate," he said.

The new editor, perhaps understandably, has not convinced everyone that he is hiring reporters who can do that. One of the latest examples pointed out by neighboring journalists is the paper's account of a federal judge's ruling on a municipal annexation lawsuit in nearby Indianola. The judge threw the town's annexation plan out of court. But the story in the *Democrat-Times* failed to bring out that point; the headline read: "Keady rules Indianola acted racially." By contrast, the banner headline in John Emmerich's Greenwood newspaper that same afternoon read: "Indianola annexation suit thrown out." Indications that the Greenville newspaper's story was more than somewhat misguided came the following day when the paper ran a meek one-column story on its front page. "Indy likes ruling," said the article.

For the *Democrat-Times* to have muffed such an important story in its circulation region was seen as convincing evidence that the paper had deteriorated under Freedom's control. But, as if compounding error with error, the *Democrat-Times* offered not a single line when a Greenville lawyer appealed the decision against Indianola to a higher court two weeks later. The appeal was reported by the Greenwood paper, a weekly in Indianola, two television stations, and two larger papers that maintain bureaus in Greenville.

The *Democrat-Times*'s stumble over the Indianola story may be due, at least in part, to the new management's decision shortly after arriving in Greenville to cut back sharply on the area that the paper would try to cover with on-the-scene reports.

In spite of the controversy that had swirled around it, the Carters' *Democrat-Times* had always had the largest circulation of any Delta-based paper. This was natural because Greenville was easily the largest community in the vast open spaces of the northeast Mississippi agricultural region. The bulk of the paper's readership had been in Greenville and Washington County, but there were also clusters of subscribers throughout the entire central and south Delta, and reporters were assigned to cover those outlying areas. Emphasis was placed on Bolivar County to the north and Sunflower County to the east, but the sparsely settled counties of Issaquena and Sharkey to the south and Chicot County, Arkansas, to the west also received the on-site attention of reporters from the Greenville newsroom. The result was a paper that bulged at the seams with hard news and features from a six-county area, with the use of United Press International wire copy held to the minimum necessary to give readers an adequate summary of the day's national and world events.

But the Freedom management took one look at the paper's far-flung coverage and decided it should be curtailed. The number of readers in outlying counties might not have been sufficient to justify, from a financial standpoint, the extensive news coverage given those counties over the years. But the Carters felt obligated to provide some coverage wherever the paper circulated. Freedom felt no such obligation; it limited on-site coverage to Greenville and Washington County and kept track of the other counties only by phone calls to local law enforcement officials. "We've just decided that our news coverage should be where most of our advertisers and readers are," Grunder explained after the pull-in.

Freedom had taken over the *Democrat-Times* during the early stages of a severe recession, and the geographically restrictive reporting was perhaps a response to financial realities. The new management shut down the paper's long-standing Cleveland bureau and brought back into the main office the reporter who had staffed it. Gruner explained that the man in the bureau was one of the paper's most experienced reporters. "It seemed silly to have him covering an area where we didn't have a lot of circulation," he said. After several months without the bureau to the north, Grunder changed his mind, and the reporter was sent back to try to re-establish coverage in the neglected area.

Although Cleveland does have its own five-day-a-week paper, the other areas where Freedom's *Democrat-Times* cut back on reporting were no longer covered on a regular basis by any daily. The *Commercial Appeal* of Memphis is read widely in the old *Democrat-Times* circulation area, but has only a single staffer to cover the entire region. In October 1982, the *Clarion-Ledger,* Mississippi's statewide newspaper based in the capital city of Jackson, opened a bureau in Greenville. Even with some additional attention being given the area, however, there are at least five county and city governing boards once covered on a fairly regular basis by the *Democrat-Times* that are no longer getting the scrutiny they did during the Carter years. Even one of the paper's nearby competitors was sorry about the curtailment of area coverage.

"As soon as they came in, Freedom withdrew their people from here," said Jim Abbott, editor of the *Enterprise-Tocsin* in Indianola, the Sunflower County seat twenty miles east of Greenville. "In a way, we enjoy that, but there were some stories they did that we just couldn't do with the limited staff of a weekly newspaper. Trials that may go on for several days are a good example. I think our county misses that coverage. I know I do."

Although Freedom reversed itself on its Cleveland bureau, there are few signs that the paper will move back into other areas it has abandoned. When efforts are made to cover events in those counties, the information is gathered for the most part by telephone. That was the case with the Indianola annexation story.

Apart from the reduction in the coverage area, some readers have complained that there are fewer local stories in a paper that historically had thrived on anything and everything local. But Fischer says that the facts do not support such observations. "I expect we're running 15 to 20 percent more local news now than the paper was a few years ago," he says.

The publisher also says Freedom has spent more than $500,000 updating the editorial department by installing a front-end system and a high-speed wire that provides a better selection of stories than was available under the Carters. Freedom also dropped its contract with United Press International and switched to the Associated Press, a move that would never have taken place under the Carters because of Big Hodding's ignominious dismissal by the Associated Press almost fifty years earlier. The new ownership went a step further, moreover, when it promptly redesigned the paper and scrapped the modified Old English flag that had greeted readers, with only one interruption, for about ninety years. Curiously, the Old English flag belonged to the *Daily Democrat-Times* and was dropped briefly when Big Hodding's *Delta Star* took over that paper in 1938. The flag Freedom chose for the revamped *Democrat-Times* bore an uncanny resemblance, ironically, to the one Big Hodding experimented with forty-two years earlier when he took over Greenville's established paper. But Carter quickly abandoned his experiment in favor of continuing with tradition.

The sweeping changes that began at the Greenville paper in 1980 pleased some elements of the community, including those people whom the years had not mellowed. They still thought of the Carters as a scourge and were glad to be rid of them. Publisher Fischer had been talking about those people when he said, after the first year of Freedom ownership, that the new management had been accepted by the community because "our views are more in line with the way people think around this area than were those of the previous owners." Going into his third year in Greenville, Fischer is still optimistic. "We've been accepted better here than in any other town I've ever seen," he said.

Advertisers, it almost goes without saying, were soon opening their arms to the new management because of the flexible and accommodating attitude in the business department, which had been absent under the irascible John Gibson. Fischer said the payoff from improved relations with advertisers has been an increase in advertising linage and gains in circulation. The Audit Bureau of Circulations record of circulation for six months ending June 30, 1982, showed the *Democrat-Times* with 15,695 subscribers for the daily paper and 16,258 for the Sunday morning edition. "We've shown growth ever since I've been here," maintains the publisher, who adds that actual paid circulation at the time of the takeover, "if you look at it real close, probably was closer to 14,000" than 15,000.

He also insists there is no way to substantiate the claim that the newshole has gradually shrunk under Freedom. For the first month of 1983, the paper averaged almost 44 percent advertising, leaving 56 percent of its space for news, he said.

"December [1982] was the best month the *Democrat-Times* has had in a long time, and we ran right at 50 percent advertising and 50 percent news," he said, "and remember, that was with one of the best months we've ever had."

Dennis Gilliam, an advertising salesman who worked at the paper under both the Carters and Freedom, agreed that the ratio of news to advertising had improved under the new owner. But, he added, that may not mean readers are getting more news in their daily paper. "In the old days we'd have 75 percent advertising content in Wednesday's paper. That left 25 for news. But we were running forty-eight pages so that there was just a whole lot more space in there for news."

An editorial employee, who remained at the paper after the sale to Freedom, said the Carters strived to keep the paper at about 56 percent advertising. "But under the Carters we were given three open pages for news everyday. Now the only page that we know we're going to get without any advertising is page one." That employee also said that papers under the Carters on Sunday and Wednesday were anywhere from forty-eight to sixty pages. Thursday's paper was usually twenty-eight to thirty-six pages, the employee said, adding, "A big paper now is thirty pages."

But Fischer said the Greenville paper enjoyed an eight-thousand-inch gain in advertising linage in 1982. "There's a lot more cooperation with the retail community," said Jesse Griggers, manager of the local J. C. Penney outlet. "They're a lot more efficient," reported the manager of a car dealership.

Fischer said the paper makes an effort to "cater to what the ᴊness people want. We realize that without them we couldn't put out a newspaper."

The new owner also has tried to use more process color in the newspaper than had been the case under the Carters. And, in an attempt to upgrade editorial performance, Freedom hired a Texas journalism professor in 1981 to critique its newspapers. The result is a monthly newsletter distributed to staffers, where Martin L. "Red" Gibson, Freedom's "Newspaper Tuner," offers tips on writing, headlines, and photos.

The most striking change that has occurred as a result of Freedom's takeover has been on the editorial page, where the Carters had enlightened or antagonized their readers, but rarely bored them. The moderately liberal editorial tone of four decades gave way overnight to the doctrinaire libertarianism of the new ownership.

It took several weeks to get a new Freedom editor in Greenville, but Fischer instructed the staff in the interim to fill the editorial hole with material culled from other Freedom papers. *Democrat-Times* lower-level editors had become accustomed to a similar practice under Philip Carter, who had split his time between Greenville and New Orleans, writing fewer and fewer editorials during his three years as editor. There was one difference, however. Philip Carter had always insisted that reprinted editorials—even those from *Editorial Research Reports*—be credited to their source. After a short period of that under the new management, holdover *Democrat-Times* editors were instructed to drop the credit line from the borrowed editorials. When the editorials contained the name of a community, it was "localized" to leave readers with the impression that someone was writing local editorials every day, when in fact practically all the early Freedom editorials originated elsewhere.

But that has changed. Most editorials in the Greenville paper now are locally written, virtually all of them on local or state subjects. After persistent prodding by lower-level editors, Grunder has even started identifying the source of all nonstaff editorials with a credit line.

The change of heart about credit lines helped save some embarrassment. In the early months of Freedom management, there were dead giveaways that uncredited editorials were not locally written. A summer 1980 editorial explaining the paper's policy against political endorsements was an example. It began: "A candidate for state office came by the other day. He never said so directly, but the gentleman was seeking this paper's backing in his upcoming election." The trouble was, there were no elections for state office in

Mississippi that year; the next scheduled elections were three years away.

But Grunder did not shy away from controversy or balk at antagonizing local government officials when the opportunity arose.

The most notable editorial crusade of Freedom's first year was against the Washington County Board of Supervisors, which had constantly flouted the spirit of the state open meetings law by conducting frequent closed-door sessions. Openness in government remains a big editorial issue on the pages of the *Democrat-Times*.

Approaching subjects from a libertarian viewpoint, the paper occasionally offered surprises to readers who thought they had the new guys pegged as traditional conservatives. A fairly typical week of editorials in January 1982 included harsh words against a proposed state tax increase to fund public kindergartens, a position likely to please old-style conservatives, but also offered opposition to drug laws and draft registration as well. Antigovernment consistency is no less valued at the *Democrat-Times* than at other Freedom papers.

It is not surprising that local government officials, as wary as they often were about what the Carters might write about them, grew even more unhappy with an editorial line that was automatically antigovernment in almost every instance. The new editorial policy, many local politicians felt, was unfair because it reacted in a knee-jerk fashion to any action by government rather than giving sober and thoughtful evaluation to what government does and whether or not it is good for the community. So fervent was the new management's ideological commitment to the elimination of government that it once jumped on a group of senior citizens for approaching the board of supervisors for help in buying a second-hand van for transportation to a federally funded meals program at a local church. The old folks should find friends or relatives to give them a ride, the editorial said, without getting into what obviously would be the paper's editorial opposition to the meals program itself.

The new *Democrat-Times*'s antigovernment stance did not do much for its credibility among Greenville's blacks, who make up more than half the town's inhabitants. Although race is not a motivating factor in the kind of libertarianism the paper espoused, some of its editorial rhetoric was to many black readers reminiscent of the old racist arguments that were couched in terms of promoting individual initiative and responsibility, but whose aims were to deny blacks whatever benefits or advantages government programs could provide. Sarah Johnson, who became, with the Carters' editorial backing, the first black member of the Greenville City Council in 1974, was one who did not make any distinction between the libertarians and the segregationists in their views about government. "I'm one of the people who's quit taking the paper because it's gotten so bad," she said. "There were some editorials I considered a vehicle to create dissension in the community." Since the Carters were so obviously ahead of the times in Mississippi on racial issues, pioneering the equal treatment of blacks in the paper's news column as well as on its editorial page, comparisons to the new ownership in that area were inevitable. If some blacks have read racial attitudes into the Freedom editorials that are not there, so have some unreconstructed white racists gleaned the same impression and taken comfort in it, feeling they have been vindicated after years of complaining that the Carters "always cater to the niggers."

Grunder was sensitive to how certain libertarian positions would be interpreted in a Mississippi Delta area that is heavily black and poor and still polarized in many ways along racial lines. He avoided espousing one position that is dear to most libertarians' hearts—the abolition of public schools—because of an awareness that to many Mississippians, white and black, support for integrated public education is the litmus test for commitment to racial quality of opportunity. "If I was to tout private education in Greenville, I might very well be accused of being racist," Grunder said. "Until this community becomes accustomed to us and our philosophy and understands that it's not racial, that subject will be taboo."

But Grunder points with pride to an editorial the paper ran in early 1980 protesting the Mississippi legislature's action in raising fivefold the tuition of Iranian students enrolled at state universities. "I think that tended to show our position on racial issues," he said.

Ironically, Freedom's only printed acknowledgement of the Carter legacy it has otherwise ignored came in an advertisement purchased by the group in response to articles lamenting the sale of the paper and the loss of a journalistic voice for civil rights. The ad, which ran on the cover of *Editor & Publisher* magazine, brushed aside the editorial boldness of the senior Carter, exercised at the risk of life and limb. It suggested Freedom's own commitment to civil rights was superior because its papers had editorialized against the incarceration of Japanese Americans in California during World War II. The ad also revealed Freedom's ignorance of Carter's accomplishments. Big Hodding won the Pulitzer Prize for a body of writing calling for human justice, but the Pulitzer selection committee singled out for special recognition an editorial entitled "Go for Broke" in which the Greenville editor had espoused fair and just treatment for the Japanese Americans.

Freedom dropped several of the *Democrat-Times*'s regular syndicated columnists when it took over, including Jack Anderson, David Broder, and William Raspberry, a native Mississippian. Grunder pointed out that while Raspberry was discontinued because he disagreed too often with the libertarian line, another black columnist—economist Walter Williams—was picked to replace him. William F. Buckley and Patrick Buchanan had been run by the Carters for editorial-page "balance," something not highly valued by the new management. Buckley and a Mississippi political columnist are the only editorial-page holdovers; Williams, James J. Kilpatrick, Lewis Grizzard, and Louis Rukeyser are among those added. Brodie Crump, an elderly local character who had written yarns and reminiscences about the Delta for thirty-four years, was dropped from the editorial page when his health prohibited him from continuing his column.

Although Grunder viewed race as the one thorny area where the paper must tread lightly in espousing the party line, there are those who believe that the Freedom philosophy may wear thin on a lot of currently content white readers when they realize its full implications. One local politician noted that the Delta was carved out of swampland and made livable thanks in great degree to the government. He shuddered in recalling a conversation with the Freedom folks in which they expressed the view that the levees protecting the town of Greenville from the Mississippi River's wrath should have been built and maintained by private, not government, interests. "Anybody who says those levees could have been built without the government just doesn't know what he's talking about," the politician said.

As David Saltz, who stayed for four months after the sale, put it: "I can't believe there won't be a negative reaction in the community when people realize they oppose so much of the government assistance that the Delta depends on to survive. They're against the very life-support systems of their own community."

The elder Hodding Carter credited the survival and profitability of his newspaper in part to his own involvement in and loyalty to Greenville. "I have no right to be the town scold without taking part in the town's life," he wrote in a *Look* magazine article. "I could have no better defense against our critics than to prove that I am as much a citizen of Greenville as is any other person who dwells here."

The devotion to the community of Carter, his wife, and Hodding III muted the voices of denunciation and made life tolerable for the family in the Greenville they loved. It is also what people most recall when they become nostalgic about the Carters and lament the loss of the hometown paper to outsiders. "At least the Carters were local people with a stake in and a commitment to Greenville," even the Carters' old adversaries can bring themselves to say.

The Freedom people are doing their best to convince the local people that they, too, want to be a contributing part of the town. Charlie Fischer is on the board of directors of the local United Way and an industrial development group. He accepts every speaking engagement and has made the rounds of the Greenville civic clubs more than once.

Eric Grunder is a member of the local Lions Club and likes to spend time "down at the coffee shop jawboning with political types." He reacts a bit defensively when asked about his own commitment to Greenville, but has an effective rejoinder: He has bought a house in town and is in the office every day, which is more than could be said for Philip Carter in the three years he edited the paper more or less long-distance from New Orleans.

"I realize," said Grunder, "that to some people, unless you've been here since '01, you're a newcomer, but we hope as quickly as possible to be considered Greenvilleans. We're vitally interested in seeing this community grow and prosper. We're here to stay."

Some people, of course, will always hope that Grunder is wrong. In mid-1982, Walker Percy, a descendant of the man who had helped bring the Carters to Greenville, was decrying the loss of the home-owned paper. "What Greenville needs most right now is a good newspaper," he told a New Orleans reporter at a bash for former *Democrat-Times* staffers. "I haven't seen many issues of the newspaper under the present ownership, but the ones I have seen lead me to believe it is a mediocre newspaper.

"I feel very strongly that journalism, a newspaper, actually creates the essence, the spirit of a community. I have noticed that where you have a good community, you have a good newspaper. . . . So since I am by nature a pessimist, I would say that Greenville in a few years will probably not be out of the ordinary."

Those are strong words for the Freedom folks. And perhaps they will choose to take their counsel from Big Hodding's first *Democrat-Times* editorial some forty-five years ago. In that editorial, he tried to put his finger on just what it was that made Greenville different, "and different in a way we like.

"Tolerance, respect for the individual soul's right to its own privacy, and dignity are rare virtues, but they are sown fairly liberally within our city limits.

"Last, but not least, in times of peril—and what times are not perilous?—we have always had our leaders who unselfishly fought to make our way of life honest and honorable and happy. The names change, the great-hearted pass, but the tradition endures and the ranks are refilled."

Manchester Herald

Bill Williams

After ninety years as an independent newspaper, the *Manchester Herald* in Connecticut was sold in 1971 to Hagadone Newspapers, a division of Scripps League Newspapers. By 1981, only a decade later, circulation had plunged 30 percent, and advertising linage had dropped an estimated 30 to 35 percent. Some had begun to ask whether the *Herald* could survive another decade.

The sale of the newspaper came as a shock to many readers and employees. The *Herald* had been locally owned for three generations by the Fergusons, a family well known and respected in the community. Among readers, there was a feeling of loyalty and closeness to the hometown newspaper and its owners, who had lived their lives in the community and had been active in town affairs. The feeling of loss was intensified, perhaps, by the fact that the new owners lived in Idaho and California, a continent away.

The *Herald* was founded as a weekly on October 1, 1881, by Elwood S. Ela, the son of a Methodist minister. Within a few years, Ela hired a teen-ager named Thomas Ferguson, who eventually would gain control of the newspaper, to write news items as a part-time correspondent. At age ten, Ferguson had emigrated with his family from Belfast, Ireland, and settled in the Talcottville section of Vernon, near Manchester. After completing grade school, he worked in a local woolen mill while also selling subscriptions and writing for the *Herald*.

"The thrill that I had from seeing my items of news in the paper encouraged me to continue getting more and more news every week," he wrote years later. In 1889, at age nineteen, Ferguson joined the newspaper full time as a "printer's devil" in the pressroom, where he ran errands for three dollars a week. During the next three decades, he learned all aspects of the newspaper business as foreman of the paper's job printing shop, mechanical superintendent, and city editor. The *Herald* became a semiweekly in 1896, and in 1907 it was incorporated. Ferguson became a stockholder and secretary of the new corporation. Seven years later, in 1914, the *Herald* became a daily with a circulation of 4,168.

By the early 1920s, Ela's health had begun to decline. Heart disease forced him to cut back his hours and transfer more responsibility to Ferguson. When Ela died in 1924, Ferguson became publisher, though he did not yet own the paper. Ela had left most of his stock to his son-in-law, C. Dennison Talcott, who became *Herald* president. Talcott was an executive with Talcott woolen mills and did not play an active role at the newspaper. Gradually, Ferguson acquired more and more stock; in 1945, at age seventy-five, he gained full control.

In 1928 Ferguson had moved the *Herald* into its present plant, just off Main Street. The building had been constructed by the Knights of Columbus as a lodge hall. The Knights were unable, however, to raise sufficient money to pay for the building and were forced to sell it at a loss. Meanwhile, Ferguson's only son, Ronald, had joined the newspaper after college as a reporter (later he became city editor and then managing editor).

Thomas Ferguson guided the newspaper until his death in 1951 at age eighty-one. By then, he had worked at the *Herald* for sixty-two years and was widely known as the dean of Connecticut publishers. The business passed to Ronald, who was gravely ill in a hospital. In a quirk of history, Ronald died exactly two weeks later, and the paper passed to his sons, Thomas F. Ferguson, twenty-six, and Walter R. Ferguson, twenty-five, who ran it as copublishers for two decades, until the sale in 1971.

Manchester is a town of just under fifty thousand, located nine miles east of Hartford, the state capital, and about halfway between Boston and New York City. An interstate highway linking Boston and Hartford slices through the northern edge of town. During the early part of this century, Manchester grew rapidly as large industrial companies opened factories. The largest was Cheney Mills, which became one of the world's major silk companies and manufactured much of the silk used to make parachutes for U.S. forces during World War II. But after the war, many factories, including Cheney Mills, folded or reduced their operations. Manchester gradually became a bedroom community for blue-collar workers at Pratt & Whitney Aircraft in nearby East Hartford and for white-collar employees at the many national insurance companies with headquarters in Hartford.

Under the Ferguson brothers, the *Herald* was, perhaps, typical of many small daily newspapers. There was heavy emphasis on local government coverage, but little serious investigative reporting or analysis. "We did a thorough job of reporting," recalled Thomas F. Ferguson. "Sometimes, we assigned two reporters to a Board of Directors [the local town governing body] meeting to be sure of thorough coverage. We were dedicated to quality." Ferguson pointed out that the paper won several awards for editorial quality and layout during the 1950s, including a New England Associated Press award for a series of articles on the state juvenile court system. Local news rarely made page one, although there were several pages of town news inside the paper. Ferguson said he made a deliberate decision to emphasize national and foreign news on the front page. "We had a minimum of local stories on page one," he said. "My philosophy was predicated on the fact that we were nine miles from Hartford. We had to print a product that was equal to or superior to the Hartford papers."

The Fergusons knew the community intimately and cared about education, medical care, and other issues important to the town. Thomas Ferguson, for example, had been a director of Manchester Hospital for fourteen years when the paper was sold.

Herald employees said the Fergusons also displayed a personal interest in the staff and were generous with benefits. "It was a typical family operation," an editor recalled. "They took care of people. There was liberal sick pay." The editor recalled that one employee, who died of cancer, had no eligibility in the pension plan, but the Fergusons paid the family his salary for six months after his death.

During the 1950s and 1960s the *Herald*, like most newspapers in one-newspaper towns, prospered. It operated in the black every year from 1951 to 1971 and saw its circulation increase from about ten thousand to sixteen thousand.

Politically, the *Herald* was rabidly Republican, and invariably endorsed Republican candidates. Local Democratic leaders charged that news stories were slanted in favor of Republican candidates. The first Thomas Ferguson was a member of the Republican Town Committee from 1898 until his death in 1951. He also served twenty years as Manchester's Republican registrar of voters and attended several Republican National Conventions as an alternate delegate or guest. Thomas Ferguson, the grandson, also was active in Republican politics. After the sale of the newspaper, he was elected chairman of the Manchester Republican party and later was elected to the Republican State Central Committee. His wife, Vivian, served three terms as a Republican member of the town's Board of Directors.

The decision to sell was not an easy one for the Ferguson brothers. Both had been associated with the newspaper most of their adult lives. Like many independent newspaper owners, however, Thomas Ferguson worried about the crushing burden of inheritance taxes if he tried to pass the newspaper to his only son, who was fourteen in 1971.

"We were meeting a squeeze," he recalled. "We couldn't put aside enough money for inheritance taxes without having to liquidate the property. Many small newspaper publishers find themselves in this situation. I was very happy in the newspaper business, but I had to be practical and look at the future. If I died and my will called for my stock to go to my wife and children, the inheritance taxes would have to be paid. But we were not able to build up sufficient assets to pay inheritance taxes. We couldn't pay sufficient dividends to put money aside for taxes. If people want independent daily newspapers to continue to exist, they'll have to find a way to allow newspapers to be passed to heirs without this tremendous inheritance tax problem. Unless some tax relief is afforded to closely held newspaper corporations, the trend [to group ownership] will continue. I loved the newspaper business. If I could do it over again and find a way around this problem, I would."

Although they were copublishers of the *Herald*, Thomas and Walter Ferguson were remarkably different in style, responsibilities, and interests. Thomas served as president, general manager, and executive editor and played an active role in journalistic organizations. He was elected president of the Connecticut Daily Newspaper Association and president of the New England circuit of the Associated Press. He also was a founding member of the Connecticut Council on Freedom of Information, and at the time of the sale served as national treasurer of the Associated Press Managing Editors Association. Colleagues described him as out-going and friendly—a man who thoroughly enjoyed his life as a smalltown newspaper editor.

His brother, Walter, was more reserved and conservative. He was the *Herald*'s vice-president and mechanical foreman. He had no role in the newsroom. Thomas graduated from Trinity College, a respected liberal arts college in Hartford, but Walter dropped out of Trinity after one year to work in the backshop at the Herald, where he was a linotype operator, stereotyper, and pressman. Even after he became copublisher in 1951, Walter continued the work he loved in the backshop, where he set type on a linotype machine. He gradually gave up the work, however, as he assumed more administrative duties.

The brothers' differences in style and interests eventually led to strong disagreements about the future direction of the *Herald*. One editor who knew both men said, "They just couldn't get along. Tom was a big spender. Walter was very thrifty. They had some words over money. It was really cat and dog for a while." Another editor recalled, "They were very different in approach. Tom was a little more elegant in dress, in demeanor, in habits. He was more of a spender, personally and in the business. Walter encouraged the image of being a tightwad. I don't think he really was, but it was an image he liked to project."

Money became a sore issue that led to a widening gulf between them. The newspaper had been spending more and more to modernize. In 1967, four years before the paper was sold, the Fergusons constructed an addition to the newspaper building and installed a new Goss Urbanite offset press with a forty-eight-page capacity. Thomas wanted the corporation to branch out and become a multimedia enterprise, in part to generate more revenue for inheritance tax purposes. "There was a difference in philosophy," he said. "I wanted to expand by buying other investments, but he [Walter] didn't want to." Thomas suggested that they purchase other newspapers and move into radio and television, but Walter steadfastly opposed expansion. The disagreement could not be resolved.

Like many owners of small newspapers, the Fergusons had been approached often by prospective buyers. Inquiries came about once a month. "They were blind feelers that came from brokers. We never knew if they were for real," Thomas Ferguson said. In 1971 a broker approached the Fergusons with an offer from Hagadone division of Scripps League Newspapers, a chain of newspapers with headquarters in Hillsborough, California. Scripps League is a private corporation owned and operated by Edward W. Scripps, who became chairman in 1931 and still held that title fifty-one years later in 1982, though much of the day-to-day responsibility by then had been turned over to his son, Barry H. Scripps. Until 1971 Scripps's newspapers were scattered in small, one-newspaper towns across the Midwest and West in places like Flagstaff, Arizona; DeKalb, Illinois; Coos Bay, Oregon; and Napa, California. The *Manchester Herald* was the first newspaper purchased in the East, although three others were purchased later.

The sale of the *Herald* was completed in November 1972. Thomas Ferguson said it was a case of someone approaching them "with the right price at the right time." The sale price reportedly was $2.5 million, though no figure was made public at the time.

During the years following the change in ownership, editors and readers complained about a gradual, but palpable, decline in the newspaper's quality. Theodore Cummings, chairman of the Democratic party in Manchester, said he realized in hindsight that the paper had high standards under the Fergusons. "It went downhill very fast after the sale," he said. "It's one of those cases where you don't know a good thing until you don't have it anymore. They had some decent reporters who cared about their work. They had a sense of journalism and a sense of the power of the press and a sense of self-respect and accuracy. Sure, they [the Fergusons] were Republicans, but they would give credit to Democrats, and they were more accurate. Sometimes it was slanted, but they covered the Democratic party. The new owners ran it right into the ground. They weren't interested in news. They just wanted to sell ads. They were not journalists. They didn't encourage good journalism."

Under Scripps League, the *Herald* dropped the Los Angeles Times-Washington Post News Service almost immediately. An Associated Press wire was canceled and replaced with a less complete and less expensive wire from United Press International. The newsroom staff was reduced from twenty-two to fourteen, though some of the reduction involved part-time positions. Travel by reporters was virtually eliminated.

Under the Fergusons, reporters often were sent on out-of-state assignments. One reporter covered the 1968 Democratic National Convention in Chicago. Another traveled to Atlantic City when a Manchester woman was Miss Connecticut in the Miss America contest. Sports Editor Earl Yost covered baseball spring training in Florida for twenty-three years and the World Series each fall. He also drove once a week to New York or Boston to cover the Red Sox, the Rangers, and other professional sporting events. After the sale, out-of-town sports coverage was eliminated. Yost even was told not to cover the Hartford Whalers hockey games because the newspaper could save money by using United Press International wire copy, even though Hartford is less than ten miles from Manchester and the Whalers are the only major league sports team in Connecticut. Yost continued to cover the hockey games, however, doing so on his own time for no extra pay.

Less than a year after the change in ownership, longtime *Herald* editor Alan H. Olmstead resigned. Olmstead had written the *Herald*'s editorials for nearly thirty-one years. When he departed, local editorials disappeared from the editorial page. They were replaced by vacuous, canned editorials, mailed to the *Herald* from Scripps League offices in California, on such subjects as the contribution of small businesses to the American economy, the fiftieth anniversary of the Empire State Building, and the value of daylight savings time.

A prolific writer, Olmstead was widely known in Connecticut for his editorials and columns. While *Herald* editor, he began writing free-lance for the *New Yorker* magazine and contributed thirty-two pieces in thirteen years. During interviews, many readers and editors cited the departure of Olmstead as the event that most symbolized the *Herald*'s deterioration and gradual loss of editorial quality.

Born in Bridgeport, Connecticut, and educated at Yale University, Olmstead landed his first newspaper job at the now-defunct *Bridgeport Times-Star*, where he reported news and later wrote editorials. In 1941 *Herald* Publisher Thomas Ferguson hired him as associate editor of the *Herald* and editor of its editorial page. Soon the associate editor title was changed to editor. Although Olmstead was the *Herald*'s top editor for more than three decades, his sole responsibility was the editorial page. He wrote daily editorials and, three times a week, a column called "Connecticut Yankee." Unlike most newspaper editors, he had no newsroom responsibilities. The Fergusons gave him complete freedom to work full-time writing his column and the editorials and laying out the editorial page.

Olmstead brought to the newspaper a felicitous writing style not often found in smalltown publications. "He wrote attractively," recalled William Sleith, a retired Manchester businessman. "Everyone who read him appreciated his writing. He was a top-flight editorial writer. The editorial page was as good as that of the *New York Times*." Clemewell Young, a poet who studied under Olmstead, wrote after Olmstead's death in 1980, "His descriptions of the seasonal return of red-winged blackbirds, or an unusually prodigious flowering of vervain, were as evocative as any poetry." Olmstead loved the outdoors and often wrote about nature. When he moved to Manchester in 1941, he and his wife, Catherine, purchased thirty-five acres of land in the northern end of town and operated a farm. They raised cows, pigs, and chickens, and grew corn and other crops. Each December they sold Christmas trees from the property. "He'd do a beautiful nature column," said Stephen A. Collins, editorial page editor of the *News-Times* in Danbury, Connecticut. "His boyhood love for the outdoors never left him. He was a real pro at putting words together. He was a master. He had a love for the land, a love for New England."

Olmstead's style is illustrated by this passage about a windy Sunday in mid-October:

> The wind began before breakfast. It blew out of the north and it blew through the house, awakening the thermostat from its long summer holiday. It lashed the trees in the yard and it tormented the foliage landscape, so that all day long the leaves of many colors, near what the New England state development commissions label their peak display, had to fight to hold to their branch and not give up, this day at least, their summer lease on life. . . . All day it drove on past, sweeping the blue October sky clean of cloud and dust, beating the reds and yellows of the swamps and hillsides into a frenzy of resistance, striking through compromise clothing into old man's marrow, signaling, at last, the change of seasons which comes not by calendar, but by how we live.

Olmstead left the *Herald* in September 1972, less than a year after it was sold. The new owners said they could not afford a full-time editor on the editorial page. They wanted Olmstead to assume additional duties in the newsroom, but he refused and left the paper with a mixture of bitterness and sadness, according to people who knew him well.

Although the *Herald* changed in many ways after the sale, there was no sudden shift in direction or dramatic turning point that signaled a decline. Rather, a series of cuts and economies and editorial decisions gradually diminished the quality of the product. "Initially, there was no great change," recalled a town official. "I saw reporters every day. But after a while, there was no more daily contact. A lot of the reporting was done by phone."

The first new publisher after the sale generally received high marks from employees and readers. Burl L. Lyons came to Manchester from the *Daily Inter Lake*, a ten-thousand-circulation Hagadone newspaper in Kalispell, Montana, where he had been managing editor and later publisher. At the

Herald, Lyons continued the plant modernization program started by the Fergusons a few years earlier. An eight-thousand-foot addition was constructed, and the newsroom was moved into the new wing in November 1972. The paper also shifted from hot type to cold type, and in the transition the production staff was sliced from twenty-seven to ten. At the nonunion *Herald*, there was no need to negotiate the reduction. *Evaluating the Press: The New England Daily Newspaper Survey*, a 1973 book that evaluated every daily newspaper in the six-state region, said of Lyons and the *Herald*: "By January 1973, he had what surely must qualify as one of the most modern and attractive small-newspaper plants in New England. His production facilities and equipment are from the leading edge of technology—cathode ray tube (CRT) equipment for type production and proofreading, and optical character recognition (OCR) scanners for producing type directly from the typewritten copy of reporters and ad men."

While he was trimming the staff and modernizing the production facilities, Lyons also was making a good impression in the community. He became active in community groups and wrote a chatty weekly column called "Hi Neighbor." The *New England Daily Newspaper Survey* reported Lyons's involvement with the local Shriners, the Chamber of Commerce, a savings bank, the United Fund, and a downtown action committee.

Lyons also was popular with the paper's editorial staff. When he left the *Herald* in July 1975, to take a political job as administrative assistant to the attorney general of Montana, many at the newspaper said they were losing a friend. "There was some sadness when he left," recalled Sports Editor Earl Yost. "We had a get-together. Everyone came. He was well liked. He was interested in everybody." But some editors said Lyons was not oriented strongly enough toward maximizing profits to suit Hagadone executives. "One of the reasons he left was because of his desire to keep the editorial quality high," a *Herald* editor said, "It didn't square with their desire to cut costs."

Lyons, now publisher of a ninety-two-hundred-circulation Scripps League daily newspaper in Flagstaff, Arizona, confirmed that view. "There were some budget constraints I felt I could no longer live with. I didn't feel that I could turn out the type of product I thought Manchester deserved. I told them [Scripps officials] I was going into politics for a while." Lyons said, however, that Scripps set no specific profit goals for the *Herald* while he was publisher.

Lyons's successor was Raymond F. Robinson, a publisher-businessman with little background or interest in editorial aspects of the business. He came to the *Herald* from DeKalb, Illinois, where he had been publisher of the *Chronicle*, an eleven-thousand-circulation Scripps League daily. Robinson was quiet, almost reclusive, with a penchant for neatness. "He once inspected our desk drawers to see if they were neat," a longtime reporter said. "He always wanted the desk top clean. The phone had to be in the right-hand corner at a ninety-degree angle."

In 1976, the year after Robinson arrived at the *Herald*, there was a split between Scripps League and its Hagadone division. As part of the division of properties, Scripps assumed full control of the *Herald*. After the split Scripps owned twenty-one daily newspapers in thirteen states from California to Vermont, while Hagadone was left with six daily newspapers in six states.

Robinson stayed on as publisher at the *Herald*, but there was growing pressure to adopt economies that would increase the *Herald*'s profit margin. For years *Herald* employees had received free home delivery of the paper, but Robinson eliminated that benefit. He also reduced the number of pages in the paper, shrank the newshole, and cut the staff further. The paper carried fewer staff-written stories and readers noted that United Press International stories with Manchester date lines began to appear. Robinson received a steady barrage of memorandums from Scripps League headquarters on advertising, circulation, page-one layout, masthead changes, and other details. One editor recalled preparing reports at home for Scripps League. "There was always some new gimmick or packaging concept," another editor said. "It might be a new box on the front page, or all-cap heads, or down-head style."

During a 1979 interview, Robinson defended the staff reductions as necessary economy moves. "You have to be financially strong to stay in business," he said. "Labor is a very high cost. You produce a quality newspaper with what you can afford. No publisher has enough editorial people. There's no way today you can satisfy everybody. A paper this size can't afford to have one person writing editorials." Regarding complaints about staff morale, the publisher said, "If people are not satisfied, they can leave. My people aren't chained to their desks. People here have gone on to better jobs. This paper has produced some great opportunities for young people."

Robinson had been publisher for less than a year when the *Hartford Times* folded, leaving the *Herald* as the only afternoon newspaper available in Manchester. (The March 31, 1976, figures of the Audit Bureau of Circulations showed that the *Herald* sold 10,365 papers in Manchester, compared with 2,803 for the afternoon *Hartford Times,* and 9,448 for the morning *Hartford Courant.*) Despite the sudden loss of afternoon competition in October 1976, the *Herald*'s slide continued.

A year and a half later in May 1978, another afternoon daily, the *Journal Inquirer*, a spunky, ten-year-old tabloid that circulated in towns north of Manchester, entered Manchester for a head-to-head circulation battle with the *Herald*—a bold move that would force the *Herald* to fight for survival.

The *Journal Inquirer* was founded in 1968 by a local contractor, Neil H.

Ellis, who combined two weekly newspapers to create a six-day-a-week tabloid. The paper's circulation area comprised several rapidly growing towns between Manchester and the Massachusetts border twenty miles to the north. The *Journal Inquirer*'s circulation climbed steadily year after year during the 1970s. By 1978 circulation exceeded twenty-five thousand, and by 1982 it stood just under forty thousand. The feisty tabloid succeeded with a formula that emphasized local news and investigative reporting.

The *Journal Inquirer*'s publisher is Elizabeth Ellis, the wife of owner Neil Ellis. Under her direction, the editors give strong backing to reporters on investigative assignments, often taking open-meeting and public-record complaints to the state Freedom of Information Commission. In one case a *Journal Inquirer* reporter was arrested when he refused to leave a town council work session. Acting on instructions from his editors, the reporter argued that, under state law, the meeting was public because there had been no vote to go into executive session. The charges against him were later dropped in court.

The *Journal Inquirer*'s decision to challenge the *Herald* in Manchester was an agonizing one that was carefully considered for many months. "We never would have tackled the *Herald* before the change in ownership," Publisher Ellis said. "I'm a native of Manchester, and we were proud of the *Herald* as the hometown newspaper, but it has diminished in quality. It's filled with wire copy and handouts. There is no investigative reporting. It lost some guts or something." The *Journal Inquirer* entered Manchester neighborhood by neighborhood, distributing the newspaper free to every household for five to six weeks before asking people to sign up as subscribers. Three reporters were assigned to cover the town full time. Within a year the *Journal Inquirer* had five thousand subscribers in Manchester. Many readers switched from the *Herald* to the *Journal Inquirer*. A few advertisers also switched, though most of the larger advertisers purchased ad space in both newspapers.

Although readers of the *Herald* complained to reporters and editors about its declining quality, there was a strong sense of loyalty to a paper readers had grown up with—a paper that had been part of Manchester history for almost a century. "People are loyal to what the *Herald* was," Ellis said. "There's a tradition of loyalty. Newspapers are such a habit. They have to do a lot wrong before people turn against them. People tell me that the *Journal Inquirer* is a great newspaper, but the *Herald* is their hometown newspaper. Some say there's nothing in it [the *Herald*], but others say it does a better job on club news. The DAR is having a strawberry festival. Things like that. If you want a child's picture in the paper, or a list of names, you go to the *Herald*. People say we're not as attentive. To a degree, it's true. If someone wins a contest, they might get a photo on the front page of the *Herald*."

Christopher Powell, the *Journal Inquirer*'s editor, spoke with emotion about what happened to the *Herald*, although he said he was a biased observer. "I am not against chains per se, but it was the worst thing that ever happened to the *Herald*. They gutted the paper. I grew up in Manchester, and I can remember the anticipation I had when it was sold. But it has no guts, no spirit, no intelligence. They're just in business to send money to California."

Three executives of Scripps League Newspapers, who could be expected to have a different view of their company's purchase of the *Herald*, declined to be interviewed. Barry H. Scripps, executive vice-president, asked through his secretary that questions be submitted in writing. In response to a written question about Scripps League's philosophy for a local newspaper and the group's goals for news coverage and quality, he wrote: "Each newspaper affiliated with Scripps League has wide latitude and authority. It is assumed that the highest ethical and professional standards of American journalism will be followed. The newspapers are dedicated to truth and to a free society in which liberty of expression will make a truly democrat: government a living reality. Both sides of a story must be fairly presented. The essentially creative work of publishing a newspaper would be stifled by any policy based on attempting to ascertain the most desirable forms and patterns and then standardizing."

Some current and former *Herald* employees, reflecting on the change in ownership at the newspaper, contended that the sale by local owners to a remote, California-based newspaper chain changed the newspaper in many ways.

"We don't have any close ties between employees and management," one editor said in 1979. "They couldn't care less. It's absentee ownership. It's a cold, hard thing when you work for a chain. Their only concern is making money. They are strictly interested in the bottom line." Another longtime editor said, "Basically, I think the family operation is probably better. The chain is always remote from the community it's supposed to be serving. Once you make 15 to 17 percent, you set a goal of 20 percent. There's a built-in danger that a chain will exist for the sole purpose of making money. A paper doesn't have to be good to make money."

In response to a written question about criticism of group-owned newspapers, Barry Scripps wrote: "A newspaper is as good or bad as its people. Newspaper groups have made a valuable contribution to the economic health of many small newspapers, which could not afford the costs of modernization. Our philosophy is that the local editorial product is the single most important factor to the success of a community newspaper. This philosophy has been successful for fifty years and will continue to be."

Nevertheless, readers, advertisers, town officials, and reporters for the newspaper complained about cutbacks in local news and a continuing loss of quality. "There was a noticeable decline [under Scripps League]," said

Manchester Mayor Stephen T. Penny. "I thought they drove it into the ground. The staff was down to nothing. It appeared they weren't interested in quality. There was a constant turnover in staff. I was constantly dealing with new reporters. I recall the night a new reporter sat through an entire, four-hour meeting and then asked me who I was."

As the *Herald*'s circulation and advertising declined, employees became increasingly worried. Robinson tried a series of changes involving the masthead, layout, and graphics to make the *Herald* more appealing, but nothing worked. "The *Journal Inquirer* seemed to create such a scare," a *Herald* reporter said. "There was a paranoia about it. Everything we did was in reaction to what the *Journal Inquirer* was doing."

A year after the *Journal Inquirer* moved into Manchester, the *Herald* decided it would have to expand into new towns to reverse the continuing drop in circulation. The newspaper had printed only one edition until then, but in 1978 Robinson decided to add editions for East Hartford, an industrial town of fifty-four thousand people between Hartford and Manchester, and for Glastonbury, a bedroom community of twenty-three thousand south of Manchester. One reporter was assigned to each town, and each had to fill a full page with news every day. Under increasing pressure to turn out copy, reporters worked overtime without extra pay to meet their quotas. Despite an aggressive promotional campaign, the newspaper sold only about a thousand copies in East Hartford and fewer than that in Glastonbury, while circulation continued to slide in Manchester.

Scripps League executives recognized that the *Journal Inquirer* was threatening the *Herald*'s survival. In a letter dated December 27, 1975, addressed to *Journal Inquirer* Publisher Elizabeth Ellis, Scripps League offered to buy the *Journal Inquirer*. The letter was signed by Barry H. Scripps, who at the time was vice-president of Scripps League. In the letter, Scripps said he had given a lot of thought to newspaper markets and regarded the *Journal Inquirer* as a prime opportunity for Scripps League. He said he wanted to discuss with Ellis the sale of the *Journal Inquirer* and the possibility that current *Journal Inquirer* management would remain with Scripps League after a sale. Asked in writing about the 1975 offer, Barry Scripps said Scripps League "never offered to buy the *Journal Inquirer* to the best of my knowledge," although a copy of the letter signed by him remains in Ellis's files.

Meanwhile, Robinson imported editors to try to find a formula to revive the sagging *Herald*. A new managing editor, Frank Burbank, arrived in September 1978 from another Scripps League newspaper, the twenty-thousand-circulation *Gazette* of Haverhill, Massachusetts. A year after Burbank's arrival, another *Gazette* editor, Steven M. Harry, was transferred to Manchester, where he was named executive editor. But Harry only contributed to the decline in staff morale, according to a number of present and former editorial employees.

Staff turnover was rapid. Young reporters fresh out of journalism school worked six months to a year at the *Herald*, then quit and moved to other newspapers. Susan Vaughan, a reporter who stayed two and a half years, remembered, "There was so much strain on everyone to meet the early deadlines when we moved into East Hartford and Glastonbury. We felt the quality was suffering. Everyone was overloaded with work. We got so many complaints from people saying the paper was going downhill. We got tired of having to apologize for the paper. The staff was very loyal, but we felt like the publisher didn't care about the image of the newspaper."

Vaughan, who covered business as part of her beat, also was disturbed that advertising considerations affected news judgment. "Everything was geared toward the advertiser. If a new business was an advertiser, I'd have to do a story on it," she said. *Journal Inquirer* Editor Christopher Powell cited an example of advertising pressure from a local bank, Savings Bank of Manchester. The bank purchased full-page ads in the *Journal Inquirer* and the *Herald* and asked each newspaper to carry a package of five news releases on the page facing the advertisement in each paper. The *Journal Inquirer*, Powell said, ignored the request. He said a reporter reduced the five releases to one five-inch story, which was carried on another inside page. The *Herald*, however, ran all five releases, without revision, on a page facing the bank's advertisement, as the bank requested.

By early 1981, the *Herald*'s fortunes were at a low point. The move into East Hartford and Glastonbury had not stemmed circulation losses. Circulation had plunged 30 percent in ten years, from about sixteen thousand to under eleven thousand. Advertising also continued to drop. On most days during the first half of 1981, the newspaper comprised either twenty or twenty-four pages, though it sometimes was as thin as sixteen pages. Before the change in ownership, it had carried as many as forty pages. The decline, however, was even sharper than those figures indicate. Advertising as a percentage of total space during 1981 usually was between 20 and 30 percent; on some days it was as low as 15 percent.

The *Herald*'s continuing loss of circulation and advertising eventually led to talk in the community and in newspaper circles that the *Herald* might fold.

In March 1981, however, there was a surprise announcement that Scripps League had removed Raymond Robinson as publisher (he was assigned to an advertising position with Scripps) and appointed Richard M. Diamond, fifty-three, former owner-publisher of a weekly in Trumbull, Connecticut, to succeed him. Diamond, a well-known Connecticut publisher and coauthor of a syndicated current events column, had founded *Trumbull Times* and built it into a successful weekly in prosperous Fairfield County, fifty miles north of

New York City. In 1979 he sold the newspaper to the Journal Company, publisher of the *Milwaukee Journal*, and moved to Florida, where he entered the real estate business. In Connecticut, Diamond had been a director of the Connecticut Council on Freedom of Information and an outspoken advocate of access to public records. After local police told his reporters they could not inspect an arrest blotter, he took the case to the state supreme court and won.

Diamond and Edward Scripps had known each other since 1976 when Diamond contacted Scripps to discuss the possibility of launching a new newspaper to fill the void left by the collapse of the *Hartford Times*. Nothing came of the talks, but the two struck up a friendship. Five years later, Diamond got a phone call from Scripps, who offered him the job as *Herald* publisher. "I missed the newspaper business. I never really wanted to be completely out of it," Diamond said, in explaining his decision to return to Connecticut. To lure Diamond to the *Herald*, Scripps reportedly offered him the chance to become a part-owner of the newspaper if he could save it. Diamond declined to discuss the precise terms of the arrangement. Diamond also was given broader authority than previous publishers, over both day-to-day operations and long-range direction. "It's evident he has a different status," a *Herald* editor said a few months after Diamond's arrival. "He's exercising authority other publishers did not have. The key is that he's calling the shots."

Diamond moved quickly to change the paper's direction. Within a week of his arrival, he fired Steven Harry, the executive editor. Shortly thereafter, he announced that the paper would end regular news coverage of East Hartford, Glastonbury, South Windsor, and Vernon and concentrate on Manchester and three small suburbs the paper had always covered— Andover, Coventry, and Bolton.

In a letter to readers, the new publisher explained: "The people of Manchester want their own newspaper, one that addresses itself to community issues and one in which they can take pride. Despite this mandate to produce a community newspaper for Manchester, the *Herald* has marched to a different drummer in recent years. An expansion effort undertaken four years ago did not succeed. In recent weeks we have curtailed full news coverage of four area towns to concentrate on comprehensive news coverage of Manchester." To emphasize the new direction, Diamond changed the paper's name from the *Evening Herald* to *Manchester Herald*. (Scripps League had changed the name from *Manchester Evening Herald* to the *Evening Herald* when the paper moved into Glastonbury and East Hartford.)

As part of the campaign to increase circulation, the *Herald* was distributed each Wednesday to every household in Manchester. An extra eight thousand copies were printed for the nonsubscribers. As a further inducement for new subscriptions, the newspaper carried coupons for prize drawings. Prizes included a trip to Disney World, two hundred dollars worth of groceries, movie tickets, dinners, lawnmowers, and cash.

Diamond conceded it would not be easy to win back subscribers who had soured on the paper and canceled their subscriptions. "People have long memories. If you go to a restaurant and order roast beef and it's bad roast beef, you'll remember that years later. It's the same thing with a newspaper. Some people gave up on the paper. Now I have to get it back in their hands. The biggest complaint was that there was no Manchester news. They didn't need the paper. It will take one to two years to convince people that this is a Manchester paper and if they want Manchester news, they have to read it."

Diamond promised more local editorials, more investigative reporting, and more comprehensive news coverage of Manchester. "I want to cover the hard news, but also to be analytical," he said. "The town has no police commission. Is that the best way to function? We want to ask these questions. Is the hospital meeting the needs of the community? Are the schools? One of the functions of a paper is to examine how well the institutions of the community are serving the community. We want to put a microscope on this town."

Diamond said his goal for the editorial page was to have locally written editorials and columns appear each day. The new publisher also said he wanted more investigative reporting. "We're digging," he said. "I don't want to come out punching wildly, but I want people to know we can do some digging. We're checking the public records on a regular basis now." As an example of more aggressive reporting, Diamond said the newspaper reported that the town assessor had a real estate office on the side and that the telephone at his real estate office also rang at town hall. When he was not at the real estate office, the assessor would take his real estate calls in the assessor's office.

A few months after his arrival, Diamond hired Daniel Fitts as editor. Fitts had worked as a reporter for Diamond at the *Trumbull Times* and had gone on to become managing editor of the *West Hartford News,* an award-winning Connecticut weekly. Before Diamond announced Fitts's appointment to the staff, however, word leaked to the rival *Journal Inquirer*, which broke the story. Managing Editor Frank Burbank, who had been the *Herald*'s top news executive, was incensed when he learned about the appointment of Fitts from a *Journal Inquirer* reporter who telephoned him for his reaction. Furious, Burbank, the last Scripps editor, resigned.

By early 1982 it appeared that Diamond was making progress toward his goal of publishing a more professional newspaper. The paper displayed a crisp, clean layout. Local news stories were displayed prominently on page one when they had significant local news value. On most days page one carried a mixture of local, state, national, and foreign news. Sometimes, however, important international stories were downplayed. When Pope Paul II was shot on May 13, 1981 (two months after Diamond became publisher, but before Fitts was named editor), the *Herald* carried the story as a one-column item at the top-left side of page one. Most other afternoon newspapers carried the shooting of the pope as the lead and many completely remade page one to accommodate the late-breaking story from Rome. A month later, the *Herald* similarly underplayed news about the raid by Israeli planes against an Iraqi atomic reactor.

The *Herald* is divided into four sections. The first includes foreign, national, and local news, plus the editorial page. The other sections are "Focus," sports, and business. Soon after he became editor, Fitts named a new "Focus" editor and added a reporter, giving the section a three-person staff. "Focus" rotates among five themes: food, family, people, leisure, and weekend. The section carries columnists Dear Abby and Andy Rooney, plus a blend of features and news items similar to that found in many large-city daily newspapers.

The sports section, with a staff of two, is edited by Earl Yost, who has been with the paper as a sports reporter since 1945. Coverage of local high school teams receives a lot of space. Yost has nearly four full pages to fill with photos, wire copy, and material written by him and sports writer Len Auster.

The business section appears to be the weakest part of the paper. It consists of one page of news, followed by three pages of classified and display advertising. The lead page typically includes a Sylvia Porter column, several news briefs, and one or two wire stories about business.

The most evident change in the newspaper since the arrival of Fitts and Diamond occurred on the editorial page. Three or four times each week the page carries a local column, written either by Fitts, Diamond, City Editor Alexander Girelli, or a reporter. The columns generally touch on local themes, such as politics, zoning, the schools, or economic development. The page also carries staff-written editorials about local issues on most days. Fitts stopped using editorials supplied by Scripps League. Diamond said Scripps makes no attempt to dictate local editorial policy. "There's very little in the way of editorial direction," he said. "I have a feeling they're fairly pro-Reagan, but I think they're more interested in the bottom line. They expect a certain profit."

Six months after he became editor, Fitts said he had made progress in upgrading the *Herald*. "The emphasis is on good, solid, comprehensive local news coverage," he said. "We're trying to stay on top of the big local stories. We now have a good stable of reporters who are getting to know the town well and develop sources. The real emphasis is on solid day-to-day coverage to build up credibility." Fitts said he was sensitive to the charge that his reporters—most of them recent college graduates with no previous journalism experience—were not familiar with Manchester issues. "A big criticism is that so many of our reporters are new to town, and little mistakes creep into the copy. The reporting tends to be shallow." He said, however, that the writing and depth of coverage were improving with time.

Despite the gains in editorial quality, Diamond faced a formidable challenge in trying to win back readers and advertisers. When he took the job as publisher, he confidently set a two-year timetable to boost the *Herald*'s circulation to twelve thousand, but he later set more modest goals and talked of holding circulation between ten and eleven thousand.

Diamond conceded the struggle to gain circulation and advertising was proving tougher than he had anticipated. "I thought I'd be further along than we are, but we're making some strides," he said in early 1982. "It's tough. Around the country, newspapers aren't taking off anywhere." During the ten months since his arrival at the newspaper, Diamond said circulation had dropped by about three hundred. Circulation fell by about one thousand in East Hartford, Glastonbury, and other suburbs when the *Herald* pulled out of those towns and picked up about seven hundred in Manchester. Diamond said the newspaper was selling about eighty-two hundred copies a day in Manchester by early 1982. A factor that made the drive for circulation difficult, he said, was that of 18,500 homes in Manchester, 35 percent consisted of rental apartments and condominiums. While 60 percent of the owners of single-family homes bought the newspaper, only 15 percent of condominium owners and apartment dwellers did so. Nevertheless, Diamond remained sanguine. To reduce costs, Diamond said he had cut the full-time staff at the newspaper from fifty to forty-seven, and planned to cut it further to forty-five. Despite the cuts in the overall staff, Diamond said the news staff increased slightly with the addition of new reporters. He said editorial expenses represented about 20 percent of the newspaper's budget, an indication, Diamond asserts, of the *Herald*'s strong commitment to news.

Initial reaction to Diamond among employees and readers appeared to be favorable. A town official who had followed the newspaper for a number of years said, "He seems to be turning it around. I see a new direction, a real attempt to get back the local flavor. I'm impressed with him. He says the *Journal Inquirer* beat the pants off the *Herald* because the *Journal Inquirer* did a better job. He's a realist." *Journal Inquirer* Editor Christopher Powell said, "I think Diamond is far smarter than anyone they've had there before. I've spoken to him a few times and I think he understands the causes of the *Herald*'s deterioration." Diamond, however, said he would feel better if readers and advertisers were responding in bigger numbers. "Talk is cheap," he said. "It takes time. It takes time for people's favorable reactions to filter down."

As circulation declined slightly in 1981, advertising also dipped about 2 percent to 4.5 million lines, compared with 9.8 million lines of advertising in the rival *Journal Inquirer*. The *Herald* also carried about 150 preprinted advertising inserts for the year, compared with 354 in the *Journal Inquirer*. Excluding the inserts, Diamond said the *Herald*'s advertising/news ratio was, on average, about twenty-eight to seventy-two, compared with an advertising/news ratio of fifty to fifty at the *Journal Inquirer*.

Diamond predicted that advertising would pick up as the editorial product improved. "Local advertisers like to identify with the paper they're advertising in. If they're not reading the paper themselves, it's a hell of a lot harder to get them to advertise in it." Advertisers seemed to back that view. Al Sieffert, Jr., who runs an appliance store in Manchester, said, "The *Herald* has become a lot more aggressive under Diamond. He's brought the paper back to life. It's stronger for us as an advertising vehicle. It was a local joke before." As a result of the changes, Sieffert said he was advertising in the *Herald* more often. William Hale, president of the Heritage Savings Bank in Manchester, said he was pleased with the emphasis on local news. "I think the paper should be dedicated to local news," Hale said. "If I want news from the Middle East, I'll buy the *Hartford Courant*." Advertisers said the *Herald* ad rates were competitive. In early 1982 the *Herald* charged $3.85 per column inch for a little more than ten thousand circulation, compared with $5.60 per column inch at the *Journal Inquirer* for nearly four times the circulation. Advertisers, however, had to weigh the fact that 80 percent of the *Herald*'s circulation was in Manchester, while 85 percent of the *Journal Inquirer*'s circulation was outside the town.

Despite the obvious difficulties, Diamond was upbeat about the future. "I feel I can stop the slide and show a little growth in two years. The basic concept of pulling in our horns and trying to be a local Manchester paper is a good one. We can't be a third regional paper. I think I can make a small, cost-efficient paper with ten thousand circulation, with 90 percent of it Manchester circulation. That's my formula."

Midland
Reporter-Telegram

Griff Singer

You race westward from Dallas and Fort Worth in your Lear jet, and quickly the cross timbers section of the state turns to mesquite and brush country, then suddenly to desert.

Below, you notice strange shapes—something like bomb craters. But no war has been fought here, at least not in modern times. For miles and miles, there are only a few fences and ranch roads, plus some stock ponds and small oil storage tanks. Occasionally, a brilliant green patch appears, obviously some farmer's irrigation project.

As quickly as the tree-covered ground turns to desert, an oasis comes into view.

No palm trees, no camels. This is a 1983-model, oil-spewing oasis called Midland.

This is Tall City. Modern buildings, soon to be dwarfed by a forty-story bank tower, glisten in the bright sun. Transportation is in the form of shiny Cadillacs, Lincolns, Mercedes, or fancy pickup trucks. Or maybe an airplane or helicopter.

While cities in the northern United States suffered through recession, Midland continued to live its traditional yo-yo experience: a few months as a boom town on the verge of exploding, then a few months with employment dropping. As the world oil and energy market goes, so goes Midland.

In the heart of the oil-rich Permian Basin, this western Texas city of seventy-five thousand is home base for more than seven hundred oil companies and affiliated businesses.

But Midland, so named because it sits at the midpoint on the Texas and Pacific Railway between Fort Worth and El Paso (Midland to Fort Worth or Midland to El Paso—307 miles), is not a city of roughnecks and drillers in dirty clothes and muddy boots.

Executives work and play here. If need be, they will take a day off and fly to "Big D" with their spouses to shop at Neiman-Marcus. If there is no time for that, then Bill Blass or Oscar de la Renta will just have to come to town for a special showing. After all, a town of seventy-five thousand that includes two billionaires and who knows how many millionaires obviously has money to spend.

That has been part of the Midland story since oil companies first came to this ranching and agricultural center in 1926.

Those spots that from the air looked like bomb craters are old, dried slush pits. They mark each one of the thousands of oil wells drilled in the region.

When the world energy crisis became what was thought to be an unending problem and when the lid on domestic oil prices was lifted, Midland boomed. But as a world oil glut developed, it was slowdown time again.

Oil was first discovered in this region more than fifty years ago. The cattle barons and sheep raisers reluctantly had to stand back and let the high rollers take the lead. The economic times have been good or bad with them over the years here. On several occasions during the past two decades, tenants for office space in downtown Midland were as scarce as teeth in a scrawny prairie chicken. At other times businesses would almost jump at the chance to lease space, even if it resembled a chicken coop.

The January 1982 unemployment rate was the second lowest in Texas, just about 3 percent. And while jobs of all sorts were available (one bank reportedly was short fifty secretaries), finding a place to live was a formidable task. That all changed, however, within two months. The boom was over, and oil businesses felt the crunch.

But still it was not that bad. Some bankers were concerned about all the money on loan for now-idled drilling rigs. Unemployment in Midland in January 1983 was 5.6 percent, again one of the lowest rates in the state. In comparison, neighboring Odessa's January 1983 unemployment rate was 8.2 percent. (Odessa also lives and dies by the oil business.)

The hordes from the north, seeking fast, big bucks in the Midland area, soon disappeared. No longer were people forced to live in cars or in virtual shacks as they had been only months before.

More than twenty would-be newspaper purchasers must have had a notion that business generally would be good, even though up and down, when in 1978 they went calling on Mrs. James Allison, Sr., after she announced the *Midland Reporter-Telegram* and the *Plainview Daily Herald* were for sale.

Her husband had published the *Reporter-Telegram* from 1940 until he died in 1975. He was succeeded by James Allison, Jr., who scrapped a career as an advisor for the national Republican politicians in the eastern United States.

The younger Allison made improvements in the newspaper—adding wire services, changing the paper's dress to modular makeup, upgrading production facilities, and installing computerized editing and typesetting equipment and new offset presses.

Three years later, he also was dead, a victim of leukemia at forty-six. The elder Mrs. Allison reluctantly decided it was time to sell the *Reporter-Telegram,* and the *Daily Herald* in Plainview, a Panhandle town of ten thousand north of Lubbock. The Allison family had owned that property for many years, too.

Among the unlikely shoppers for the two-newspaper package was the Hearst Corporation.

Hearst had not bought a newspaper in almost twenty years. And it just seemed strange for the big-city-oriented Hearst to want two newspapers in isolated West Texas.

But Hearst wanted the properties badly enough to shell out a reported $35 million—$30 million for the *Reporter-Telegram* and $5 million for the *Daily Herald.* The firm has since purchased two other community newspapers in Midland, Michigan, and Edwardsville, Illinois, as well as thirty suburban newspapers—two dailies and twenty-eight weeklies—in California.

Is Hearst happy that it expanded its Texas holdings (the *San Antonio Light* also is a Hearst property) and bought into smaller community newspaper markets for the first time?

"Yes," says William C. Thomas, who moved from San Antonio to become Hearst's first president and publisher of the *Reporter-Telegram.* "Frank Bennack [chief executive officer of Hearst and former publisher of the *Light* in San Antonio] must have had a great feel about what was going to happen in Midland and Plainview," Thomas said.

While Plainview's economy continued to be very stable, Midland's exploded after Hearst came to town. Advertising linage increased. Major shopping centers opened. Buyers no longer needed to drive twenty-two miles to Odessa to make big purchases. And even after the boom sounded more like a pop, sources said advertising linage was still higher than in previous years, though short of budget projections.

During the height of the boom in 1981 and early 1982, 51 percent of the *Reporter-Telegram* classified section was for help wanted. That all changed, but because of strong classified sales work the slack was taken up, and then some, with property sale and rental advertising. Midland's classified advertising in mid-1983 reached record levels.

And circulation was up. Audit Bureau of Circulations figures for 1978, just before Hearst came to town, showed a daily circulation of 20,544 and a Sunday circulation of 22,448. The March 31, 1982, total was 22,118 daily and 25,025 Sunday for a city with just over 26,000 households. The current management is confident that daily circulation for 1983 will reach 27,000, and Sunday circulation, 30,500.

Business has been so good that another press unit was installed, increasing black-and-white capacity to ninety-six pages.

With business good, the *Reporter-Telegram* could be tempted to maintain the status quo. But the Hearst management has talked improvement. "I want to make this the best community newspaper in the country," Thomas said in early 1982, proudly describing improvements made on the *Reporter-Telegram* since Hearst took over in January 1979.

Thomas did not get the chance to fulfill his dream, although he did get to pick up an armload of plaques and certificates for recognition in the Texas Press Association competition for 1982. Thomas has been promoted to a far more challenging position as publisher of the afternoon *San Antonio Light*, warring with Australian Rupert Murdoch's *Express and News*, a morning-evening-Sunday combination. Thomas was dispatched to San Antonio in March 1982 to replace William B. Bellamy, who in turn was named president of the *Light*.

Thomas clearly was not sent to Midland "to retire" and enjoy an easygoing smalltown life. Hearst does not do business that way. Midland definitely could be called a stepping stone for Hearst executives on the way up. Thomas's successor is George Irish, a thirty-nine-year-old transplant from Hearst's smaller *Midland Daily News* in Michigan. He has taken hold where Thomas left off, even to the point of assuming many of Thomas's civic responsibilities.

Despite Thomas's (and now Irish's) plans to make the *Reporter-Telegram* the best community newspaper possible, some old-time readers complain that the paper is "just not like it used to be." Others note improvements, particularly the move from the chamber-of-commerce approach to news. And still others perceive little or no change in coverage or appearance since the big-city boys came to town.

Thomas was the only member of the Hearst executive family to move to Midland, which relieved the local business community; they feared a complete turnover in personnel at the newspaper. (Irish has brought in one "outlander," Ray Dumont, to serve as his general manager. He was rescued from Hearst's *Boston Herald American*, which was sold to rival Murdoch who also publishes the *New York Post* and the *Times* of London, among other publications.)

The move of only Thomas to Midland was viewed as reassurance to Mrs. Allison, who died in 1980, that the *Reporter-Telegram* would remain the same old *Reporter-Telegram*, at least in spirit. "That was one of the primary concerns Mrs. Allison had," Thomas said. "She didn't want the newspaper to lose touch with the community."

One source said that another newspaper group offered a higher price for the Midland-Plainview package but that Mrs. Allison turned it down "because it was one of those over-the-transom deals after the Hearst bid had come through and the price had become known to some individuals. Apparently she didn't want to do business with someone who would be involved in any sort of underhanded scheme."

Irish echoes what Thomas said earlier about life as president and publisher in Midland and Plainview. The boss has autonomy in running the newspapers, particularly when it comes to news and editorial matters. While Thomas was also publisher in Plainview, Irish carries only the title of president there. James Thomas (no relation to William C. Thomas), a longtime Plainview news executive, was named publisher.

Despite Bill Thomas's background in advertising (he was advertising director at the *Light* when Bennack called him home from a Mexico vacation to tell him he would soon become a publisher if the Midland deal could be consummated), he says his long career in newspapering has included some of everything.

"The time has passed when this will be referred to as the '*Repeater-Telegram,*'" Thomas said before returning to San Antonio. "I have a flair for the news as well as an interest in advertising."

Thomas, fifty-six, served in the right spots to become a publisher. The Chicago native went from World War II Navy duty to the dispatch department of the *St. Petersburg Times* in Florida in 1946. He ended up in the *Times*'s management training program and in 1960 became vice-president and advertising director of the *Bristol Herald-Courier* in Tennessee. He then was named publisher of the *Suffolk Daily Herald* in Virginia. Following the sale of his interest in that newspaper, he accepted the post of general manager and advertising director of the *Miami News*. He joined the *Light* in 1968, becoming advertising manager in 1975, and in 1978 director of advertising and marketing, responsible for all advertising, research, promotion, and marketing functions.

Unlike Thomas, Irish makes no claim to a flair for news. Irish's strengths are in personnel and management, though his first newspaper job was in advertising.

After graduating from Millikin University in his hometown of Decatur, Illinois, in 1966, Irish worked at the *Decatur Herald and Review* as a classified advertising salesman for a little more than a year. Then he joined the Lindsay-Schaub Newspapers as a personnel assistant and served as personnel manager from 1972 to 1976.

Irish moved to Michigan's *Midland Daily News* as office manager in April 1976, became business manager in 1977, general manager in 1979, and publisher in 1980, after Hearst acquired the property.

Midland townsfolk could not criticize Thomas for being aloof from the community. He served on the board of directors of the Midland Chamber of Commerce, Industrial Foundation, United Way, High Sky Girls Ranch,

Midland Objectives for the '80s, Leadership Midland, and Junior Achievement. He also was chairman of the Palmer Drug Abuse Program and was on the advisory board of the Texas Tech University Department of Mass Communications and the Permian Merit Scholarship Board.

Irish, in less than a year, had moved in to become vice-president of the United Way; board member of the Chamber of Commerce, Junior Achievement, High Sky Girls Ranch, and Palmer Drug Abuse; and a member of United Way's New Horizons (for developing new programs) and the Rotary Club.

Based on his activities in Decatur, Irish can be expected to keep a close tab on city development plans. He was chairman of the Decatur Plan Commission for four years, until moving to Michigan.

While wanting to carry on what Thomas and the *Reporter-Telegram* organization have started under Hearst, Irish says his main challenge is in planning for the newspaper. "We have got to determine how we can best serve a community that indeed is unlike any I know of anywhere else," he said.

"Midland's economy can change quickly. There doesn't seem to be a good bellwether to predict what is going to occur, at least not very far in the future." As an example, Irish recalled that in 1981 Midland was caught up in what he termed a "super-heated" economic situation. It was not following the national situation at all.

"When I came in on March 15 [1982], I thought this community was still in that super-hot economic situation and started working with that in mind. Then I soon realized that we also had fallen into a recession situation, something that actually started a month earlier.

"What we need is to develop a way to initiate alternative plans to best serve the needs of our customers. I have talked to many of my friends in similar newspaper situations, but none can explain what is going on in Midland," Irish said.

While advertising linage is up, Irish notes, "It's not enough to write New York about."

One method being seriously considered to bolster advertising revenue is a total market approach, providing advertisers mail service to households not subscribing to the *Reporter-Telegram*. That possibility and the need to bolster the paper's business and circulation data processing capabilities have caused Irish to temporarily delay plans initiated by Thomas to purchase a new front-end system for the news department.

Irish decided to purchase a new system for the business office, combining the existing news and business computers and adding some terminals for the news side. He said the move to improve the business-circulation effectiveness does not mean that he is not interested in improving the news product. "I'm very satisfied with the staff that I inherited," he said. "But we need to do better—to improve our writing and editing, to get a new spirit."

Irish is mindful of the *Reporter-Telegram*'s competition—"That's anybody who reports news and sells advertising"—which he describes as all the area media: three television stations, sixteen radio stations, and the larger circulation *Odessa American*, which the Audit Bureau of Circulations says distributes 37,200 copies every afternoon and 46,300 on Sunday.

While complimenting Freedom Newspapers's *Odessa American*, particularly its packaging of news, Irish said, "We do better in Odessa than they do in Midland on advertising."

Also creating competition from the news side is the *San Angelo Standard-Times*, which distributes 1,777 newspapers every morning in Midland. Irish is aware that the Harte-Hanks paper is looking to make some move at getting a larger part of the Midland-Odessa market by implementing its own total market package.

At the editorial helm of the *Reporter-Telegram* is Jim Servatius. He and Thomas and Irish are convinced that the *Reporter-Telegram* is doing a better job under the Hearst flag. But the three quickly note they do not fault the job done by the Allison family, particularly by the younger Jimmy Allison.

It made sense to Thomas to make the soft-spoken Servatius the editor in January 1980. Servatius had been keeping an eye on Midland while working as editor at Plainview for seventeen years. And he was new enough on the scene as managing editor in Midland—he arrived in August 1978—so as not to be labeled part of the *Reporter-Telegram*'s old guard.

He succeeded a man who knows Midland well. W. H. Bill Collyns had been editor of the *Reporter-Telegram* for thirty-three years. And before that, he was manager of the Midland Chamber of Commerce for ten years.

When Hearst bought the *Reporter-Telegram*, it was, as Collyns puts it, "suggested that I retire," even though he had only a year to go on his contract. Thomas kept Collyns on as a member of the newspaper's editorial board and gave him the title of "editor emeritus."

Collyns later took a position with the First National Bank of Midland as the chairman's advisor on community and regional affairs. He also kept the newspaper title. But when a *Reporter-Telegram* story about the bank's involvement in a lawsuit created controversy, Thomas said it was time to sever the relationship with Collyns. The crowning blow was that the bank refused to talk to the newspaper's reporters and responded instead with a full-page ad.

One policy that is different is the handling of local news. "That's changed, all new," Servatius said. "We were covering it all along, but now we are showing our readers that it is in the paper by displaying it the way it deserves," Servatius said. In the old days, some local stories, particularly those of a controversial or uncomplimentary nature, were buried behind the classified advertising pages. Now, on Sundays, the *Reporter-Telegram* has a complete local section with a local front; on weekends, the good stories are placed on page one or played at the front of the first section.

"We feel the local news must get good presentation when it is warranted," Servatius said. He considers the *Reporter-Telegram*'s biggest news competitors in this executive-oriented city as the *Dallas Morning News* and the *Wall Street Journal*. But there is more competition. The nearby *Odessa American*'s circulation area covers seventeen counties, primarily to the west and south. The *San Angelo Standard-Times,* one of the original Harte-Hanks publications, at one time maintained a two-person news bureau in the Midland-Odessa area but has since closed it. Still, a morning edition of that newspaper is hauled more than a hundred miles into the market to compete against the afternoon *Reporter-Telegram* and the *Odessa American.*

Phil Schoch, editor of the *San Angelo Standard-Times,* said its Midland bureau was discontinued when circulation did not deliver the subscribers necessary to justify the bureau economically.

"We don't try to compete with Midland on Midland news now. If something interesting develops on a spot basis, we will staff the story," he said, noting that the *Standard-Times* gives strong coverage to twenty of the forty-six counties in its circulation area.

"Some of those subscribers we have in Midland have been regulars for years. They want our oil page news in the morning, rather than wait for Midland or Odessa in the afternoon," Schoch said.

Because oil, energy, and business are such important parts of the Midland scene, the *Reporter-Telegram* has increased its coverage of those activities. "We have reorganized our oil reporting, trying to make it as informative and meaningful as possible. We can't fool these people. They know when we do a good job and when we don't. We went to the oil people to find out what they needed to know and we have tried to deliver that information," Servatius said. Sunday editions include at least five pages of oil and business coverage while each weekday at least one page is devoted to oil and business.

Editorially, Hearst has given the *Reporter-Telegram* complete freedom. Thomas and Irish kept the Associated Press, Los Angeles Times-Washington Post News Service, a state capital bureau service, and Copley News Service. A natural addition was the Hearst Feature Service. Servatius said virtually all editorials are locally written, and the gloves are now off when it comes to local politics.

After Hearst arrived, a forty-year *Reporter-Telegram* tradition was abolished when the editorial board—Thomas and Servatius and his editorial assistant—decided political endorsements should be made in local races, not just national and state contests. "We lost the mayor's race by eight votes, but at least our readers knew how we stood, and we presented them with some thoughts on why we thought one candidate was better qualified than another," Thomas recalled.

Collyns was a member of the editorial board at the time the change was made, but he did not attend the meeting. He still believes the decision was unwise, saying, "It was done without enough thought." But Servatius counters that a great deal of discussion went into the endorsement question. "We didn't do it as gods we know all. We investigate any matter that we editorialize on."

"We have attempted to expand our coverage and comments on issues and events. Sometimes the readers don't particularly like what they see in print. But we feel it is our responsibility to call attention to problems that arise," Servatius said.

"Midland people for years have had the attitude that 'we can take care of our own.' And in many instances, the city did. But with such tremendous growth, some of the people who need help have been ignored. Our local government has rejected funds to help some of these folks who can't help themselves. As conservative as we are, the *Reporter-Telegram* has taken some positive stands on accepting federal funds to help solve some local problems."

One such problem dealt with low-cost and low-rent housing. The *Reporter-Telegram* ran two series bringing to light the shortage of housing for low-income residents as well as the condition of some available rental property. The *Reporter-Telegram* confessed to owning a rundown rental house across the street from the back parking lot of the newspaper and published a photograph of it along with pictures of similar houses in other parts of town. "We knew we had to admit that we were part of the problem of being a less-than-interested landlord," Thomas said.

While some Midland residents might view such series as "anti-Midland," Thomas said that just is not the case. "It is our responsibility to report news situations that are good and bad, and if the things we see are bad, we call them to the community's attention so that they can be corrected."

Servatius added that the *Reporter-Telegram* has not swayed from supporting the Midland community. "If anything, we have increased our support of community affairs and projects. The old ownership was noted for its boosterism and we still like that role to a point."

But earlier generations of Hearst newspapers were noted for a different role—that of gee-whiz sensationalism's purveyor. W. A. Swanberg, William Randolph Hearst's biographer, wrote that Hearst "turned journalism into a mad, mass-production world combining elements of the peep-show, the Grand Guignol, and the foghorn." Some Midland citizens feared that Citizen Hearst's old tactics still lived.

Reporter-Telegram readers criticized the newspaper for publishing a photograph from the local graveside service of a resident killed in the January

1982 crash of an Air Florida jet at Washington. One reader felt it invaded the privacy of the family and was just not the thing that nice newspaper editors do. A flood of letters also went to the newspaper when earlier it ran a crash-scene photo of a body in the icy waters of the Potomac River. Readers complained that while the *Reporter-Telegram* had the freedom to run such photos, it should be accountable.

Servatius agreed in an editor's note, saying:

> Rights cannot be separated from responsibility.
>
> Many of the events of life are not pleasant. Airplane crashes, soldiers wounded, dying or dead on the battlefield, My Lai, and the assassination of a president in a motorcade in Dallas are among them. Photographic coverage of such events expresses, in ways stories cannot, the tragedy and horror of them. . . .
>
> Sometimes the picture is not a pretty one. On those occasions, decisions are not made lightly. While we believe the public wants and deserves complete coverage, even when it may illustrate the violent or tragic side of life, we have no intention of sensationalizing the news or emphasizing the morbid and have no respect for publications that do.

Even when readers' reactions are negative, Thomas said it is important that the newspaper listen. "People make the newspaper, and we are trying to talk to the people of Midland, our 'family of readers.' We want to find out what they like and don't like."

Thomas added that in his roles as a publisher he has avoided a practice of making rules on "don't do this and do that." One veteran staff member backed up that statement, noting that few if any "sacred cows" are known to the news staff.

The lack of "sacred cows" is one new *Reporter-Telegram* trait that caught the eye of Mrs. H. B. Johnson. She has been reading the newspaper for more than thirty years, and likes it better under Hearst management.

"It's not biased like it used to be," said Johnson, now retired after working in the jewelry business for many years. "In the past, the newspaper slanted too much of the news. It seemed to play ball with the monied people. Now that's changed. There is a lot more local news in the paper now. The paper is larger, but of course there is much more advertising than in the past," she said.

Johnson said it appears that the newspaper is staffing meetings of governmental bodies while formerly those were left uncovered. "Now we are getting some insight into what things they are doing, and who's doing what," she said.

Hank Avery, an oilman and former mayor of Midland, has a different view. "We used to have a newspaper. The only good thing about it now is the rubber band around it," Avery said. "It is amazing how things have evolved. There's nobody there anymore who knows a thing about Midland. All of the old ties are gone, and it has hurt the newspaper. They don't know what Midland is today, and they certainly do not know about its past."

To make his point about the newspaper staff not understanding the city's past, Avery cited an obituary. The newspaper carried a short story on the death of Mrs. Marvin C. Ulmer, basically listing survivors and funeral services.

Avery said the newspaper failed to report that she was the widow of a former Midland mayor who had served on the city council more than twenty years. And the paper also failed to note that the Ulmer family took money from its personal bank account to buy the land for Midland City Hall when the city treasury could not afford it.

Former editor Collyns indicated one reason he was scheduled to stay with the paper, even if in an advisory role, was to look out for such problems as the Ulmer death story. But with him gone, Collyns said few people at the paper recognize those names and places that are a part of Midland's past.

One person with such knowledge is Betty Simmons, but she has been busy serving as an executive administrative assistant, first to Thomas and now to Irish. Simmons has been associated with the Allisons and the *Reporter-Telegram* administration for thirty years. She is quick to brag that under her new bosses the newspaper is just as community-oriented as before, but without boosterism—what she described as the "chamber-of-commerce approach. Our editorial content is more complete in every aspect, not just what is good," she said.

If the *Reporter-Telegram* shows a weakness in recognizing old names and ties, it has exhibited strength in taking on old-line Midland from time to time. The First National Bank skirmish is a good example.

Rumors started floating in mid-October 1981 that First National was involved in a multimillion-dollar suit involving an oil company. Servatius and Thomas said the newspaper attempted to get information from the bank. But the paper was waved off. "Nothing to it," the bank said.

Rumors persisted, however, and finally the *Reporter-Telegram* learned that something was brewing in Dallas. The Associated Press was contacted. But it could find nothing. Finally, Thomas told Servatius to send one of his best people to Dallas and determine what was going on.

Longtime police reporter Richard Orr hit a gusher, discovering the suit in federal bankruptcy court. The *Reporter-Telegram* ran the copyrighted story as a banner in November 6, 1982, editions. The story reported that the bank had been hit with an injunction three weeks earlier. The court ordered the bank to stay foreclosure and restore more than $5 million in assets the bank had offset from various accounts of GMW Corporation of Midland, an oil company facing financial problems. The bank had held a $25 million promissory note from GMW and had foreclosed by taking over some of the accounts, including a payroll account. GMW lawyers were successful in their argument for an injunction to keep the bank from foreclosing, noting the bank action had damaged the personal lives and businesses of their employees. The bank had appropriated the salary account of GMW, then debited employee accounts the amount previously credited, thus causing checks to be returned for insufficient funds.

While declining to talk to *Reporter-Telegram* reporters, the bank took out a full-page ad addressed to the public. The ad claimed, among other things, that there were major errors in the reporting and that the newspaper was three weeks late reporting the story labeled "exclusive." But Thomas stood by Orr's account, once again pointing out that the newspaper had attempted to track down the story while bank officials denied it.

Other actions regarding GMW and the bank have hit the courts in recent months. Thomas and Irish plan to continue reporting what happens. In the meantime, Thomas said, the lawsuits now total in the hundreds of millions of dollars. With obvious pride in the newspaper's decision to pursue and print the story, Servatius noted, "and the TV people have yet to touch it."

Asked about his relationship with the bank, Irish said one of the first people he met and lunched with after arriving in Midland was the president of First National. "It was a cordial meeting. We just happen to have differences of opinion on how stories should be handled. They still don't like to see their name in print associated with lawsuits. We instruct our people to be fair, regardless of who is involved," Irish said.

How do working pros in the area view the *Midland Reporter-Telegram*?

A media consultant and journalism educator, who has kept a close eye on West Texas journalism for years, views the newspaper as "a pretty decent mid-size daily. There's no doubt, the newspaper has beefed up its coverage since Hearst came to town. The local coverage definitely has improved. It is done more professionally," he said.

But when comparing the work of the *Reporter-Telegram* with the Odessa and San Angelo papers, the consultant said Midland does not score as well. "Odessa in particular does more hard-hitting stories these days. That staff does more investigative work. The *American* looks better, the coverage is better. And when you mention the *San Angelo Standard-Times*, generally people respond that the publication merits respect."

The consultant lauded the efforts of new publisher Irish, noting, "He seems to be a genuine person. Bill Thomas was effective, but he came off to some people as being too hard-nosed and impersonal."

The source especially was complimentary of reporters Lana Cunningham and Hallye Jordan—"she's a good educational writer"—and Gail Burke of the lifestyle section, who recently received a writing award from the American Cancer Society.

"The Hearst people haven't done that badly by Midland. It is pretty obvious they want to produce a good product," the consultant said.

"My contacts indicate that the staff generally is happy with the current leadership, although some of them seem to have some difficulty understanding Jim Servatius."

A *Reporter-Telegram* city editor under the Allison ownership acknowledged that he and Servatius did not see eye-to-eye on news. But he lauded the editor's ability at organization and planning. "He is an intelligent man and an excellent organizer," said Tom Nickell, now managing editor of the competing *Odessa American*.

Nickell was at Midland from 1977 to 1979 before heading off for Nevada and a stint of smalltown newspapering and fiction writing. He moved to Odessa in 1982 and quickly rose from city editor to news editor to managing editor through a series of departures and promotions.

Nickell said before the untimely death of Jimmy Allison and before Hearst arrived, the *Reporter-Telegram* was making strong moves at being a very good local newspaper.

"Jimmy Allison was a grand man to work for. He told us we would continue to be procommunity, but we would not be blind either. That was quite a bit of evolution from the old man [the elder James Allison] to Jimmy," Nickell said.

Nickell said the *Reporter-Telegram* was making great strides under then managing editor Tom Rutland. "And we had some good reporters, such as Linda Hill [now press aide to United States Senator John Tower (Republican, Texas)] and Mark Vogler, who won several awards for his investigative reporting."

In making comparisons, Nickell said Rutland never shook off the police-reporter mentality he developed in Oklahoma City. He never worried about packaging the newspaper or planning for Sunday editions. On the other hand, Servatius takes pains to make the newspaper an orderly product. Planning for a Sunday edition starts at least ten days in advance.

"No doubt, the *Reporter-Telegram* is much more attractive under Servatius than it ever was with Rutland. That was just the difference in the two men. The problem with Rutland was that he never worried about what we were going to do for Sunday. He just expected one of those good police-type stories to come along. Of course, sometimes they didn't materialize and then we were in for a dull Sunday. But otherwise, we were doing exciting things."

Shortly after Hearst arrived, Nickell said there was a heavy loss of staff. For one, some of the staff did not care for the Hearst operation or reputation.

Nickell, for instance, had worked on the opposing *Express-News* in San Antonio before going to Midland, so he was not too keen about his new bosses coming from a former competitor.

But, Nickell admitted, "Under George Irish I detect a difference at Midland from what it was like under Thomas. I'd say everything now is for the good for them. Their instituting a daily local page is good. It shows part of the Servatius organization," Nickell said.

San Angelo Standard-Times editor Phil Schoch probably disagrees with Nickell of Odessa on who is leading the West Texas newspaper pack as of now. But they agree Midland has been less aggressive than their papers. "From what I have seen," Schoch says, "Midland has been content to stay almost solely within the Midland County area. (Midland has once again put a full-time regional reporter into the field, moving beyond the bounds of Midland County.)

"Odessa has got my attention. But whatever Midland or Odessa does, that's good. Competition breeds better writing, better editing—a better product. We welcome such competition," Schoch said.

Midland's new publisher is concerned about the newspaper's performance, image, and credibility. To get a feel for how the news staff is performing, Irish established a "Bureau of Accuracy" program. On a daily basis, some five stories are clipped and sent to the primary news source in the story. The source is asked to respond to questions and return them in a postage-paid envelope. "We ask them to comment on accuracy of facts and things like that," Irish said. "We have been getting about 90 percent response, and most are favorable."

Another practice Irish has instituted to get better acquainted with the community is weekly luncheons at the newspaper, where various community leaders and primary news sources are brought in to meet with news and advertising executives. "We are looking for their comments and suggestions about the newspaper, and we have the opportunity to get better acquainted in an informal situation," he explained. "It is a good way to meet sources and a good public relations tool."

Irish said the *Reporter-Telegram* is considering a telephone call-in program in which readers are allowed to express opinions on various subjects.

With the growth of advertising linage, the *Reporter-Telegram* newshole has proportionately kept pace. But the news staff has gained little since Hearst arrived. And a problem that has plagued many West Texas newspapers for years—employee turnover—continues at Midland, though it was slowed considerably by the economy and improved benefits at the newspaper.

The pattern is for young journalists, most of them fresh out of college, to start at a newspaper the size of Midland. Some stay as long as two or three years, some less. Part of the problem may be their desire to join a larger newspaper. But when Midland transforms itself periodically into a boom town, low newspaper salaries versus big oil-company paychecks becomes the biggest problem.

Servatius said an inexperienced reporter at Midland now starts at $235 a week, plus a 7.5 percent annual bonus (that is up 2.5 percent since Hearst took over). The company also pays health insurance and retirement plus other normal fringes, such as paid holidays and vacations. New employees are reviewed after three months and then every six months. A pay raise is almost assured after the first three months.

Other employees are lured from the newspaper during good times. Thomas said there was a problem with classified ad department employees spotting ads for better wages before they got into print and leaving to take advantage. Experienced staffers in the energy and business news department are especially vulnerable to raids by oil companies.

The news department numbers thirty-four, two more than when Hearst came in 1979. The paper has added a regional reporter and another person on the oil-business desk.

Servatius said turnover for the past year has been low—four of thirty-four, amounting to about 12 percent. The editor said he has seen some years when turnover was as high as 33 percent.

The lower turnover may be tied to the economy. But Servatius also credits improved employee benefits, brought about by Hearst and scheduled for further improvement under Irish, as one of the principal reasons for people wanting to stay.

As for the rest of the newspaper staff, little has changed. There have been no reductions. A few "old-timers" did decide to find employment elsewhere, however.

"We attempted to give some of the people (most of them in production areas) more responsibility, and some decided on their own that they would be better off somewhere else," Thomas said. "It was a situation where they did not choose to maintain the pace that we felt the *Reporter-Telegram* must keep now."

One problem area involved circulation, where as many as half of the routes were not being served by regular carriers. Thomas said he cured that with an advertising campaign aimed at adults interested in making twelve dollars an hour—the time required to handle the afternoon job by car.

Collyns, however, said that pressure was put on some longtime employees who decided too much was being demanded of them. "You couldn't blame the oil editor for leaving to join an oil company. He was forced to work twelve hours a day, doing business news in addition to the oil news he had been responsible for all along."

Assessing morale is not easy. But Irish and Servatius noted the staff works hard and attempts to carry out its responsibilities. "Basically, we have a happy group of people now," Servatius said. When asked if the personnel background of Irish has been a factor in improving morale, he responded with a wide smile.

That may have been borne out by the fact that current staffers generally were reluctant to talk negatively about life with the *Reporter-Telegram*. A relatively senior member of the news team, however, said the staff is "hungry for direction. They [the editors] want us to do enterprise work, but they don't encourage us that much. The newspaper needs more heart and spirit. Without that, it is just a shell," the staffer said.

"The biggest problems are low pay [top scale reportedly is about three hundred dollars a week for reporters] and lack of direction. . . . Servatius is too busy to get out and meet people, and some of the other leaders are passive—they don't stir up the folks the way they could."

Irish may have detected the need for Servatius and his lieutenants to get out of the shop more. For one, he dispatched Servatius to the American Press Institute, well known for reviving overworked editors caught up in the daily grind of "getting out the paper," for a ten-day seminar at Reston, Virginia. "He [Servatius] hadn't been out of the state for years. So it was great for him to get some new ideas and to get some revitalization to go along with some things we already were discussing and planning," Irish said.

Irish also has directed his subeditors and department heads to get more involved in community life. "If we are going to adequately report and cover this city, we must get out into it to know what our readers are doing and thinking," Irish said.

Servatius sees no problem with his editors and other department heads becoming active in such things as service clubs. "Midland is a civic-oriented community to the point that some pretty outstanding speakers are brought for service club meetings. We cover the meetings almost as news because of the quality of the programs. In that respect, our city probably is not the norm for cities of comparable size in other parts of the country."

Servatius said he is aware that many newspaper editors believe that their staffs should not be associated with such organizations because of possible conflicts of interest. "We believe there is a conflict if an organization attempts to give an editorial staff member responsibility for club publicity or is expected to participate in promoting some major community program such as the United Way," Servatius said. But he noted that news people must become a part of their community, and so long as they are not covering meetings and handling publicity, that is just fine.

Irish is convinced that being part of Hearst has helped the *Reporter-Telegram* grow, improve, and be more independent. "Because we are privately held, we don't have to worry constantly about the quarterly earnings statement. We can put in more, not just take it out to satisfy the shareholders," he said.

"The Allisons did a good job. But it must be difficult to deal with people in some [difficult or touchy] situations when for years you have served with them on the board at the bank, in the schools, and things like that."

Irish, echoing Thomas, says that Midland has a good newspaper, but that it can be better—it will be better.

And Servatius agrees. He is pushing for a "new dress" for the publication—new headline and body type and the use of color photos. "Some people say you should be careful about changing the looks of a newspaper. You don't want to scare off or confuse your longtime subscribers. But with the number of new residents coming into the area, I don't think changing our appearance to make the *Reporter-Telegram* more readable will be offensive," Servatius said.

Irish also looks for better organization and packaging. He notes, "We want to make it a little easier for the readers to get through our newspaper. We want them to make the best use of that twenty-three minutes they spend with a newspaper every day."

Irish has a lot at stake. He wants to succeed as a newspaper publisher. So he, like Thomas, wants the *Midland Reporter-Telegram* to be the best community newspaper in the country.

Based on what readers, some of his staff, and even critics seem to be saying, George Irish just may be able to go a long way in accomplishing that goal at the tall oasis.

The New Mexican

Peter Katel

I t was a long courtship, but when Gannett Company and the *New Mexican* of Sante Fe married on February 27, 1976, there was on the surface no reason to expect that the union of one of the nation's largest media companies and Robert M. McKinney, the newspaper's publisher and former owner, would be anything but happy.

Gannett acquired (for $11.7 million of its stock) the weekly *Taos News* and, more importantly, a long-established state capital paper, the only daily in a growing Sun Belt city. McKinney gave up ownership of the *New Mexican* without, so he thought, giving up the power to run it.

From the point of view of readers, Gannett's acquisition seemed beneficial. The commonly expressed opinion was that the quality of the paper had fallen off since the 1960s, when the *New Mexican* was in some respects the most influential paper in the state, assiduously read by the people who ran New Mexico. Gannett, reporters were often told by acquaintances and news sources, might revitalize the paper.

That would depend, of course, on the success of the Gannett-McKinney relationship. And when the merger occurred, there were already signs, though only a handful of people were in positions to see them, that each side had a different understanding of who would run the *New Mexican*.

The tall, silver-haired McKinney—a former stockbroker, an ambassador to Switzerland during the Kennedy administration, and a board member of Trans World Airlines and Martin Marietta—has the bearing and somewhat aloof air of a man who considers himself in charge wherever he is. He clearly saw himself still the leader of the paper he had owned since 1949. By necessity, the leadership was often long-distance. Although McKinney kept a house in Santa Fe, he spent most of his time elsewhere during the last years of his ownership, keeping in touch with the newspaper by telephone and letter.

Gannett initially pronounced itself satisfied with McKinney's helmsmanship. In the *New Mexican*'s front-page announcement of the merger, Allen H. Neuharth, Gannett's president, said McKinney had "laid the groundwork for continuing growth." The statement continued, "We look forward to his further leadership."

Two years later, however, the marriage was on the rocks, over the very question of McKinney's continued "leadership." On September 30, 1978, McKinney filed a lawsuit in federal court in Albuquerque to end the relationship. He charged that Gannett broke the contract guaranteeing his executive authority, that Gannett had intended to do so when the agreement was signed, and that consequently the *New Mexican* should be returned to him. (McKinney's daughter, Robin, had bought the *Taos News* from Gannett for $350,000 in April 1978, under an agreement between McKinney and Gannett.) And, McKinney said, Gannett had lowered the quality of the newspaper.

That is an assertion that Santa Feans in growing numbers have accepted. Circulation has dropped steadily under Gannett's management. The paper has made glaring errors; and Santa Feans now have a basis for comparison, for the *New Mexican* faces competition not only from an energetic weekly, but also from a zoned edition of the state's biggest daily.

The trial of McKinney's lawsuit was held before a six-member jury in Santa Fe from March 28 to June 30, 1980, and decided, at the district court level, the question of ownership in favor of McKinney.

The differences between Gannett and McKinney went back to the fundamental question of what kind of agreement they had made. Although Gannett had referred to it as a merger, the company's lawyers called it a sale throughout the trial, underlining their position that McKinney had given up the paper for good in 1976. That assertion seemed to have some common-sense logic to it, despite the technical accuracy of the term *merger* for a transaction that took the form of a tax-free exchange of stock—three hundred thousand shares of Gannett for all of the *New Mexican*'s shares. However, Gannett's position was eroded by the evidence of what McKinney believed he was agreeing to—and of what Gannett promised.

Gannett's acquisition ended a series of talks that began in 1970, when according to a Gannett document, McKinney was "hesitant to sell" because he believed the value of the paper would increase. In that belief he was correct. By 1975, when serious negotiations began, Gannett was willing to pay thirty times the paper's annual pretax earnings—$10 million; five years earlier the company had offered $3.6 million in stock or $4.3 million in cash.

McKinney said he decided to give up ownership of the *New Mexican* when he developed serious heart trouble in 1975. McKinney, who was born in 1910, did not want to be responsible anymore for such matters as assuring a supply of newsprint. By giving up control of business details, however, he had no intention of relinquishing control of the paper. He planned to stay in power even though he would no longer live even part time in Santa Fe because of the effect of the city's seven-thousand-foot altitude on his heart. Thus, McKinney said, he negotiated only with Gannett because of the company's "local autonomy" policy. "A world of different voices where freedom speaks," Gannett describes itself in an advertisement. "There is no single Gannett editorial voice."

"McKinney seeks 'continuous association' with the *New Mexican*," a Gannett memo says in summary of a June 4, 1975, meeting in New York between McKinney and Neuharth, the Gannett president. But by July 9, when McKinney concluded a two-day meeting in Santa Fe with Paul Miller, then chairman of Gannett, and Jack Purcell, vice-president for finance, Purcell wrote that McKinney's position was that he "expected that Gannett would really run things from Rochester notwithstanding his titles."

If that was Gannett's understanding of McKinney's position, it evidently was not McKinney's. On November 26, 1975, McKinney angrily broke off negotiations because of a Gannett redraft of the contract that was to spell out McKinney's authority at the paper after the merger. Douglas H. McCorkindale, Gannett vice-president and general counsel, did the rewrite and said in a cover letter that McKinney would report to the Gannett-controlled board of directors of the *New Mexican* and to Neuharth. McKinney would have "the same duties and responsibilities as any other publisher and chief executive of a company owned by Gannett," McCorkindale said. McKinney was not willing to settle for that, however, and by December 8, Gannett had backed down, deleting the section that made McKinney subordinate to Neuharth and specifying the considerable authority that McKinney wanted.

During the trial, Neuharth testified that it had been McKinney's idea to report to the Gannett president, on the grounds that such a status would be prestigious. But the language of the employment contract that accompanied the merger agreement confirms McKinney's account of his negotiating position. He got the considerable authority he wanted.

For five years after the merger, McKinney was to be chairman of the board of the *New Mexican,* chief executive officer, publisher, and editor in chief. For the next five years, he was to be editor in chief only. For the ten years, McKinney was to be paid thirty thousand dollars a year and allowed to keep his office at the newspaper, a company car, and a secretary. After the ten years had elapsed, McKinney could continue, on a month-to-month basis in whatever capacity, if any, on which both sides agreed.

For those first five years, McKinney's power was to be nearly unchecked. Subject only to budget limitations imposed by the newspaper's board of directors, McKinney was—according to the language of the contract—in "complete charge" of news and editorial policies and in charge of "all operations" of any company publication with "complete authority" over all employees.

Furthermore, McKinney was explicitly freed from any obligation to spend all his time on newspaper business. "In accordance with his customary past practice," decisions on how much he would do and from where he would do it were "individually and solely" McKinney's.

McKinney was an infrequent visitor to his newspaper, and to Santa Fe itself, for more than five years before he relinquished ownership. Several times a year, reporters would be told to get their scrapbooks of clips up-to-date (and in some cases to get their hair cut)—directives that presaged the publisher's arrival. Within a few days, McKinney would appear; he would spend a week or two at the paper and then depart. But, subordinates testified at trial, he kept in constant touch from afar by letter and telephone; his mail was forwarded to him. After Gannett took over, McKinney directed political endorsements and was consulted on at least one major story, by long-distance telephone.

Not surprisingly, Gannett's position in the lawsuit was that the contract did not say what it seemed to say. Neuharth, in a pretrial deposition, parts of which were read aloud in court, said the "only meaningful thing in the entire contract [is], or was intended to be" the provision that McKinney is responsible to the board of directors. The rest, Neuharth said, is "window dressing."

The board of directors never met before Gannett and McKinney came into serious conflict, which occurred less than a month before McKinney filed suit. Neuharth testified that actions he took concerning the *New Mexican* were performed in his capacity as a director. But Judge Campos instructed the jury that the board had never delegated any authority to Neuharth.

A Gannett executive analyzed the McKinney contract differently from Neuharth. And that analysis, unlike Neuharth's, was not expressed to opposing counsel in a lawsuit, but offered in a letter to a colleague in December 1977, before McKinney sued.

Robert B. Whittington, then vice-president of the Gannett-West division, wrote to his immediate superior, "the terms of the sale . . . on paper seem to say, 'I, McKinney, have sold the paper to Gannett, but I really still run it and they just got whatever money comes through.'" Then, referring to Stephen E. Watkins, a McKinney associate who was then president and general manager of the *New Mexican,* Whittington wrote: "Don't know if Paul Miller or AHN [Neuharth] would want to admit that [contract] gets in the way of Watkins. It obviously would not get in the way of some replacement from the outside who could be told, 'Look, this is the way the contract reads, so be nice to the old coot and tell him what you've done after you've done it and be sure that his empty office is kept dusted in case he ever does drop in.'"

Rollan D. Melton, then president of Gannett-West and the man to whom Whittington wrote, took a similar view of the contract. In a November 1977 letter to Whittington, Melton said of the "absurd demands" by McKinney to which Gannett had acquiesced: "Increasingly as I'm exposed to Miller and Neuharth in acq [acquisition] stuff, I think they both fail to think thru [sic] the consequences of getting papers at any price. Feel they believe the most important thing is to get the property(ies) and cope with the debris later."

These and other equally frank letters and memorandums between Gannett officials were introduced as evidence in the trial and gone over at length, often projected on a screen so that the jury could follow passages as witnesses and the lawyers referred to them.

In a May 17, 1978, memo, John C. Quinn, vice-president for news, told Neuharth, referring to N. Walter Ryals, the Gannett-installed president and general manager, "Walt Ryals is pressing his campaign to move towards severing the McKinney relationship with the *New Mexican,* which I told him he was launching even sooner than I had expected he would. . . . From the view of the News Division and the readers, the sooner we get McKinney's name off the masthead, the better." At the bottom of the typed memo, Neuharth wrote, "I agree, *but* let's make sure we remember he has a contract."

Whether or not Gannett remembered, top-level personnel changes at the *New Mexican* were directed by Gannett, despite McKinney's possession on paper of full authority over all employees.

Watkins was fired on March 28, 1978. After his departure, other McKinney holdovers, including the production manager and composing room foreman, left or were fired. (Advertising Director Wayne Vann had departed in June 1976 for another Gannett paper; McKinney also had been unhappy with that move, believing Gannett should not have transferred one of the paper's most able executives; Vann returned five years later and is now president and general manager.)

In arguing that Gannett broke the contract guaranteeing his executive authority, McKinney alleged five breaches: the firing of Watkins; the hiring of Ryals to replace Watkins; the refusal to follow McKinney's order to fire Managing Editor Barclay Jameson; the refusal to follow McKinney's order two days later to fire Ryals because he would not fire Jameson; and the suspension by the newspaper's board of directors of McKinney's authority pending resolution of his lawsuit.

Before the trial opened, Campos concluded as a matter of law that the contract had been broken when the *New Mexican* published a June 4, 1978, political endorsement. The editorial included criticism of the chosen gubernatorial candidate, Democrat Bruce King, which McKinney had ordered deleted. It was because of the editorial that he had ordered Managing Editor Jameson fired.

A considerable part of the trial was devoted to whether Gannett was justified in firing Watkins. The evidence concerning his termination led to the larger question of what Gannett's intentions were toward the *New Mexican*—whether Gannett intended simply to milk the paper.

It was undisputed that at a December 14, 1977, session in Chicago, during the annual meeting of Gannett publishers, Melton and Whittington of Gannett-West told Watkins that the *New Mexican*'s pretax profit margin should be in the 36 to 38 percent range, as it was for the Gannett papers in Olympia and Bellingham, Washington. The *New Mexican* then had a profit margin of 22 to 23 percent, Whittington testified, asserting that Watkins was not expected immediately to increase the margin by 14 to 15 percent; he would have four to five years for that. But Watkins was expected to boost the newspaper's pretax profit margin to the Gannett average of 26 to 27 percent in short order.

Watkins listed "general improvement in cost control" as one item in an eighteen-point summary of what he was told in Chicago. By the time of that meeting, Gannett had already cut some costs. In the spring of 1976, for example, the width of the paper was reduced one inch. Later, in 1978, the *New Mexican* canceled United Press International (the Associated Press wire was kept, and Gannett News Service and the New York Times wires were added).

Watkins was reprimanded in Chicago not only for the shortfall in profit, but also for poor "housekeeping" in the newsroom, mailroom, and advertising office and the "possible disallowance" of circulation numbers by the Audit Bureau of Circulations. Three months later, the circulation problem exploded when the circulation manager was found to have been misstating sales to the extent that the company had to write off seventy-five thousand dollars in losses. The writeoff was the final straw, Gannett executives testified, and Watkins was fired.

But his days with Gannett were evidently numbered anyway. McKinney's lawyers stressed that Watkins delivered on the bottom line; in 1977 the *New Mexican* ranked sixteenth of the fifty-three Gannett daily papers in the category of increase over the previous year's profit, eleventh in the percentage of profit over budget, and forty-first in the ratio of profit to sales. Gannett executives, however, found Watkins "impossible to deal with," in the words of one internal memo. For one thing, Watkins persisted in regarding McKinney, not Gannett, as his boss.

Watkins's adherence to the contract giving McKinney full power contributed to the general manager's downfall. But Gannett's flouting of the agreement contributed to the downfall of its defense against McKinney's suit.

Gannett, Campos stated in a fifty-two-page memorandum opinion filed on March 17, 1981, had made a deal it did not plan to keep. "Gannett went into this deal with its eyes wide open," Campos wrote. "It knew the Employment Agreement would interfere with how it wanted to run the *New*

Mexican. It also knew that McKinney was old and physically infirm. It knew that he would be residing in Virginia. It wanted the *New Mexican* very badly. Gannett took a gamble." The company, Campos said, "lost its gamble."

The jury verdict had imposed no requirement on Campos to order return of the paper. Gannett lawyers had argued that that step would be unfair and that all the verdict called for was a court order that Gannett abide by the contract it had, according to the jury, broken.

But such an order would be impractical, Campos said, noting the length and "unusual contentiousness" of the case he was completing. He had no intention of generating more litigation—possibly contempt proceedings over compliance—with the kind of order Gannett suggested. In any case, Gannett had "deliberately and wrongfully destroyed" the possibility of peaceful coexistence between Gannett and McKinney, the judge said.

Practicalities aside, return of the paper was legally appropriate, Campos said, because the contract that Gannett broke was at the heart of the newspaper deal. McKinney would not have given up the paper without assurance of the right to control it for some time. Furthermore, Gannett was not merely a contract-breaker, but a wrongdoer, the judge asserted. "There is no market where McKinney can replace what Gannett has wrongfully taken from him," Campos declared. "Considering McKinney's age, his health, and all other circumstances, Gannett has already wrought, and daily continues, an unconscionable and malicious deprivation of precious rights belonging to McKinney. . . . It was a unique right for which no commodity or other property can serve as a substitute."

The judge's memorandum opinion sought to legally justify his key ruling. On June 30, 1980, Campos had decided that the paper should be returned to McKinney. Campos insisted that his decision was not a punishment of Gannett. The company, he acknowledged, "may feel it suffers too much from this remedy." But it is "the fairest remedy and the only adequate remedy." Gannett's Neuharth immediately blasted the decision as one "based on politics and provincialism."

Campos let Gannett know that he did not appreciate Neuharth's attack. In court on September 3, 1981, Campos said frostily, referring to Neuharth's characterization of the decision as political, "Out here in the provinces, we have a three-letter word that describes that kind of distortion and a four-letter word to describe people that traffic in that kind of distortion." The judge declined to use the actual word, "liar," in describing Neuharth.

Campos's order was appealed to the Tenth Circuit Court of Appeals in Denver not only by Gannett—which was hardly surprising—but also by McKinney. Campos's decree—called the "unscrambling of the egg" during the trial—directed Gannett to return the 700 shares of the *New Mexican* to McKinney and about $4.3 million in profits the company had made during its ownership, with reasonable business expenses deducted. McKinney was to return his 450,000 shares of Gannett stock, which some five years after the merger had risen in value by $4.5 million. Campos denied Gannett's request for credit of five hundred thousand dollars in interest that Gannett would have earned if it had not had to pay income taxes on the *New Mexican.*

McKinney's appeal challenged Campos's denial of a motion for a new jury trial. McKinney wanted to go back to court to demand damages from Gannett, contending it had lowered the value of the paper by mismanagement.

Gannett officials have denied that contention. In any case, Gannett will continue to run the paper until appeals are decided. That may be a long time. Whoever loses in the circuit court probably will go one step higher to the Supreme Court.

The debate over what Gannett has done to the *New Mexican* is not limited to the would-be owners of the paper. The paper's employees and readers also have an interest, though not of the multimillion-dollar kind.

Gannett clearly has improved the lot of newsroom employees. McKinney paid poorly. When Gannett took over, the average news-side salary, including that of the city editor, was $8,892 a year. Clerical workers in the Los Alamos and Espanola bureaus made $105 to $110 a week; reporters and photographers made $140 to $210 a week; and the city editor made $250 a week. Raises were granted once a year.

Four years after the Gannett acquisition, news-side salaries ranged from $200 a week to $330 a week. For employees with less than five years of experience, raises were given twice a year; employees on "senior" status got annual raises.

During the trial a group of employees filed an affidavit in court in protest of McKinney's attacks on Gannett's management. For their part, they said, they appreciated Gannett. Eight employees who had worked for both owners said in an accompanying affidavit that "management under McKinney discouraged employee tenure, contributed to a high rate of turnover, and tended to undermine employee morale."

Turnover, particularly at the managerial level, did not cease with Gannett's takeover. After the flurry of voluntary and involuntary departures of McKinney loyalists, Gannett replaced Ryals with Vann (McKinney's former advertising chief) in February 1981. And Michael Stepanovich, who had been imported from Gannett's *El Paso Times* to replace Gannett's Jameson as managing editor, was himself replaced in August 1981 by another *El Paso Times* editor, Larry Sanders.

The following year City Editor George Welles departed, as did Editorial Page Editor David Roybal. Of the eight holdovers who had testified to high turnover under McKinney, three had left the paper less than three years later. Although the turnover rate may be slightly lower than under McKinney, Gannett was in no position to make an issue of it.

Nevertheless, if the affidavits by employees showed that Gannett had won their hearts, there is evidence that the company had failed to achieve such acceptance in Santa Fe.

One measure of that failure may be circulation. When Gannett took over, the *New Mexican* had a daily circulation of 17,404 and a Sunday circulation of 20,932. The numbers climbed steadily until, in the first quarter of 1977, they reached 18,874 daily and 21,549 Sunday. But audited figures for 1981 show a drop of 15 percent in daily circulation (to 16,034) and of 9 percent in Sunday circulation (to 19,564). An unaudited publisher's statement of September 30, 1982, shows slight improvement: 16,383 daily and 19,646 Sunday.

In 1979 the *New Mexican* began publishing a Saturday paper (promoted with the slogan, "I get it on Saturday morning"). The circulation of the morning paper started at 16,388, according to a 1979 audit, and dropped by December 27, 1981, to 15,199. Nine months into 1982, circulation was reported at 15,856.

Neuharth, in a telephone interview, challenged the use of circulation figures to show that Gannett has not been accepted in the Santa Fe area. He asserted that circulation had been artificially boosted under McKinney by selling the paper outside its natural market zone and by underpricing it. "Those are ways to build up numbers," he said, "but that doesn't necessarily reflect the acceptance of the paper by the readers, nor does it reflect the rewards that advertisers get."

The paper's chief executive echoed the theme. In a September 30, 1981, letter to advertisers, Vann trumpeted city zone circulation increases between the 1980 audit and the September 1981 publisher's statement: from 11,622 to 12,043 daily and from 13,165 to 13,707 Sunday. The 1981 audit reduced the magnitude of the achievement—to 11,787 daily and 13,445 Sunday.

As Neuharth suggested, part of the overall circulation drop is in areas outside the paper's market zone. Clearly, Gannett has concentrated on the *New Mexican*'s primary market area. In 1977, 94 percent of circulation was within the area; four years later the area had 96 percent of circulation.

Nevertheless, the bulk of the 1977 to 1981 circulation drop was concentrated within the market area; only 21.5 percent of the reduction involved circulation outside the zone. Furthermore, despite Vann's emphasis on circulation gains within the city, the *New Mexican* has not kept pace with population growth there. In 1977 circulation was 25 percent of the 46,400 population estimated by the audit bureau. In 1981 the estimated population rose to 56,900, but the *New Mexican*'s share fell to slightly under 21 percent.

Neuharth also rejected a comparison between the circulation drop and the population increase. The 1980 census, which state authorities insist erred on the low side, shows a 19 percent population increase—to 48,914 people—for the city of Santa Fe from 1970 to 1980. That is "very low" in relation to increases elsewhere in the West, Neuharth said. Census figures for cities in California, Arizona, and Texas in which Gannett has newspapers bear him out. But the population of Santa Fe County rose by almost 40 percent, to 75,041 people, during the decade. None of the comparison cities showed such a dramatic increase. And Santa Fe County is part of the *New Mexican*'s primary market area.

In charging McKinney with having pumped up circulation, Neuharth also asserted that the *New Mexican* had been "force-fed at cut rates" to people who do not read newspapers in English. In fact, while Spanish and Pueblo Indian languages are widely spoken in northern New Mexico, they are barely read. Schooling has long been conducted in English, and those people who seldom speak English have long depended on English-language papers, particularly because for years there have not been any in their mother tongues.

Neuharth's commentary on the sociology of northern New Mexico only underscores his company's newcomer status.

For any outsider, acceptance is harder won in Santa Fe than in most other cities. Santa Fe and environs are extraordinarily sensitive to newcomers. The sensitivity is particularly strong among Hispanics—56 percent of the Santa Fe population—whose ancestors began settling in northern New Mexico in the sixteenth century. Over the years, land owned by Hispanics has gone into Anglo-American hands, and English has become the main language; economic power is held predominantly by Anglo-Americans.

Resentment of the *New Mexican* by Hispanics was documented in the pages of the newspaper. "A common complaint was that the newspaper was insensitive due to ignorance," the *New Mexican* reported, quoting from a Gannett-financed study of Hispanic views of the media in Santa Fe and five other cities where Gannett owns newspapers. Citizens interviewed attributed insensitivity to "absentee owners" controlling the newspapers. And, the study said, "In Santa Fe it was said that the paper was 'just a bad paper.'"

But the tension between oldtimers and newcomers is not simply an ethnic matter. Santa Feans of all ethnic backgrounds have grown fearful about what they perceive as the creeping loss of their town to monied pleasure-seekers drawn to Santa Fe in large part by national publications. "The right place to live! We've found it: great women, great weather, and plenty to do. Pack your bags!" *Esquire* proclaimed on its May 1980 cover. In New York, Saks Fifth Avenue opened a "Santa Fe" boutique featuring such items as a beaded suede tunic for $725. The *Washington Post* put Santa Fe first on its 1982 "in" list.

Reflecting a resentment that was evident throughout the city, the Santa

Fe City Council took the unusual step in December 1981 of adopting a resolution condemning *National Geographic* for an article on Santa Fe; the magazine had sent page proofs to Mayor Art Trujillo, who was angered by, among other things, the absence of Hispanics in the photos.

Unfortunately for the *New Mexican,* residents seem to see the paper as neither an opponent nor a reliable chronicler of the fundamental change—toward ultrahigh-priced chicness and incongruous architectural trendiness—the oldtimers oppose.

"I think the *New Mexican* went through a very glorious period when Oliver La Farge was writing in it," said Orlando Romero, a novelist, historian, and Southwest resources librarian at the State Library, where his duties include cataloguing the state's newspapers. He was referring to the Pulitzer Prize–winning novelist, who was arts editor and a columnist for the *New Mexican* in the 1950s and 1960s. "A lot of Santa Feans dreadfully miss that independent, semipoetic, righteous lashing out. The *New Mexican* is not zeroing in on the fact that Santa Fe is undergoing such a dramatic change. Everything has become artsy-fartsy, fast lane–cocaine. The *New Mexican* seems to be avoiding the issue or missing the issue. I can only surmise why."

One possible reason, Romero said, is that the *New Mexican* is part of the very change in question. "The *New Mexican* may be symptomatic of what is happening to Santa Fe," Romero said, putting the newspaper's acquisition by a chain into the same class of events as former Treasury Secretary John Connally of Texas buying a house in Santa Fe and the expensive Texas department store, Neiman-Marcus, considering a store in the city.

However, despite the perception among many Santa Feans that their city is being raped, a strong argument can be made that the city needs an economic boost. There is a feeling among some Hispanic business people, a feeling well represented on the same city council that attacked the *National Geographic,* that many Santa Fe preservationists simply want the luxury of living in a picturesque town—one in which they, with their inherited wealth, do not have to scrape to make a living.

Generally considered to represent this tendency is the Old Santa Fe Association, an organization single-mindedly devoted to preserving the charms of the "historic zone," where most of its members live. Some feel the association tries to be "more native" than others. That view of the association has prevailed for some time. Oliver La Farge, writing in 1952 about the Santa Fe Fiesta, observed tongue-in-cheek: "A few dishes do remain pretty well constant; among these are chocolate and tamales, the consumption of which on festive occasions is an old Aztec custom. The Aztecs learned it from the Toltecs, the Toltecs learned it from the Mayas, and the Mayas learned it from the Old Santa Fe Association."

McKinney made the *New Mexican* a voice for preservation. A principal aim of the paper, he stated on its 125th anniversary in 1974, was to "do all it can to help preserve the distinctive flavor of Santa Fe as the 'City Different.'"

Under McKinney the *New Mexican* campaigned in the 1960s for alteration of the design of the new State Capitol—McKinney called the original design a "plate glass, southern-California-style stadium." In the 1970s the paper at McKinney's directive fought government plans to chop down salt cedar trees growing along the banks of the Rio Grande; environmentalists said they were essential to the ecology of the riverbanks.

McKinney had made his money in the stock market and the airline and military-contracting industries, but he was particular about what kinds of businesses he encouraged to move to Santa Fe. He took credit for helping to influence St. John's College of Annapolis, Maryland, to build its second campus in Santa Fe, a move that the *New Mexican* hailed triumphantly. And McKinney also spoke publicly of playing a hand in the Interior Department's decision to make Santa Fe the home of the Institute of American Indian Art.

McKinney's protectionist stance was felt throughout the paper in the 1950s and 1960s. Jess Price, city editor from 1960 to 1962, said, "We disdained industry. I think the paper helped people maintain the feeling that they were in a different place—a kooky small town that was also cosmopolitan."

However, the *New Mexican* was more than a force for preservation. In the 1960s, which are considered by longtime residents as the paper's best years, the *New Mexican* was *the* newspaper with the inside track on politics.

"It had a strong political influence," said Price, now public information director for the University of New Mexico in Albuquerque. "I don't believe it does anymore. Politicians always read the *New Mexican;* it had more to say about politics in the state capital."

Tony Hillerman, a journalism professor at the University of New Mexico who was editor of the paper when Price worked there, said the *New Mexican* "had a reputation for aggressive, especially political, reporting." State capital stories and columns (there was often little difference) were not only biting but authoritative. "New Mexico's out-of-shape legislature is back in session lumpy with insurance agents, lawyers, and ranchers, and so awkwardly apportioned that legislators serving 29 percent of the people can run the whole show," wrote Will Harrison, a columnist whose name is still legend, on January 10, 1961.

The *New Mexican* of that era clearly saw itself as the paper of political record. The New Year's Day edition of 1961 had ten articles on the upcoming legislative session. There were pictures and brief profiles of all legislators and a debate on the hot issue of state aid to public schools.

The paper also reported the gossipy, behind-the-scenes stories that readers in such a political town love. The staff column, "At the Capitol," ran on the front page each day, recounting what happened in the closed-door election for House speaker and revealing a mix-up over votes for candidates named Jack and Mack.

During the 1960s, Price said, McKinney vacillated between wanting to make the *New Mexican* into a southwestern *New York Times* and wanting to turn out a Santa Fe–oriented paper.

McKinney responds: "I think Price is off-base." In a telephone interview from his Virginia estate, McKinney did not dispute the observation that he had had ambitions of transforming his paper into one of the caliber and scope of the *Times;* but he added firmly, "At no time did I believe you shouldn't cover local news as much as possible." The best papers are those with the strongest possible coverage of their home regions, he said. With obvious pride McKinney said he had devoted an exceptionally big part of the paper's resources to covering local news. "Even when the town was smaller, we had twenty-five or twenty-six people on the news staff, I believe. We always had a great many more [news-side] people than the average newspaper of our size."

By the early 1970s, as McKinney acknowledged, the *New Mexican* had lost the corner on the state capital, which had been its prime news asset. The wire services and the *Albuquerque Journal* expanded their capital bureaus and the *Journal* began circulating throughout the state.

A survey of editions from 1971 showed a newspaper that covered the hard news of Santa Fe and nearby communities energetically but in no great depth. News was reported lucidly but without much analysis. No longer present were the intimate capital coverage and the clear adversary stance of much of the political reporting.

Instead, politicians received plenty of space to say what they wanted (a practice that continues today), as in front-page interviews in December 1971 with United States Congressman Manuel Lujan and Governor Bruce King.

Not only politicians had their say. On December 10, 1971, the paper ran a story about a clothing factory opening that quoted the Chamber of Commerce president in praise of the project—the chamber president being Editor Jack Sitton.

Sitton left at the end of the year, replaced by John R. Bott who joined from the *New York Post,* where he had been city editor. Bott completed the transformation from a *New Mexican* perhaps too dominated by political reporting and commentary to an unpretentious hard-news paper.

The great strength of the *New Mexican* five years before it changed hands was that it latched on early to developing stories and stayed with them day after day. In July and August 1971, for example, the paper reported almost daily on the effects of a drought—on the utility company's attempts to promote water conservation, on criticism of the utility by politicians and citizens, and on a related problem of city faucets dispensing dirty water. That sort of tenacious coverage is rarely practiced by the *New Mexican* today.

Gannett officials say they have transformed the *New Mexican* from a paper that was nothing more than McKinney's political tool into a highly professional product. In fact, the partisan cast to the paper's political reporting dropped away as early as the late 1960s, when McKinney began absenting himself from Santa Fe for longer periods.

Unquestionably, McKinney was well known for his political interests. He made no secret of his friendly relations with Democratic senators Clinton P. Anderson and Joseph M. Montoya. Furthermore, Robert E. Storey, editorial page editor under both owners, testified in court that McKinney liked political intrigue. "He liked to go behind the scenes and talk to people off the record." Storey cited consultations between McKinney and Bruce King over whom the *New Mexican* should endorse as King's running mate in the Democratic primary.

Neither Storey nor anyone else, however, gave any examples of McKinney going beyond such practices. In any case, there is little in Gannett's version of the *New Mexican* to support the company's claim of making the paper more professional.

The editing process occasionally seems to stop before headlines are written and stories set in type. On November 10, 1980, the page B-one headline "Women better off staying away from men's jobs: activist" ran over a story in which Graciela Olivarez, a former federal and state official, indicated that she holds precisely the opposite opinion. Nearly one year later, on November 21, 1981, the paper ran a front-page story about the city of Santa Fe billing Santa Fe County for utility services, with no explanation of why the city would be providing gas, electricity, and water to county government when none of the utilities are city-owned.

Problems with stories cannot all be blamed on the copy desk. Articles are often simply inaccurate. On November 14, 1981, a front-page story reported that two former penitentiary prisoners had been pardoned after testifying against a fellow prisoner. In fact, they had been paroled—a considerably different action. On December 3, 1981, the *New Mexican* ran a story with photos on page A-three about the decline of the city's railway station; the city attorney was quoted as saying that the Atchison, Topeka, and Santa Fe Railway wanted to shut down the station. The lawyer had said that, but had been corrected by another city official who said the railway wanted only to eliminate its agent at the station. The station remained open.

Equally serious is the newspaper's occasional failure to gather information from its area independently. A front-page, 650-word story on November 10, 1980, described a U.S. Bureau of Land Management program to resolve land title problems in northern New Mexico. "Presides Vigil had faith in the government," the lead said. The story recounted Mrs. Vigil's success in obtaining title to land on which she then opened a modest drive-in restaurant. "We've got a lot of thanks to give to those Bureau of Land Management people for all the help they've been," Mrs. Vigil was quoted as saying. The story came verbatim from a Bureau of Land Management press release. The *New Mexican* gave no indication of the story's origin.

The *New Mexican*'s lack of restraint in running government handouts serves readers poorly. On November 19, 1981, the paper ran on page A-five a story concerning attainment of a "milestone in the development of efficient fuels for breeder reactors" at Los Alamos National Laboratory. The story seemed to be important, but that was impossible to judge by someone unfamiliar with nuclear technology. The story was simply a rearranged and lightly edited handout from the laboratory.

On other occasions the *New Mexican* evidently takes information from other papers. The November 26, 1980, *Albuquerque Journal* ran a prominently displayed story on page B-one about a Santa Fe liquor license auction in which the winner, according to the headline, paid $51,000 for a license. The *Journal* story, however, had a typo, and the price was misstated as $51,005. The same day, the *New Mexican* ran a story about the auction—and reported the price as $51,005. The *Journal* corrected its error the next day; the *New Mexican* did not.

As the liquor license story shows, the *New Mexican,* despite its position as the state capital daily and its history as the leader in political coverage, is now usually the follower not the leader. Thus, though the state penitentiary, where one of the worst riots in United States penal history occurred, stands only five miles from the city limits, the *New Mexican,* while it did an adequate job during the riot, has effectively left most of the major investigative work in the riot's aftermath to other papers. The *Albuquerque Journal* has followed each step in the drawn-out federal court proceedings concerning a prisoner's class-action lawsuit filed three years before the riot. Those proceedings have included thoroughly documented reports by court-appointed monitors damning conditions at the penitentiary. The *New Mexican* has been content, for the most part, to run rewrites by the Associated Press of the *Journal* stories.

For its part, immediately after the riot the *New Mexican* collaborated on a publication about the event with one C. F. Boone of Lubbock, Texas, who has made a business of publishing "quickie" magazine-format "books" about disasters. (His past works include *Lubbock Tornado* and *Richmond Flood*.) This one was entitled *Holocaust at New Mexico State Penitentiary*.

The news content of *Holocaust* was based entirely on early information about the riot, much of which turned out to be wrong—for example, the initial official explanation of the riot's beginning.

Holocaust ended with a sort of sermon saying that perhaps the "real story" of the riot lay in the fact that the Catholic chapel was unharmed.

"Somehow, in even the most chaotic circumstances of human inhumanity, there is a thread of respect and reverence." Unmentioned was the fact that the Protestant chapel next door was a gutted wreck. And it turned out, when the state attorney general released a report on the riot in June, that the body of one of the slain prisoners was found—in the Catholic chapel.

However, the *New Mexican* did take the commendable step in 1981 of joining with a competitor that has attacked it fiercely, the *Santa Fe Reporter,* in a six-month investigation of the penitentiary that resulted in some solid exposes (also participating in the investigation were an Albuquerque radio station and a television outlet). The *Reporter* initiated the cooperative investigation, and though the *New Mexican* is to be congratulated for joining, its subordinate role in the enterprise reflected once again the paper's lack of news leadership.

Even when the paper does show initiative, it does not follow up satisfactorily. On April 2, 1981, the *New Mexican* broke on its front page the story of older businesses—a fabric store, a five-and-ten, and a pharmacy—forced away from the downtown plaza by steep rent hikes. The well-documented article focused on the social implications. "The change is well under way, and it promises to alter the character of downtown shopping forever." Chic stores were expected to take over. A storeowner who managed to remain near the plaza was quoted as saying of the older, departing businesses, "The landlords are killing them." Of the area, he said, "It's going to end up as one big tourist trap." A bank vice-president agreed, saying, "The area has been a community shopping area. But as the use of the properties becomes more limited, the tendency is away from that and more oriented toward tourism."

But the *New Mexican* let the story languish. On November 7, 1981, *Journal-North,* the *Journal*'s zoned Santa Fe edition, ran a full page headlined: "The Plaza; Old Stores Giving Way to Trendy Ones." In five photos and seven hundred words, the *Journal* covered essentially the same story. But when the *New Mexican* next returned to the subject on January 3, 1982, to report further developments, the meaning of the trend for ordinary Santa Feans was left out. The only people quoted were those with reason to be happy about the changes. "I want to improve Santa Fe," said one of the real estate men behind the upheaval. A gallery owner turned developer said about the businesses she would bring in that "the emphasis . . . will be to serve Santa Fe."

The *Santa Fe Reporter,* in a year-end story, predicted sarcastically that in five years Hispanics would be barred from downtown.

The *New Mexican* did report critically the publication of the *Esquire* article that so offended many townspeople, and the paper was right on top of the city council's anger over the forthcoming *National Geographic* article.

When the spirit of chic came closer to home, however, the paper seemed to draw back.

Criticism of that aspect of the *New Mexican*'s coverage is not limited to Hispanic artists, like Romero, who might be so shocked at what they consider a threat to their beloved Santa Fe that they would lash out against any institution that did not fight the trend.

Peggy Hemmendinger, state board member of the League of Women Voters and president of the Santa Fe Concert Association, says of the new tone in Santa Fe, "The *New Mexican* seems to be wanting to capitalize on that. They seem to not only condone it but encourage it. I wonder if the paper is behind it."

The same thought, expressed more forcefully by another Santa Fean—Oliver La Farge's son, John Pen—was published in the *New Mexican* on June 19, 1983, and drew a response by Vann one week later in his Sunday op-ed column. The reply did nothing to allay fears that the *New Mexican* sided with the developers who are transforming Santa Fe. ". . . [S]ince the downtown area has changed toward predominantly tourist-oriented business, and since tourists have responded by ever-increasing numbers favorably to that change, we should promote it," Vann wrote. And he went on to attack La Farge. "Who asked you to be the conscience for all Santa Feans?" The attack drew a rebuke from another reader which was also published.

Hemmendinger publicly criticized the *New Mexican,* not for the way in which it covered the changes in Santa Fe, but for a city elections campaign story.

On January 6, 1982, the *New Mexican* ran a front-page story about the involvement of City Councillor Dora Battle, the only woman running for mayor, in a messy divorce. The wife of a man Battle had been seeing obtained two restraining orders in divorce proceedings prohibiting the candidate from signing for meals in the name of the store the man owned. The article, however, went considerably beyond the court orders, which were of no great political significance.

Citing a deposition Battle had given in the divorce case, the *New Mexican* reported, "Battle said she had met David Parker first in April 1979. . . . It was not until May or June 1980, however, that Battle said she spent nights with Parker at the Inn of Loretto [the hotel's name is the Inn at Loretto] and La Posada." Further, "Battle said under oath she had temporarily severed her relationship with Parker . . . until he had decided something about his marriage." But, "Battle said she later returned to Albuquerque and she and Parker stayed for about four nights in the Albuquerque Hilton at Parker's expense."

Battle was given an opportunity to respond, on the morning of publication, to the evidence unearthed by the *New Mexican*. The article provoked twelve angry letters to the *New Mexican,* with no response from the paper, which never did explain why it displayed the story so prominently.

For ex-editor Bott, the newspaper erred in running the story across the top of the front page in the home-delivery edition. Detailing the nature of Battle's relationship with the store owner was justified, Bott reasoned, because the romance was integral to the credit arrangement that led to the court orders. But, said Bott, "That type of story, in my newspaper you don't lead the paper with it. It's not a Watergate story; there's no indication it changed her vote or influenced her vote. Spread across page one, it's a little much." He probably would have run the story on the front page, but below the fold.

Despite its failings, the *New Mexican* should not be dismissed completely. Photographs are consistently lively and imaginative. Soft-news features and profiles are often engaging. Coverage of Los Alamos, despite the occasional reliance on laboratory press releases, is energetic. The paper has an exclusive Sunday column by John Hightower, the Pulitzer Prize–winning former diplomatic correspondent of the Associated Press and a Santa Fe resident.

Critics of the *New Mexican* under Gannett express little nostalgia for the McKinney days. "I thought it was awful then," Hemmendinger said, adding a slight qualification, "Under McKinney, it was bad, but not that bad."

McKinney, however, contended in his suit that the *New Mexican* declined in quality under Gannett. To support the claim, he paid a newspaper consultant to study the paper under both owners. The analysis by John Malone of Chicago shows, in the eyes of the McKinney camp, a drop in coverage under Gannett.

Malone's content analysis, based on data from a week of papers in 1975 and a week in 1978, found: 5,064 fewer words, advertising copy excluded, in the *New Mexican* under Gannett (36,420 per issue under McKinney and 31,356 per issue under Gannett); more space per issue devoted to headlines under Gannett (337 column inches under McKinney and 720 column inches under Gannett); fewer news stories under Gannett (an average of 157 items per issue under McKinney and an average of 92 items under Gannett); and excessive "air" around headlines, photos, and cutlines (no air under McKinney and 1.48 pages of it under Gannett).

Malone defined an item as any copy with a headline. A slightly different approach toward analyzing the newshole leads to the conclusion that Gannett is publishing more stories—but not necessarily those the readers want.

In an independent count of stories of two or more paragraphs—in order to avoid counting fillers—the *New Mexican* was found to have run more international, national, and state stories under Gannett than under McKinney. During the week of April 16 to 23, 1974, the paper had 23 international, 144 national, and 67 state stories. For the same dates five years later, the number of international stories more than doubled, to 55. There were significantly more national stories, a total of 181; and a handful more state stories, 75 in all. Under both regimes, almost all the copy in these categories came from wire services, the exceptions being staff-written statehouse stories.

But while Gannett expanded the use of wire copy, the number of local stories diminished. For the week in 1974, the *New Mexican* ran 142 local stories. Five years later the volume dropped 21 percent, to 111.

Gannett's cutting of local copy is matched by its selective trimming of the news staff outside Santa Fe. In the main newsroom, there have been three additions to the roster since Gannett took over, bringing the staff up to twenty-eight. But the paper laid off its Taos staffer, halved what was a two-person bureau in Espanola, and cut back the Los Alamos bureau to one reporter (there had been two part-timers in addition).

Business-side advantages come simply from belonging to Gannett—lower costs for newsprint and equipment, for instance. There are other benefits; one Santa Fe ad man observed that the *New Mexican* carries far more national ads than it did under the previous owner, presumably as part of package deals that Gannett's national advertising office is able to offer.

But Gannett is not limiting itself to the automatic benefits of chain ownership in boosting the *New Mexican*'s revenues. Advertising rates climbed 77 percent between 1975 and 1980. More special sections geared to attracting advertisers are published, far more than under McKinney, including a weekly food section.

And in 1980 the *New Mexican* launched *Northern New Mexico Today,* a free paper that is delivered to the households of all who do not subscribe to the *New Mexican* in Santa Fe and Los Alamos counties and Espanola.

Publication of *Today* enabled Vann to say, in his September 1981 letter to advertisers, that it offered them "coverage of more than 93 percent of the tri-city households, when used in combination with the *New Mexican.*" For the coverage advertisers pay $1.50 per column inch on top of their fee to the *New Mexican.*

Audited figures for mid-1982 show a circulation of 18,249 for *Today,* according to Certified Audit of Circulations. But some in the business community question whether the numbers tell the whole story. The advertising agent who charted the increase in national ad linage said he doubts that *Today*'s actual coverage is as broad as claimed. For one merchant, there is no doubt that *Today* does not live up to its billing. "Circulation and readership are two completely different things," said Matthew Schwartzman, proprietor of the Candyman stores, which sell records, musical instruments, and stereo gear. "They may have circulation, but no readership." He said he regularly sees copies of *Today* lying in yards, not having been picked up, or discarded.

Schwartzman does not like the *New Mexican* under Gannett, though he regularly advertises there. Of *Today,* he said, "If it was a vehicle that really reached people, that I felt was going to give me my best response per unit—people who are going to come into The Candyman—I would advertise in it. I'm a businessman."

Clearly, not all advertisers share Schwartzman's acerbic views. *Today* was still being published more than two years after it began. Despite a publicly expressed charge that Gannett was subsidizing the shopper in an anticompetitive move, *Today* has advanced from running nothing but copy from the *New Mexican* to publishing some articles of its own.

The *New Mexican* as a whole appears to have done well by Gannett. Neuharth said earnings have "improved, as necessarily follows when you improve the product." By Gannett's account, the pretax, net income of the paper—before certain intercompany charges were assessed—more than doubled after Gannett's first year of ownership, from $339,749 in 1975 to $734,249 in 1976, and has climbed steadily upward. In 1979, the last year for which figures could be obtained, Gannett made $1,265,228 from the *New Mexican.*

Circumstances have changed somewhat since then. The *New Mexican* now shares its market area not only with the weekly *Santa Fe Reporter,* founded in 1974, but with the *Albuquerque Journal,* which launched its zoned edition, *Journal-North,* on November 11, 1980. The edition has a full page of news from Santa Fe and neighboring communities three times a week. Twice a week, the news is carried in an eight-page or six-page section.

T. H. Lang, publisher of the *Journal,* says the new edition was not launched because of the *New Mexican*'s legal and circulation troubles. He has heard of "dissatisfaction" in Santa Fe with Gannett, because it is an "outside entity." But, he says, "We are not practicing any sort of predatory techniques in Santa Fe."

Nor has the *New Mexican* accused the *Journal* of untoward tactics. Relations between the *New Mexican* and the *Reporter* are another matter.

The *Reporter,* a voluntary-pay tabloid with a circulation audited by Certified Audit of Circulations at 19,329, reaches almost all homes within Santa Fe city limits. The launching of the *New Mexican*'s *Today* offshoot came at a time when the *Reporter* was picking up advertisers at the daily's expense. The *Reporter,* in an article about *Today,* questioned pointedly whether the new shopper's ad rates were below cost and whether Gannett was breaking antitrust laws by trying to crush a smaller competitor. In an editorial the *Reporter* speculated that Gannett figured the weekly could not afford to file suit to block *Today,* or that if the *Reporter* did go to court, the litigation would "bleed it dry."

Neuharth, when asked about *Today,* said he was not aware of the shopper, but that it sounded like what "many if not most" Gannett papers produce in order to give advertisers total market coverage. "That's not directed at any competitor, it's directed at trying to give advertisers what they want in a market," he said. And Gannett is "very careful not to violate antitrust laws," he added.

The *Reporter* did not trust Gannett to be careful in that regard. In March 1981, one month after Gannett put Vann in charge of the *New Mexican,* the *Reporter* published a six-page special report on a newspaper war in Salem, Oregon, that had led to the filing of an antitrust lawsuit against Gannett by Community Publications, the owner of a free-distribution weekly that had folded, allegedly because of Gannett's tactics. When those tactics were employed, the marketing director of the Gannett papers, the *Oregon Statement* and *Capital Journal* (now merged), had been none other than Wayne Vann.

The *Reporter*'s article about the case was based almost entirely on internal documents obtained and filed in court by Community Publications for its case (since settled). As in McKinney's suit, Gannett's own documents did little for the company's image.

A 1976 memo from Vann to his advertising sales staff described a program he named "Operation Demolition": "The whole idea of the program is to reduce or eliminate each of the advertisers on your base list, while at the same time you keep additional advertisers from advertising in the *Community Press.*" Making the intent of that project perfectly clear, Vann's boss, publisher N. S. Hayden, said in a letter to Neuharth, "Now that I feel containment has been accomplished, our goal is to fatally cripple the *Community Press,* and to accomplish this we have instituted 'operation demolition.'"

McCord told his readers that a similar program to cripple his paper was possible in Santa Fe.

Vann, in an interview in 1981, said it was "absolutely preposterous" to think that he planned to eliminate the *Reporter.* The *New Mexican* and *Northern New Mexico Today* would, however, seek business "aggressively," he said. If the *Reporter* lost accounts, it would be from strong but clean competition, not unfair tactics. Vann also said that the *Reporter* had been "highly selective" in its publication of evidence from the court case; he did not dispute the authenticity of what was published (and after the *Columbia Journalism Review* published a tough story on the Salem fight based on the same evidence McCord had uncovered, Neuharth said the story was not unfair).

Though the *Reporter*'s story on the Salem case openly sounded the alarm, the *New Mexican* did not in the ensuing months put the weekly out of business. Nor did the *Reporter* give any sign that the attempt had been made. When the weekly dropped, after less than a year, an unprofitable Sunday edition, there were no charges that the decision stemmed from any untoward practices by the daily.

Far from stomping its competitors into the ground, the *New Mexican* seems to be running hard to stay with them. The *Reporter*'s circulation has climbed steadily from its 1980 level of 18,294; *Journal-North* reached a reported circulation (it is not separately audited) of 10,880 in early 1983, including 3,005 home-delivery copies in the city of Santa Fe.

It is hard to know the *New Mexican* inside out. Vann, president and general manager, and Sanders, managing editor, declined to answer any questions or provide any factual information about the newspaper for this chapter. "We don't grant interviews," Vann said. "I don't care to comment at all." But the decline in the paper's circulation appears to tell the story of Gannett in Santa Fe. Santa Feans have always criticized the *New Mexican*. Under McKinney, however, they usually kept buying it.

Bill Mauldin, the two-time Pulitzer Prize–winning cartoonist, a part-time Santa Fe resident for more than twenty-five years and a full-time one for twelve, is among the townspeople who dropped their subscriptions. No great fan of the *New Mexican* under McKinney, Mauldin said of the Gannett version, "I just wasn't reading it." He continued, "This is a very colorful, very special sort of a corner of the world, and I think a newspaper that represents it should represent the city and what goes on here. And it just seems to me it [the *New Mexican*] is very standard—it could be printed in Hutchinson, Kansas, or Amarillo or Pecos, Texas. Essentially, it lacks character. It particularly lacks the character of the place that it's being printed in. . . . I don't think it's all that bad a paper, I just think it's unimaginative." One year later Mauldin was asked again about the *New Mexican*. He said that just as he believed the chic takeover of Santa Fe would grind to a halt, the *New Mexican* would improve. "Something like the *Reporter* is going to force the *New Mexican* to get better."

Had Mauldin resubscribed? He had not, nor had he even read the paper in more than a year. "I talk to a lot of people who read the paper," he said. "If I heard somebody say it was getting better, I'd subscribe."

The News and Daily Advance

Ben A. Franklin

For richer *from* poorer, for better *from* worse—that bent nuptial equation says it neatly, if optimistically, for the monopoly newspapers in Lynchburg, Virginia (population, 66,700)—the *News* in the morning and its perversely named afternoon carbon copy, the *Daily Advance* (the same news under a different logo). The papers are certainly richer under a new and aggressively businesslike group ownership, Worrell Newspapers. Given their luridly atrocious history, the Lynchburg papers could not have gotten worse.

In this day of failing newspapers, anyone who can do that cannot be *all* bad. And so far that seems a fair measure of Thomas Eugene Worrell, Jr., a flashy, young, business- and law-school-trained communications chainer. Rich and getting flamboyantly richer, Worrell is forthrightly determined to continue making big bucks at small newspapers.

At the end of 1982, for a reported $47 million (a figure disputed by a Worrell executive), he sold eleven of his smaller properties—eight dailies and three weeklies—to the New York Times Regional Newspaper Group, reducing total Worrell print circulation by about a third, to 232,000 combined daily and weekly. The remaining daily readership (148,500) still ranks Worrell Newspapers fifty-fifth among 161 daily newspaper groups, and it is still far flung. The Worrell dailies (nine of the remaining sixteen) are chiefly in Virginia, but they extend west into five other states from Illinois to Texas and New Mexico. Furthermore 382,000 homes in Illinois, Virginia, and the Virgin Islands can receive his television signals.

It is consistent with Worrell's acquisitive nature that many of his chain's newspaper properties were vulnerable when he got them. The Lynchburg papers were a public shame—pariahs in the community they served. The "Worrellizing" of Lynchburg described here suggests that, due to circumstances, if not to the pure white flame of commitment, there may yet be more to Tom Worrell than the playboy who, not disagreeably, meets the eye. He would like that. He wants to be accepted, as much as possible on his terms—purple shirts, snakeskin cowboy boots, and all. In Virginia, both for his papers and for Tom Worrell, it is proving a contentious row to hoe.

On June 14, 1977, a primary election day in Virginia, the *Lynchburg News* told its twenty thousand subscribers in "the City of Seven Hills," on a bend of the James River in the steep foothills of the Appalachian mountains, how to vote. Editorial writers are forever trying to goad readers to vote, one way or another. But this endorsement was different. For one thing, it was placed in a five-word banner on top of page one, above the logo.

Among the family owners of the *News* and its afternoon cousin, the *Daily Advance*, there lurked men who proved the occasional worthiness of the radical cliche, "scions of reaction." Their patriarch had been an intellectual, a redneck, and a legend in his time—the late United States senator Carter Glass. Senator Glass was "the father of the Federal Reserve System." He was also an unreconstructed and denunciatory racist, and a bane of communists, the New Deal, and Franklin D. Roosevelt.

To the senator's heirs at the *Lynchburg News*, the Democratic primary of 1977 posed a clear and present danger to the Commonwealth. Andrew P. Miller, the former Virginia attorney general, was the Glasses' desired candidate for the gubernatorial nomination. But he was an underwhelming campaigner. Miller might actually lose to Henry E. Howell, Jr., and Howell would then march on Richmond before his Bolshevik horde.

Howell, an iconoclastic, tart-tongued perennial underdog whose liberal energy and twangy rhetoric against "the Big Boys" had given him the nickname of "Howlin' Henry," was perceived by the Glass menagerie as an enemy of the establishment, a barely disguised Marxist. In fact, Howell was and is not even remotely pink, only an anomaly in Virginia—a populist, consumerist, and pro–civil rights moderate liberal. The Glasses' perception of him came easily in Lynchburg, an outpost of hard-core orthodoxy in ultraconservative Virginia. But the Glasses' miscalculation was total. Their terror was shameless. At their newspapers, it toppled every tenet of professionalism and fairness.

Over the top of its page-one, German Gothic logo, the *Lynchburg News* on election morning bannered its five-word primary day editorial: "VOTE FOR MILLER—NOT SOCIALISM." (For good measure, the late Powell "Red" Glass, then the editor and publisher, ordered the same headline flown atop the paper's second section, too.)

Howell narrowly won the nomination anyhow—losing by only a few hundred votes even in Lynchburg, the Holy See of the Reverend Jerry Falwell's so-called Moral Majority. But he was too progressive for establishment Virginians. "Howlin' Henry" was routed in November. Not until 1981, when Charles S. Robb, the son-in-law of Lyndon B. Johnson, became the first member of his party to win since 1965, was a Democrat elected governor of Virginia. Many still blame Howell's alien liberalism for the Democrats' decade in the desert. But Howell is not that extreme; Virginia is.

The "Not Socialism" headline is recent history, after all. But it made not a stir in Virginia. The aberration was hardly a surprise. In the long context of the Glass family ownership of the Lynchburg papers—the senator bought the *News* at age thirty in 1888 for thirteen thousand dollars—it was far from the most wretched excess. Nonetheless, coming in 1977, the red-baiting of Henry Howell was a regression—a reversion to type after a period of family-enforced reform.

Since 1969, when a community outcry against the racist crudities of the *News* under its then–general manager, Carter Glass III, the dynastic founder's grandson, had finally required his removal by the family, the Lynchburg papers had been relatively tranquil. Virginia journalists who did not live in Lynchburg and did not have to depend on the Glass papers admitted to a certain sense of loss, a longing for the Gothic rococo.

For Southern dailies in a largely blue-collar industrial city (Three Mile Island's flawed reactor was designed there by Babcock & Wilcox, the city's largest employer), the Lynchburg papers had had a straightforward, solidly conservative reputation in the craft through much of the first half of the century. The papers are remembered by two alumni who trained there in the 1940s, Edward C. Burks of the *New York Times* and Guy Friddell of the *Norfolk Virginian-Pilot*, as well-edited, responsible, and dignified newspapers run by men who were, or became, some of the state's premier practitioners of that time—men who by and large isolated the news operations from the Procrustean views of Senator Glass.

"Senator Glass was crazy politically, but he ran a quality newspaper," one veteran of the Lynchburg newsroom recalls. "It was a take-care-of-your-people paper."

Quality prevailed on the Lynchburg papers until the stream of events that began with the Great Depression—the New Deal; the Truman Fair Deal; and worse, the racial liberation of the Kennedy-Johnson years, the New Frontier and the Great Society. The 1960s filled the news horizon with events that bemused and vexed the Glass heirs. Their heritage was formidable.

When the senator (and briefly secretary of the treasury, under fellow Virginian Woodrow Wilson) died in Washington in 1946 at the age of eighty-eight, illness had kept him from setting foot in the Senate or, for that matter, in Virginia for four years. He apparently gave no thought to retiring, and neither obedient Virginians nor their obedient newspapers would have asked that of him. In an obituary observation, President Truman noted the two salient aspects of the Glass years. One was that the senator had been the last member of Congress born before the Civil War. The other, as Truman put it, was that Senator Glass had "gloried to the end" in Franklin Roosevelt's soubriquet, "the Unreconstructed Rebel."

Senator Glass had won FDR's scorn for his resistance to the New Deal in the 1930s. But he had held his crusty credentials much longer.

In 1902, the year Virginia Democrats rewrote the state constitution with Jim Crow's pen—and the year the elder Glass first went to Congress—he had denounced the Reconstruction enfranchisement of Negroes in the South as "the unspeakable crime" of the post–Civil War years. Under Glass leadership, the black franchise was effectively repealed in Virginia by the imposition of a poll tax.

That was the inheritance. And under Carter Glass III, during the "massive resistance" of the 1950s—when Virginians flirted with a near-secessionist "interposition" challenge to federal authority—and on through the early and middle 1960s, the *Lynchburg News* kept alive the senator's racist cachet.

As a matter of principle, the *News* steadfastly refused to print significant news of Lynchburg blacks—23 percent of the population. Blacks were nonpersons. The commencement schedule and the football scores at Lynchburg's all-black Dunbar High School were excluded. If you died a white plumber or sewer inspector in Lynchburg, you got an obituary in the *News*. If you died a black physician or pastor in Lynchburg, you got none; your survivors could buy a paid death notice over the classified-ad counter.

Perversely, it took a sixteen-year-old black dishwasher with a sixth-grade education to put black news on the front page in Lynchburg. In 1962 a young black named Thomas Carlton Wansley was accused in the Glass press of raping and robbing an elderly white woman—"Miss Annie." *That* was news. The crime cried out for exemplary punishment. And in a one-day trial in a segregated Lynchburg courtroom, the defendant was given not one but three death sentences. His lawyer, also black, died before he could file an appeal.

But with the Glasses' unwitting help, William M. Kunstler of New York, then a rising itinerant attorney for the damned, turned the Wansley case into one of the most celebrated civil rights confrontations of the 1960s. By snatching the accused from the electric chair, Kunstler inspired the Lynchburg papers to the starkly ideological excesses that eventually drove Carter Glass III to ruin and ouster. Still later, Glass aberrations were to let the legacy of the old senator fall into alien hands. ("One thing I don't like is bigotry," says Tom Worrell, the new owner. "I would intercede if any newspaper of mine showed it.")

Kunstler defended Wansley with characteristically technicolor tactics in the courtroom of City Judge O. Raymond Cundiff. There, although Miss Annie was not sure of her assailant's identity, Wansley was tried again and resentenced to life in prison. But in the process, Glass III so completely lost his head that he lost his job. And he saved Wansley.

The Howell headline had had its Gothic antecedent in the Wansley affair. While Wansley was awaiting retrial after his first conviction had been set aside on Kunstler's successful appeal, the *Lynchburg News* repeatedly printed pictures of the black youth's face with the caption "Convicted Rapist."

That was not enough. The *News* under Glass III never failed to mention Kunstler's name, even in wire-service stories about his wholly unrelated escapades elsewhere, without noting (often in boldface) the publisher's parenthetical judgment that the "convicted rapist's" lawyer was "linked with Communist-front organizations and efforts." A *News* editorial—if readers could distinguish it from the news columns—called Kunstler "a well-known Communist fellow traveler."

During the second trial, a wholly unrelated but implicitly invidious Associated Press dispatch from England mentioning the black activist, Stokely Carmichael, appeared in the afternoon *Daily Advance* with this boldface insert: "Editor's Note: Black power advocate Stokely Carmichael spoke in Lynchburg March 12 at a Court Street Baptist Church rally to raise funds for convicted Negro rapist Thomas Carlton Wansley."

Glass III had a truly missionary zeal. The Associated Press in Virginia then relied on its members in Lynchburg and elsewhere to punch news, unedited by the Associated Press, directly into the state wire. It was a practice that made the wire service as vulnerable as the *News* and the *Daily Advance* to the Glass distortions. John F. Daffron, then the Associated Press Richmond bureau chief, says he had a standing order requiring a "must kill" interruption of Lynchburg's printer file on the Wansley case. "Carter Glass was making us and all our members as liable as he was for that crazy stuff," Daffron recalls.

Summoned to the witness stand in Kunstler's efforts to save his client at his second trial by obtaining a change of venue (it was denied), Glass III, a lawyer as well as an editor and publisher, acknowledged that the sources of his campaign to pillory the lawyer, and thus to deny Wansley an able advocate, were the "subversive files" of the late House Committee on Un-American Activities and of the late Senator James O. Eastland of Mississippi.

Striking a blow for the First Amendment, the appeals court ruled that for it to find the *News's* fanatically poisonous treatment of the defendant's lawyer prejudicial to due process "would mean that few trials could ever be held in a land where freedom of the press is considered invaluable." The court said, "It is doubtful that any pretrial reference to an accused's attorney, in the absence of any . . . prejudicial comment on the accused himself . . . can justify a finding that due process is violated."

The victims of the raw abuse of the power of the press in Lynchburg were not readily predictable. Wansley went free on parole in 1977. And to anyone who has seen the nimble Kunstler in action, it is apparent that he can take care of himself. Ultimately—ironically—it was not only the demoted Carter Glass

III who paid the highest price for this bizarre episode in American journalism. It was also his, and his grandfather's, beloved Lynchburg papers.

The followers of Senator Glass had made his newspapers pariahs, the object of scorn and hatred in their own community. And even under more temperate Glass family management, the family tree failed. Carter Glass III retired. Powell Glass died. There were unanticipated inheritance taxes. There was an inter-Glass legal shootout over disposition of the family fortune. Tom Worrell was in the wings, ready to buy. "We always know when a newspaper is for sale," he said.

Wansley had been the beginning of the end. But the coup de grâce was administered by Lynchburg's white majority.

The Virginia Supreme Court had ordered the retrial in Lynchburg that brought Wansley life in prison. Later, Kunstler and another defender of unpopular causes, a Virginia lawyer and ex-Marine named Phillip J. Hirschkop, won for the accused a further review in the federal court in Richmond. In upholding Wansley's appeal, a United States district court critiqued the *Lynchburg News* and, as far as it could in *obiter dicta*, indicted the newspaper and Glass as knowing corrupters both of justice and of journalism.

After Wansley had spent ten years of his twenty-six years in prison, United States District Judge Robert R. Merhige, Jr., ordered him set free in 1973, citing the "shocking nature and amount of prejudicial pretrial publicity" given the case and the assertedly "fellow traveler" lawyer by the *Lynchburg News*. Judge Merhige appeared to relish the irony that it was Carter Glass III who had sprung Wansley from prison. He ruled that the newspaper's repeated references to Wansley as the "convicted rapist," coupled with its relentless identification of his lawyer as "a Communist attorney," had placed upon "the most intelligent and dedicated juror a Herculean and, in the court's opinion, impossible task to decide the case solely on the evidence."

Wansley waited in prison while the state appealed Merhige's heretical decision. A year later Merhige was reversed by the United States Fourth Circuit Court of Appeals. Making a nicety of the *News*'s relatively better behavior following Carter Glass III's exile by the family in 1969, the appeals court held that the Lynchburg papers' inarguably prejudicial publication had occurred largely during Wansley's *first* trial in 1962, not then at issue. The court noted approvingly that the Glass papers had grown in restraint; that during the second Wansley trial they had spared the defendant a second exposure as the "convicted rapist," even if they had continued to describe Kunstler as "linked to Communist fronts."

Life magazine headlined the story: "When City Bites Newspaper, That's News." In the spring of 1967, Lynchburg's most prominent white business leaders—some seventy businesspeople, doctors, and lawyers "linked to" the school board, the Chamber of Commerce, the Retail Merchants Association, and the Board of Realtors—suddenly decided they had had enough of Carter Glass III. In an open letter addressed to every household in the Lynchburg phone book, members of the white establishment declared it their judgment "that the Lynchburg newspapers are contributing to frustration and bitterness. To persist in these policies can only be destructive of the general morale as well as the reputation of our community. . . . We hope that our Negro citizens will be encouraged by the knowledge that there are many white citizens in this community who appreciate their continued willingness, in spite of repeated indignities by the newspapers, to help promote a more wholesome climate throughout the city."

This was not the first shining hour of decency and dissent in Lynchburg. Earlier, after Wansley's second trial, the *Sun Dial*, the campus newspaper of Randolph-Macon Women's College, had editorially called the papers' coverage unfair. Carter Glass III replied editorially that the student editors were traveling "the red line." To the heavier judgment of the white establishment he salvoed back that this "scurrilous" attack by "frightened dupes" was "an open invitation to racial agitation," to even a mob attack by Hottentots on the newspapers' offices.

G. Everett Bond, then the president of the school board, says Carter Glass III continued to "give us a number of serious problems in the papers over the integration of the schools." Because reasonably serene schools were essential if Lynchburg's civic and commercial boomers were to succeed in their appeals to business and industrial employers, Bond, the retired president of a company that then manufactured Chapstick in Lynchburg, says he became "an instigator" of the open letter. The letter was surely a humiliation, if not to Carter Glass III, then to the social lions who were the family shareholders in Carter Glass Newspapers. But there was also an indirect financial threat—a noble, if tentative, rumble of distant free enterprise thunder and newspaper competition.

H. Gordon Leggett, Jr., a son of the late Virginia department store magnate, Harold G. Leggett, who was another shaper of the liberating open letter, recalls that Lynchburg businesspeople were also "trying their best to bring in another newspaper to give them an advertising option." Here was an option that vituperative editorials could not answer—could only make worse—and Carter Glass III was removed from the *Lynchburg News* by the Glass family. Today, when asked about the complaints against his newspaper, Carter Glass III says, "I don't remember any criticism. I know of no criticism of any sort. . . . Anything that you want . . . I am sure is still available in the newspaper's files. At least I think it is still available. I have had no connection with the newspaper for many years."

Other, frailer Glasses succeeded him and "the attitude of the papers changed completely," Bond recalls. The Lynchburg papers' moderation under less ferocious family management is remembered as a crucial factor in the city's relatively calm acceptance of court-ordered school integration, a phenomenon still pejoratively headlined "Race Mixing" in newspapers regarded as respectable by most Virginians. And at least until the Howell headline in 1977, other signers of the letter agree that there was observable improvement. But by 1979 most of the available Glass manpower had died.

Suddenly in 1979—"in five sleepless days and nights," as Tom Worrell remembers it—in a deal with him that spurred an intra-family stockholders' lawsuit over whose ox was being gored, the two Lynchburg dailies were sold in a package that included three other smaller Glass newspapers for a reported $32 million to Worrell Newspapers. The buyers were made a chosen instrument perhaps because the Worrell patriarch, T. Eugene Worrell—the conservative, monopoly owner of Bristol, Virginia's two newspapers—was ideologically acceptable to the Glasses. "Old Gene" is a former Federal Bureau of Investigation agent, a former (and losing) Republican candidate for Congress, and, according to a contemporary, "a guy who measures everything by the box office." He also was and is "very close to his son," according to the son. "Historically," says Tom Worrell of their partnership, "we have bought newspapers on the basis of personal friendship and respect, and that's what happened in Lynchburg. 'Please come help us, we'd like for you to own the newspapers,' they said. And we did."

The Worrells' friendly deal in Lynchburg was struck with Thomas R. Glass, a survivor who remains the newspapers' largely inactive vice-president, at a salary that he calls "generous" for a "period longer than ten years." Worrell also has chosen to keep the Glass imprimatur; the masthead of the Worrell-owned Lynchburg papers says they are published by "Carter Glass Newspapers, Inc."

The family dispute over the proceeds, which lawyers finally carried all the way to the Virginia Supreme Court, grew out of a Tom Glass-Tom Worrell shutout of another bidder, Robert S. Howard, of Howard Publications in Oceanside, California. Howard says that he had negotiated with other Glass shareholders a minority stock position, but on condition that he could then buy the remainder and have full control. In an interview, Howard said that he and the Glass family minority stockholders who liked his offer were thwarted by Tom Glass's preference for Worrell. Members of the Glass family who felt that the Worrell deal was below the best offer sued other Glasses for the difference. (To the Lynchburg newspapers' credit, an only slightly opaqued news report on the family lawsuit appeared in the papers.) A Worrell lawyer nonetheless insists that "the Worrell offer was higher, and was accepted only after Howard refused to raise his offer."

Tom Worrell said he does not remember comparing the business of buying and owning newspapers with "selling shoes"—a view of publishing that is widely and scornfully attributed to him. But if he did make such an infelicitous comparison—one that he described as "an unfortunate choice of words"—it seems close to the mark. "A newspaper is a business," he says assertively, "You can't operate a newspaper unless you run it like a business."

He illustrates how tough a business he thinks it is by saying that he wants none of his children in it. "Family business is not a good idea," he said, noting by way of example "the potential to drive a family apart" that he witnessed among the Glasses in his Lynchburg purchase. "A lot of the newspapers I have bought I bought because of families that came apart."

A recurring criticism of Worrell—at large in Virginia newsrooms and in published profiles of him inspired as much by his conspicuous-consumption lifestyle as his sudden publishing prominence—is that he often elevates the advertising directors of his properties to publisher and puts them on tenuous tenure, tied to profit norms set by Worrell. Does it work? Do they all make the nut and clear a profit? "You bet," according to Worrell. "All the papers make money," he replied—with the afterthought accompanied by an introspective glare. "But not all the time."

In an interview in the two-story-high living room of his palatial Charlottesville home (aptly named, for an acquisitor: "Finders Keepers"), under a dozen stuffed heads of glassy-eyed elands, cape buffalo, and other exotic trophies of his African safaris, Worrell was expansive. His tone was sometimes defensive, but only insofar as he felt his hearer did not, or could not, understand. "Listen, I've been trying for five years to develop news people into publishers. It's a hard thing to do because they just don't have the senses. It's a different perspective, not dealing with dollars all the time. But personally I don't think a newspaper ought to be run by the newsroom, anyway, any more than by the advertising department. The publisher's job is to balance the act."

To younger newsroom skeptics who, as Virginians, deplore the crass bravado of a nouveau tycoon, Tom Worrell's statements have proven a lightning rod. An announcement in the Lynchburg papers of the reportorial marriage of the A.M. and P.M. Worrell properties—the *News* would no longer bother sending a reporter out on a story covered by the *Advance*, and vice versa; and for efficiency each would pick up the columns of the other—was posted as sardonic, if not hilarious, humor on newsroom bulletin boards across the state. "The afternoon paper is just a pale copy of the morning *News*," according to Everett Bond. "How they keep it up I don't know. They must want to kill it."

That Tom Worrell was willing to wind up with one "twenty-four-hour newspaper" in Lynchburg became apparent during the interview at his

Charlottesville home. Stomping both his snakeskin cowboy boots down on a zebra skin rug in a gesture of exasperated disbelief, he said of the Glass ownership that "they were even publishing the afternoon paper in a different typeface!" That, of course, was a mechanical bar to the more efficient "all-day" operation that Worrell's Lynchburg monopoly has become.

But not everyone applauded the loss of diversity. Like scores of other practiced newspaper readers in Lynchburg, Louise Cunningham, a longtime subscriber who is a Democratic National Committeewoman from Virginia, said that "when they got so the only difference was in the editorials I stopped taking both papers." In another Worrell efficiency move that put the *Daily Advance* under a cloud, the afternoon paper briefly became unavailable to mail subscribers. When this reader's 1981 mail subscription to the *Daily Advance* expired, he received a computer-printed notice that a renewal would fetch him the *News*, an edict since withdrawn by a new circulation director. Not surprisingly, the afternoon *Advance*'s circulation has continued to decline—from more than twenty thousand in 1978 to seventeen thousand today. (Total circulation, morning and afternoon, has remained at forty-one thousand.)

Scorn has left young Worrell unusually wary of his image as a "shoe salesman"—as a make-a-buck collector of newspaper trophies who is perceived as equating them with stuffed animal heads. His un-Virginian lifestyle invites more unwelcome attention. Virginia newspaper publishers *do not* wear gold coins around their necks on heavy chains, dangling in the unbuttoned decolletage of pastel silk shirts; drive motorcycles and flotillas of Mercedes and BMWs with license plates "WNI-1," "WNI-2," et seq.; keep company airplanes, including a corporate jet for sorties to their Florida investments and their fully-crewed sloops in the Virgin Islands; or maintain corporate headquarters overlooking Monticello. Worrell Newspapers shares with the elder Worrell a multibuilding office complex on a rolling farm, Pantops, once part of the Jefferson family domain just outside Charlottesville. There, beside U. S. Route 250 in a fenced meadow, Worrell, Sr., keeps three anachronistically frolicsome llamas. They were obtained in a trade of some Worrell thoroughbred cattle from August A. Busch, Jr., the beer king.

But young Worrell remains philosophically resolute. "I am not out to reform the world like you guys," he said invidiously to a gray-haired journalist. "I am not out to impose any particular view on anyone. I am out to reflect the views of the community."

"You need to work very hard to stay out of the community, in the sense of not imposing any particular point of view in the papers," Worrell said. It is a business strategy described by one former editor of a Worrell newspaper as "a pretty slick stunt. His stunt is to move in where there is no competition, fire everyone who has been around long enough to be making a living, and then run everything on the cheap. His papers are only good enough to get past people's doors so they can carry out their real purpose. They are not really newspapers. They are platforms for peddling ads. The company has the conscience of a PR man, and if an advertiser buys a half-page ad he gets a feature story thrown in." A Worrell spokesperson says that none of this is true. "Unless you are in a special business page offered at some of our locations, you will not be featured in a news story."

A Worrell spokesperson says that the *Sanford Star* in Maine, a weekly bought in 1977, was closed solely because "it had lost money during the entire period of its operations." But former employees there say that the imminence of a newsroom union among disgruntled workers was the paper's death sentence. With rebellious workers, the paper was quickly terminated. Its subscription list was given over to another Worrell acquisition in Kennebunk, Maine: the *York County Coast Star*, part of the package recently sold to the *New York Times*. (A number of former Sanford staffers say that they won large settlements of back wages based on overtime pay withheld by the Worrell management in violation of the Federal Wage and Hour Act. The Worrell newspaper in Charlottesville also has had to make settlement of a number of overtime irregularities and discriminatory pay claims by women.)

One may say, and obviously many do, that Worrell is a blot on the escutcheon of Wilbur Storey, with his newspaper's duty to "print the news and raise Hell." But Worrell claims that raising hell is not merely what his newspapers must *not* do, it is—generically speaking—what is wrong with journalism, or anyhow with newspaper people. He said that the reporters who interviewed him separately in 1980 for two equally unflattering stories—in the *Richmond Times-Dispatch* and the *Roanoke Times*—were demonstrating "an attitude that is putting the business in jeopardy, an attitude of 'get some-one.'" Regarding the two harsh Worrell profiles—they enshrine his playboy and conspicuous-consumption image and are full of slashing quotes from embittered ex-reporters, editors, and other critics—he observed sourly to a third interviewer: "You reporters are an exclusive club. It is more important to you to go after a person's character than to find out what the truth is."

Worrell then spoke not disapprovingly of recent massive libel judgments. His voice expressed his vicarious sense of institutional justice, redeemed, against what he seemed to feel were overzealous, unethical reporters.

"Those people [the libel complainants] were *mad,*" he said. "People everywhere are mad at the press." At who in the press? he was asked. "At reporters!" he burst out quickly with half a laugh, as if it were a dumb question. Of course, *his* employees are not apt to anger anyone, not if they want to keep their jobs (many have been fired)—that is at the bottom line of critics' judgments of Tom Worrell. "If Tom Worrell had bought restaurants instead of newspapers," one Virginian exclaimed in a bitter analogy, "he would hate the chefs. His real business would be selling drinks."

Worrell admits to smarting at his treatment in the non-Worrell Virginia press. But, interestingly enough, he does not claim to have been misquoted. It is worse—a more intricately woven and profound mistrust. In the two offending interviews, he concedes that he said what he is quoted as saying. But he says that he was nonetheless "done-unto by the club." His defensiveness marks a newspaper owner's alienation from journalists.

Almost certainly this explains the high turnover in Worrell newsrooms and the periodic spates of firings. He deflects questions about that by maintaining that he is "proud that so many of our people go on to bigger newspapers" and proud, too, of the statewide Press Association awards won, somewhat inevitably, by his Virginia properties. Worrell still owns nine of Virginia's thirty-seven daily newspapers. In 1981, according to Worrell, his Virginia dailies won 67 of 121 possible reporting and news photography awards given by the Virginia Press Association. The Lynchburg papers have won five awards in four years for in-depth/investigative reporting, including a first place in each of the last three years.

But turnover has had some ludicrous results. A former reporter at the *Daily Progress*, the Worrell flagship in Charlottesville, says his eleven months of experience made him at one point the paper's senior reporter. This may explain what is widely perceived as the diminution of the importance—or the potency—of "local news" in the Worrell newspapers. "They don't know what we want," is a common complaint.

What saves that, in part, is that the news seems straight. It also often appears canned and pureed, as in the content of some of the trendy new "Living" sections and in the Lynchburg papers' ambitious annual "Central Virginia" section. On page one, the news is heavily wire copy. And although there are plainly more well-displayed local features—crossing such bold (in Lynchburg) frontiers as teen-age sex and where-are-they-now remembrances of the city's first blacks to integrate the white high school—there are still complaints that the papers "don't know the local scene." A criticism heard in two Worrell-monopoly cities, Lynchburg and Charlottesville, is that young new-hires in the newsroom often are too unfamiliar with the territory to know when to write an obit. They don't know who is, or was, important.

According to Charles Mangum, head of the Lynchburg chapter of the National Association for the Advancement of Colored People, the Worrell management "is like a breath of fresh air. They are as fair as can be expected. By that I mean there is no complaint we can tie down—they do a story, and they make an adequate number of contacts with blacks. If there was a complaint, it would be in employment discrimination. There are no blacks on the news staff."

"The reporters seem to be transients, and there are fewer of them," says Wilma Washburn of Lynchburg College, the city's only journalism professor. "The papers don't know the city. Sometimes the articles are ludicrous. There is certainly better coverage of the black community—at least the obits are there. But if you really want to know what's going on in Virginia, in the capitol at Richmond, and in the nation—in the real world—you have to take the *Washington Post* or the news magazines. To my students the papers here are a joke. I assigned some of them to do stories about the new Federal Building on Main Street, about which there has been nothing in the papers. And they said; 'Gee, we can find this out, why can't they find it out?' " A Worrell spokesperson says that the papers carried "more than thirty" Federal Building stories.

"In many ways they are still 1950s newspapers," says the Reverend Jan G. Linn, a native of Lynchburg and student of national affairs who is chaplain of Lynchburg College. "We just don't get many national stories. And they have stopped covering the city, except in little feature stories. The college had a symposium on the Holocaust with appearances by national figures, and it got very little attention. I was told our speakers were no more important to Lynchburg than those at a Kiwanis meeting. The common complaint is that you can read the paper in five minutes. There's just nothing in it."

But to William C. Cline, a Glass relative who is now the Lynchburg newspapers' executive editor and has been a news executive there for five years, the improvement in content and display has been startling under Worrell management.

In Cline's "year after the sale" survey comparing the combined Sunday edition—the *News and Advance*—of July 1979 with August 1980, the pre-Worrell paper had 411 inches of local copy, "110 inches from reporters and the rest from handouts. The Lifestyle section had no reporter-generated copy." The comparable, Worrell-run Sunday paper in 1980 had "557 inches of local copy, including 83 inches in "Lifestyle," and 114 inches of local business copy, an expanded and wholly new area of coverage," he said.

Asked to comment on the "fewer reporters" observation of Professor Washburn, the executive editor said "that's right, we are probably down about four or five [overall] in the newsroom. But we find we are able to expand our coverage with fewer people." This is made possible, he said, by not double-teaming stories—not sending reporters from both papers to the same events.

Under Tom Worrell, no newspaper owned by Worrell Newspapers will ever publish the attention-getting editorial views of the Glasses. In Lynchburg today the editorial page seems bland, only distantly topical. The opinion-editorial selection is broad. It includes James Reston, Tom Wicker, Flora Lewis, and Russell Baker from the otherwise sparingly used New York

Times News Service; and George Will, Ellen Goodman, James J. Kilpatrick, Ralph de Toledano, Evans and Novak, Jack Anderson, Patrick Buchanan, Art Buchwald, and Andy Rooney.

Some in the Lynchburg newsroom are proud that the papers under Worrell ownership have become the occasional target of a fire-eating blast from the pulpit of Jerry Falwell. But another view in Lynchburg, expressed by Rev. Linn, is that "the papers regard Falwell as 'a national newsmaker' in our midst and uncritically print everything he puts out."

"You certainly know they are different newspapers," said one community and business leader, who said he "would speak more candidly if I am not quoted by name.

"They have changed from community newspapers under the Glasses— you know, all the service club meetings and what everyone said there—to much more a feature-story and entertainment kind of thing than a news thing. There are too many frivolous features. You have the feeling that they fill the space that's left over by tearing copy off an AP printer.

"They have certainly been much more aggressive in selling advertising, and at much higher rates. And in that, too, they have changed from a community proposition to a more strictly business proposition. As a businessman, I have to say I can understand that. But the fact is that they are a prime example of the business approach to newspapering, rather than the journalism approach—I think really too transparently so."

"Billy" Cline, the executive editor in Lynchburg whose uncle was Carter Glass III, is able to take a strongly judgmental, retrospective view and at the same time make a case for optimism.

"You don't have to be a journalist to be offended by the history of these papers," he said in an interview. "Sometimes it just wasn't the American way. But we are different now. We are putting out better newspapers today, I know we are. We have a better sense of community responsibility—to the total community instead of just the power structure. The conduit from the power structure into the newsroom no longer exists, and to shut it off we have had to stand up. And we are growing. In 1981 we had the highest home delivery growth of any newspaper in the Middle Atlantic region."

That is passing a Worrell test. But Tom Worrell's taking-care-of-business persona may be a declining factor in the Worrell Newspapers management.

Decisions on what happens next in Lynchburg, and along the other remaining and potential links of the Worrell chain, passed in part during 1982 from Tom Worrell. With the reported (and, by Worrell Newspapers, disputed) $47 million from his daily and weekly sales to the *New York Times,* Worrell vacated the Worrell Newspapers presidency. He had held that post together with the Worrell Newspapers board chairmanship, which he retains. The move gave J. D. Swartz, his longtime associate and the former Worrell

Newspapers vice-president, the day-to-day presidency of a corporate operation that quickly added three central Virginia weeklies—in Orange, Madison, and Greene Counties.

"Yeah, we're going to expand," Swartz told an interviewer who inquired about the corporation's reinvestment of the cash from sales. He speaks in a loud, rapid, and forceful, "good ole' boy" manner marked by a measure of drawling repetition that supplies a certain redundant emphasis. For instance, he called the $47 million figure widely reported as the yield from the *New York Times* purchases "not simply a lie." It was, he continued, "a damned lie," and "not even in the ballpark." "That's a lie," he said again. "Whoever said that said a lie. Whoever published that published a lie."

Is Tom Worrell now less in the management picture? he was asked. And when and where will Worrell Newspapers expand?

"That's another lie," he began. "I talk to Tom Worrell nearly every day. *You* can't talk to him because you don't know where he is, and he doesn't want to talk to you, anyway. We'll expand wherever there's a good buy in newspapers. You know where there is a good buy? If you can tell me where there's a good buy in a newspaper, we'll buy it."

Redlands Daily Facts

Kenneth Rystrom

On July 1, 1981, a member of the fourth generation of the Moore family took over management of the *Redlands Daily Facts* in California. However, for the first time since 1895, the Moore family did not own the *Daily Facts*. When Graff Moore, at age forty-one, moved into the office that had been occupied by his father, he kept the general manager title he had held for two years. But for the first time in many years, the *Facts* had no publisher. Instead, it had a new president. His name was Don Reynolds, and his office was in Fort Smith, Arkansas.

The brothers and co-owners William G. Moore, publisher, and Frank E. Moore, editor, had sold their family newspaper to a group, Donrey Media. In announcing the sale to a stunned community, the Moores, both in their seventies, cited as reasons for their decision "the federal and state tax situation that confronts all small, family-owned businesses" and "the strength that group ownership lends to community newspapers in an era of rapid change, both technological and societal." They told readers that they were "familiar with the operation of our neighbor newspaper, the *Daily Report* of Ontario, and have been acquainted with those who have managed it. We believe that the Donrey group, which owns it, follows similar principles to those that have been ours."

Donrey, as of January 1983, owned forty-five daily newspapers (in small or middle-sized communities) and forty-four nondailies, from Indiana and Kentucky on westward, with the largest number in Oklahoma and Texas. The *Facts* brought Donrey's daily acquisitions in California to six. The group also owned one VHF television station, three cable systems, six radio stations, and eleven outdoor advertising agencies.

One California editor described the group as "aggressive and expansionist." Off the record, he also described them as "tight-fisted." He said Donrey had taken some poor papers and made them better, "but they don't have a really good paper anywhere." It did not take long for the *Facts* staff to realize that with Donrey the financial bottom line came first.

Parties to the sale adamantly refused to even hint at the sale price. One former *Facts* employee said he had heard figures ranging from $5 million to $12 million.

Readers and staff members were not the only ones who were shocked by news of the sale. Graff Moore was one of the most surprised. For two or three months Graff—whose full name, William Graff Moore, Jr., never appears in print and in fact is not known by most Redlanders—had been considering prospective candidates for editor of the paper, anticipating his father's and uncle's retirements. He was expecting to assume the position of publisher and, presumably, to have an opportunity to buy into the paper, which was wholly owned by the brothers and their wives (who incidentally are sisters). Frank and Sydney's children had never been associated with the *Facts*. Graff knew that he and his sister, Lucretia Irving of Redlands (children of Bill and Jo), could not raise enough money to take over even half of the shares. "Bitter" was the word Graff used to describe his feelings concerning the decision to sell. But he recognized the threat of a severe tax problem if one or more of the owners died within a short time. To pay the taxes, the family could be forced to sell under unfavorable circumstances for a substantially reduced price.

Bill Metcalf, vice-president of Donrey Western Newspaper Division, asked Graff to stay on to provide as much continuity as possible. Graff agreed to stay at least a year. In accordance with Donrey's stated policy, Graff was given freedom to run the paper as he wished, on both business and news ends, as long as the paper provided Donrey's expected return on investment.

Graff had been itching to make some changes in news and advertising policies. The previous January he had brought James Webb from the *Escondido Times-Advocate* to introduce more modern marketing methods in a 9½-person advertising staff. Frank E. Moore's retirement gave Graff the opportunity to bring in his own editor. That selection produced another surprise, not to the community so much as to the *Facts* staff and others familiar with the paper's inner workings.

Except for an absence of four years in the early 1950s, Dick West had worked for the *Facts* since he had graduated from college in 1949. He worked first as an ad salesman when no news positions were open. He left to join the Federal Bureau of Investigation in 1951, but returned four years later to fill a reporting position. In 1964 West became news editor, taking over the wire editor position Bill Moore had held on a daily basis for more than twenty years. In the late 1970s and early 1980s, as Frank's interests shifted from the newsroom to the editorial page and to other activities, West found himself, in his words, "minding the store." He administered the policies set by the Moores, hired reporters, and made decisions when Frank and Bill were not there.

West assumed that, when Frank retired, he would be the new editor. But Graff had other ideas. Graff wanted to make some changes on the news side of the paper. He considered West to be "good in his area" but not a strong enough leader to bring needed changes. Graff acknowledged that he knew little about the news side, as he had come to the general manager position through the mechanical end of the business. He recognized that he would not be able to introduce and supervise the changes, even if he knew exactly what he wanted to do. He concluded that a new policy could be established only through new leadership.

Graff also was concerned with continuity. He considered four candidates for editor. With the help of some unnamed persons familiar with the news business, he picked Terry Greenberg, age twenty-seven, who had come to the *Facts* as a reporter and sports writer immediately after graduation from California State, Northridge, in 1977. Greenberg had lived in Redlands since then, but had left the *Facts* for the *San Bernardino Sun* in 1979. On the *Sun* he had worked as assistant wire editor for one and a half years, then as a copy editor for six months. He also had written a number of features. Graff had liked some of the ideas Greenberg had suggested when he worked for the *Facts*, especially those relating to the layout of the paper. Graff thought that Greenberg's ideas, youthful aggressiveness, and prior acquaintance with the news staff would provide the needed combination for accomplishing what he had in mind. Graff got everything he counted on, and maybe more, in terms of new ideas and aggressiveness.

But relations with the news staff were not, at the beginning, all that Graff had hoped they would be. One problem was the handling of West. West first learned about June 29 that he would not be the new editor. A reporter from the *San Bernardino Sun* called West and asked him to confirm that Greenberg had been selected as editor. A few minutes later, Graff called West into his office. There, Graff told West he had an expanded position, but not the editor's job, in mind for him. Graff asked him to stay on.

Frank Moore was so angry over what he regarded as the *Sun*'s premature announcement of Greenberg's selection that he said he would not allow the announcement to appear in the *Facts* as long as he owned it. It did not.

A few days after the change of ownership, when Graff was out of town, Greenberg asked West to stay and showed him a job description that added editorial writing to his news desk job. West took a three-week vacation and then resigned the day after he returned. About a week into his vacation, West's stand-in on the news desk had called West to say she was quitting. She said she could not work with Greenberg; he was interfering too much. After the replacement of these persons, the only change in the newsroom in the following months was the layoff, in an economy move, of a part-time news clerk. (One person in advertising and one in composing also were laid off.)

Greenberg acknowledges that he closely supervises the laying out of the pages and that he makes changes, even at the last minute, if he does not like what the make-up editor has done. Some of these changes have been made after the pages have been pasted up in the composing room, to the consternation of some employees in that department. This "fiddling with the pages" has been cited by Greenberg's critics as one reason that the composing room had trouble meeting earlier deadlines.

Format is important to Greenberg. He wants the paper to project a new, more aggressive image. He sees bolder make-up and a compartmentalized news product as one way to achieve this end. He considers his first responsibility to be to work closely with the news operation. Greenberg instituted daily news planning sessions and weekly staff meetings, both digressions from the more laissez-faire days under Frank Moore. "We operated a very informal newsroom," West recalled. "Everyone knew what to do without being told." Greenberg also instituted a "hell sheet," a marked-up copy of the day's edition indicating what he liked and disliked. He thought he had received a good response to his criticisms, though not all staff members acknowledged that they looked at the "hell sheet."

As other evidence of a take-charge attitude, Greenberg told his reporters that if they were given a hard time by news sources they should come to him. He would call the sources and go to battle for his reporters.

Not many readers were aware of what was happening in the newspaper office. Greenberg was too busy at first to spend much time in the community. Few Redlanders knew West in his capacity as news editor. Many of his acquaintances in other areas had only the vaguest idea of what he did on the *Facts*. No public protest arose when he left.

But protest did arise over changes in what the readers could see—the appearance of the *Facts*. Oldtime subscribers resented that "their paper" had been changed. Continued complaints were heard by people who moved throughout the community—persons such as Jack Cummings, former mayor, former vice-president for public affairs of the University of Redlands, and now public relations director for the Bank of Redlands. Cummings said he heard complaining whether he went to "potlucks or dancing or lunch." Most of the complaints had to do with the layout of the paper.

Julia Hinckley, whose husband had been born in Redlands to an old-line family, said she was beginning to get used to the format after a few months. "But it is a little like when you rearrange your house," she said. "When you walk around in the dark, you keep bumping into furniture."

The grouping of police stories brought the comment from one woman, who asked not to be identified, that she had not been aware that the community had so much crime. But, she said, "There must have been that much all along; it was just scattered throughout the paper."

Two of the changes that Graff—and Greenberg—had in mind were more local stories on page one and more local features. One unfamiliar with the news policies of Bill and Frank might have been surprised that the sale to an out-of-towner would bring new emphasis on local news. But, as Graff Moore, Greenberg, and Webb have stressed repeatedly, a lot of the changes had nothing to do with Donrey.

From the time they were old enough to understand that they belonged to a newspaper family, Bill and Frank led lives dominated by the *Facts*. "The newspaper is an extension of your personal life," Frank said. "It's your town and your people. We have all had a common experience." "Our Town" was the phrase usually used by Frank in his editorials and personal column ("With a Grain of Salt") in reference to Redlands. The Moore family had lived in Redlands about as long as any family. They had owned the paper since Bill and Frank's grandfather, Captain William G. Moore, came to town in 1895, ostensibly for his health, but actually (in Frank's word) to "con" his son, Paul W. Moore, to come west. The *Facts*, according to the Moores the only newspaper in the country with that name until recently, had been founded as a weekly by Edgar F. Howe in 1890, two years after Redlands was incorporated as a city. It became an evening daily in 1892. Paul W. Moore joined the struggling paper in 1897, two years after its purchase by his father. It then had a circulation of two thousand. (Redlands in 1900 had a population of 4,797.)

Many of the years under Paul Moore, and under Bill and Frank as well, were tough. Only in the last four to five years did the family own property, free and clear, that was worth anything, according to Frank. "The whole damn town was bankrupt in the 1930s, like everybody else," Frank recalled.

Bill joined the *Facts* as an ad salesman in 1933 after two years at the University of Redlands, two at Stanford, and one at the Harvard Business School. Frank joined as a reporter in 1935 after two years at Redlands and three at Stanford, where he majored in political science. According to a not unadmiring description used by a former longtime *Facts* employee, Bill and Frank acquired a Stanford *noblesse oblige* self-image that never wore off. They assumed joint management of the paper when their father died in 1942.

Throughout many of the years, according to Frank, the paper would not have made it financially if there had not been two of them to do much of the work and carry the financial burden. Both of them were needed to get the paper out.

"Practically all my life I came to work at seven-thirty, six days a week," Frank said, "and I worked until three o'clock on Saturday. There are goddamn few guys in town who work that hard. I was never one of those who played golf on Wednesday or Saturday." They kept the paper going by "blood, sweat, and tears," he said. "If Bill had withdrawn, I couldn't have swung it."

Bill ran the wire desk from 1942 to 1964. In about 1963, West recalled, both Bill and Frank had been seriously ill at about the same time. The illnesses prompted them to get some additional desk help and to designate staff members to make decisions when they were not there. That is when West moved to the news desk.

Frank functioned as both reporter and editor. During the earlier years, "we shamelessly used canned copy from NEA [Newspaper Enterprise Association] as editorials," Frank said, "and we got compliments on them." One compliment on a canned editorial came from President Eisenhower. That would have been as late as the 1950s. Frank recalls that he was doing a lot of reporting in that decade.

Redlands began to come out of the Depression in about 1942, thanks to the war industry, and the town began to grow and prosper in the early 1950s. About that time, Frank and Bill realized that they needed a bigger press. They bought a rotary letterpress from the *Philadelphia Bulletin*, but they did not have room for it in their tiny five-thousand-square-foot office on a downtown street corner. So with borrowed money they built a modern, fourteen-thousand-square-foot newspaper plant in 1956. Frank said that the decision to locate the plant several blocks from downtown Redlands and to plant grass and shrubbery around it was regarded as quite daring. In 1971 a twenty-page Goss Community press and Compugraphic photo-typesetters were installed for offset printing. In 1977 an electronic system for the news and classified advertising was added. When Donrey bought the *Facts*, it acquired a highly efficient, modern production facility.

Neither Bill nor Frank ever stopped being reporters. When one of them was the only *Facts* person at an event, he would return to the office to write the story. Frank reported on events involving nearby Norton Air Force Base, where he maintained ties with the military leadership. Bill, when he was chairman of the Redlands Community Hospital Board, sometimes would come back to the office to write a story about board actions. "He figured no one could tell the story more accurately than he could," West said. "He wanted the story to be absolutely objective, and he would ask me to look it over. Sometimes I would tell him he couldn't say something."

Just as the newspaper was an extension of Frank's and Bill's lives, so was community involvement an extension of their newspaper jobs. Bill especially was active in civic and political organizations. Bill retired in 1981 after thirty-six years as president of the library board, a position he held with great pride and without public controversy—until his last year. Then the board got caught in the middle of a brouhaha over refurbishing the exterior of the eighty-three-year-old building. The board wanted to sandblast the decaying paint and repaint the building the same color it had been for several decades. Just before the work got under way with a federal grant, members of the Redlands Historical and Scenic Preservation Commission raised concerns about possible damage from sandblasting and proposed that it be painted the color it originally had been. The battle waged for months. The result was a compromise—the most recent color, but no sandblasting. Instead of lasting twenty years, the repainting was expected to be good for only four or five. The controversy embarrassed Bill and other library board members. Redlanders had always spoken of the A.K. Smiley Library only in reverential tones, just as they had spoken in reverential tones about the two Smiley brothers and most other wealthy winter visitors from the East, who in the late nineteenth century built huge Victorian mansions in Redlands and helped bring a Victorian atmosphere to the community. That atmosphere—in which one did not speak evilly in public of another community member and, in fact, did not even acknowledge the existence of evil in the community—has persisted in Redlands, at least in the social and political set that until recently ran the library and hospital boards, the school board, the city council—and the daily newspaper.

Some longtime readers of the *Facts* had the impression that until recent years Frank and Bill refrained from printing much of the community's crime news. But West insisted that this impression was wrong. He said policies on printing crime news had not been changed over the years. He did recall, however, that sometimes Frank would express concern over the relatively large amount of crime news in Monday's paper. West said he would assure Frank that it merely represented the accumulation of weekend activities that had occurred since the Saturday edition of the *Facts*. He said Frank never suggested that crimes not be reported. The *Facts* even reported three burglaries in Frank's own home. The *Facts* insisted on printing the names and addresses of burglary victims so that neighbors would know about crimes that had occurred in their area.

The Moores did make one exception to the full reporting of crime. Until the late 1960s or early 1970s, the *Facts* had reported the names of all persons arrested by police. A change in policy came as an indirect result of a police crackdown on homosexual activities in public places, West recalled. One of the persons arrested was a public school teacher. His name was published even though he protested that he was innocent. Subsequently, all charges against him were dropped. But the man felt that his professional career and his family life had been destroyed. He moved from the community and several months later committed suicide. The *Facts* shortly thereafter adopted a policy not to publish the name of a person who had been arrested until formal charges had been filed by the district attorney.

The policy resulted in the anomaly of having the *Facts* report in its afternoon paper that a forty-year-old unnamed man had been arrested for drunk driving the night before and that another person in the car, whose name was published, had been injured. The *San Bernardino Sun* the next morning would report the names of both the accused driver and the passenger. West said that the policy was based on the recognition that sometimes persons who have been arrested are subsequently charged with lesser crimes than those indicated in police reports, and that sometimes the district attorney decides that no charges should be filed at all. "In a small town," West said, "police are not always well educated or highly trained in the law. All you have to do to know that is to read the reports they write." Within a few months Greenberg began publishing names of arrested persons, except in cases involving sex.

If the Moores did not withhold news about crime, they certainly tried to keep from sensationalizing it. A local crime had to be of extraordinary magnitude to make page one. In fact, any local story had to be highly unusual to make the front page. The practice of devoting the front page to wire stories is not unique with the *Facts*. Small dailies, probably more in the past than now, sometimes keep wire and local news separate, partly because different desk people handle the two types of news. The wire editor can plan pages early in the work day without having to worry about what local reporters bring back to the office late in the morning. The city editor, who knows what reporters are working on, can plan the local page. The practice probably was more prevalent before readers began getting most of their national and international news on television. The principal asset of the dailies, especially the small dailies, has become local news.

But, through the last day of Bill and Frank's ownership, the *Facts* persisted in assigning local news to pages three and four. In a sample week in January 1981, under the old management, the *Facts* published forty-eight wire stories and no local stories on page one in six days of publication. A year later the *Facts*, under Greenberg's editorship, published twelve local stories and three local pictures.

Why did the *Facts* continue emphasizing wire stories on page one when it could not hope to compete in quantity of stories with the *San Bernardino Sun* and the *Los Angeles Times* or in timeliness with the evening television news?

West said that periodically he and the Moores would discuss whether to start placing local stories on the front page. They decided not to, he said, because they were concerned with retaining readers who bought no other newspaper. If national and international news were reduced, he said, readers, most of whom wanted only one paper, might switch to the *Sun* or the *Times*.

One reason, of course, might have been that the Moores were comfortable with their news product and saw no reason to change. They might also have anticipated the criticism that Graff and Greenberg got when they began introducing local news into the *Facts*'s traditional front page.

There may have been another reason, a subtle one, underlying the Moores' reluctance to allow local news on page one: the town's Victorian attitude. One characteristic that is sometimes associated with news is that it comes suddenly; it surprises the reader. Another characteristic is that it often involves controversy or bears ill tidings. These characteristics are out-of-place in a community that prides itself on a wholesome atmosphere, high morals, and unbroken continuity with its past. Redlands—with its Victorian mansions, Spanish architecture, orange groves and palm trees, and a Lincoln Shrine with its own resident archivist—perceived itself to be just such a community. Halfway between Los Angeles and Palm Springs, Redlands was able to dissociate itself from the evils of those cities. It was close enough to San Bernardino and Riverside to allow middle-class workers to commute to jobs, but too far for those who needed to live near their work or rely on public transportation.

When the state of California began planning to build Interstate 10 from Los Angeles east to Palm Springs, generally along the line of U.S. Highway 99, which passed through the heart of Redlands, some local business executives were concerned that a freeway would take away the business they were getting from travelers. But another group of citizens saw the interstate as presenting an opportunity to get the highway out of town by locating it in San Timoteo Canyon, a few miles south, along the natural grade followed by the Southern Pacific Railroad. Frank Moore recalls that editorially he took a middle ground. He saw that it was important to get the highway off the city streets because people were being killed by hurrying motorists and, on occasion, runaway semitrucks. But he didn't want Redlands to be bypassed. "Redlands is not a Carmel," he said, looking back. The interstate ended up slicing through the town a couple of blocks from the business district. But, except for stopping at Edwards Mansion, an elegant Victorian restaurant on one end of town, or Griswold's Scandinavian restaurant at the other end, most motorists on the way to and from Palm Springs give Redlands little more than a glance.

Many Redlanders, including those at the *Facts*, faced a similar dilemma when a group of citizens, most of whom were not prominent, put an initiative on the city election ballot that would limit to 450 the number of homes that could be constructed each year in tracts of six or more units. For most of Redlands's history the 450 limit would have been ample, but in the two years immediately preceding the initiative, new houses numbered nearly three times that. The construction of homes was rapidly converting orange groves into treeless tracts. Gentle hills were being sliced off to make flat pads for houses. Old Redlands families, such as the Moores, were distressed to see the transformation. Yet, a number of them (though not the Moores) owned the land that was being subdivided. Houses were proving to be a far better source of income than the depressed and expensive orange business.

The *Facts* covered the campaign for and against the initiative, Proposition R, but Greenberg, who was then a reporter, recalls that he was instructed to cover only the meetings and not to dig into the issues. Frank wrote several editorials. None of them took a specific stand on the proposition, but readers who were familiar with Frank's style of writing could tell that he had his doubts. The measure was approved overwhelmingly. A year and a half later, the president of the group behind the proposition, the Friends of Redlands, was elected to the five-person city council. So was a political ally. Another council member in sympathy with their cause won reelection at the same time. The *Facts* took no stand in that election either. But, in subsequent editorials over the months and years, Frank included a number of sentences that cast aspersions on Proposition R and those behind it. The implication seemed to be that something as upstart as an initiative, pushed by political unknowns, was not the way the decisions should be made in a community of good will, continuity, and tradition.

The Friends of Redlands candidates would never have been elected, or quite likely even been on the ballot, in earlier days. Horace Hinckley, a Redlands native, whose community influence far exceeded his formal position as manager of the Bear Valley Mutual Water Company, recalls that he used to drop by the *Facts* to discuss with Bill and Frank who ought to be put up as candidates for local office. Frank recalls, sounding more than a little nostalgic, that "newspapers used to be regarded by politicians as important." Officials from city hall and the courthouse were always coming by to see what newspaper people thought. "We were just standing there; the politicians came to us," Frank said. "There was a lot more politics in politics then."

Frank did not become directly involved in party politics, but Bill did. He served as county Republican chairman and once as delegate to the party's national convention. One of his duties was to find candidates to run for the state assembly when no one else undertook the task. Bill served as county chairman for Richard Nixon and William F. Knowland in their campaigns for the United States Senate. Knowland would call for advice on such things, Frank said, as who should be the new rural mail carrier in Cucamonga.

Frank attended Republican conventions in 1948, 1950, 1952, and 1956, but only as an observer and reporter. One of Frank's major ventures into community affairs was as a member of a 1946 San Bernardino County grand jury whose work eventually ended in the writing of a new county charter. After the grand jury had completed all of its hearings and investigations, the complete record of minutes got lost. At the last minute, Frank was called to draw up the final report from memory. It took him three hours. The first effort at a new charter failed; two years later, Frank, as chairman of a charter committee, wrote the ballot measures and made speeches around the county in favor of passage. This time the effort succeeded. Frank said he spent a good part of three years around the courthouse working on this and other projects.

After that Frank tended to direct his political interests to the editorial columns of the *Facts*. He prides himself on the attention he paid to state issues, especially those before the legislature and on the ballot. "I did more on ballot propositions than anyone else in California," he said. He was unstinting in his efforts to seek out experts who could tell him what was really behind the proposals and what the likely effects were. West said that other editors, as well as politicians, looked to the *Facts* for reliable information and sound judgment on state issues.

The *Facts* owners prided themselves on their sound, conservative views and readily acknowledged their strong inclination toward the Republican party. But the conservatism was blended with common sense and perhaps with a sense of the inevitable. Some observers of *Facts* editorials thought they became somewhat more liberal in later years. The Moores may have been a little embarrassed when an analysis of their endorsement for ballot propositions in 1980 ranked the *Facts* among the most liberal papers in the state. The endorsement pattern was identical to that of the *Los Angeles Times,* but anyone who knew Frank Moore knew that he arrived at each recommendation on his own. The Moores' editorial policy remained essentially conservative and usually resulted in endorsements of Republican candidates.

At a dinner on the eve of the change of ownership, West included in a speech this tribute to Frank: "Frank is a deep thinker and, in my mind, one of the most talented editorial writers in the country. We have been fortunate to have him in Redlands because he could have chosen to write for anyone."

One of the writing qualities Frank developed was the ability not to say more than he intended. He might write on almost any topic in the news, but he did not feel he had to share a final opinion with his readers. On local controversial issues he seemed reluctant to take a firm stand, even though subsequent events might reveal that he did have his own ideas.

A few days before Proposition R appeared on the ballot, the *Facts* noted that the city council, which was lined up four to one against the proposition, was working on an alternative that, if Proposition R failed, would impose some growth limits under extreme circumstances. After comparing the two proposals, the editorial noted that "voter opinion is strongly polarized" and "probably the die is already cast." It did not say which way. It then concluded: "But citizens who are still in the 'uncertain' category will want to consider the expressed intentions of the council as well as the concrete terms of Proposition R." It made no suggestion about what they should conclude. A few days before the election, the *Facts* published an editorial presenting arguments for Proposition R; the next day it presented arguments against. A tabulation of endorsements before the election showed no recommendation. But, in an editorial that was primarily about a nasty campaign for lieutenant governor, the writer slipped in these two sentences about the local issue: "In the debate over Proposition R, there was little disposition to get down to cases and debate how the initiative would actually operate. There was a great deal of enthusiasm, however, for seeing a mote in the eye of those on the opposing side." Then the editorial went back to the state race.

The day after the election, in which Proposition R won by a landslide, the *Facts* complimented the proponents, "all novices in politics," for drafting a moderate measure and expressed gratitude that Proposition R had not been accompanied by a recall movement, which "would have been exceedingly bitter." Yet the writer could not keep from noting that the "spectre of the initiative [had] motivated every developer who could to beat the deadline by taking out building permits."

A year and a half later, when the president of Friends of Redlands and his ally got elected to the council, the *Facts* made no endorsements and offered no comment before the election. After these two had won, an editorial began, "A vision for Redlands won Round II in the city election yesterday." But "the meaning of the Friends of Redlands victory yesterday comes with a rather different emphasis from Round I in 1978" (Proposition R). Round I had emphasized *quantity* control, but the threat of Proposition R had actually brought "a tidal wave of building" that had left many homes unsold and unoccupied. "For the present, inflation and a glutted market appear to be the real factors moderating construction—not Proposition R." Round II, on the other hand, stressed *quality*. "Surely the message from the voters yesterday was that they cherish the values of Redlands and support those who champion their preservation," the editorial concluded.

So, a year and a half later, Proposition R still rankled. A year after the council election, in an editorial on the official 1980 census, the writer noted that the population of Redlands had boomed in the 1920s, held stable in the 1930s, and boomed again in the 1940s. "And so it has always gone. That is why it was difficult for many oldtimers to believe that a Growth Moderation Initiative was necessary. The historical experience of 'Our Town' has been that booms bust. The only question is when they will do so."

Perhaps it was this long view of Redlands history that kept Frank from getting excited in print over all but a few problems, personalities, or changes. His intimate acquaintance with Redlands history was especially evident in a daily column, usually written by Frank, called "With a Grain of Salt." On most days it was evident that Frank spent more effort on the column than on the editorials, and it probably had a more devoted readership, especially among longtime Redlanders. Someone might call Frank's attention to a last remaining ring, embedded in a curb, that had been used for tying horses. That might launch a column on the heyday of horses in downtown Redlands or on the history of that particular street or on the story of the person who had lived at that address.

A few days before the vote on Proposition R, Frank began a column, "When did the growth of Redlands first begin to concern the residents?" He quoted a local historian as identifying the year 1902. Six houses were built that year. That lead to a discussion of building costs in those days, including a comparison of costs on the flatland with those part way up the ridge. One pattern set in 1902, he said, helped explain why one street to this day has no room for off-street parking.

Frank and Bill continued writing an occasional "With a Grain of Salt" column after they sold the *Facts*. They seemed to alternate with Andy Rooney. One column, published in January 1982, was written to prepare Redlanders for the coming of Halley's comet in 1986. Frank had been up on the ridges above the city and had scouted out the best possible views for spotting the comet. But he warned that it was not likely to be much above the horizon for many evenings, that the moon's light would interfere on certain nights, and that the lights of nearby cities would dim it further. He guessed, seriously, that the best night for a comet party would be January 13, 1986.

Even though Frank's thought processes did not take to a VDT that was temporarily in his office, he probably would have liked to have been an engineer if he had not been an editor. In recognition of many columns relating to engineering, the American Society of Civil Engineers awarded Frank the "1980 Journalism Award." A plaque was given to him in the presence of two hundred engineers. He guessed that the engineers were "far more aware of their number who appear in the 'Grain' than I am." Then he noted he had quoted Mel Green, a construction engineer, on preservation of the library exterior walls; two highway department engineers on a big landslide removal job; and aeronautical engineer Bill Williams on soaring and hang gliding. He then noted, "Horace Hinckley, civil engineer and manager of the Bear Valley Mutual Water Company, is often in the 'Grain.' "

Some of the "Grains," especially those written by Bill, related extensive travel adventures, some to Europe, some to Baja California. Both Bill and Graff own airplanes and from time to time fly them to Mexico, where Graff has a vacation home. Graff also pursues a hobby of cross-country racing, sometimes down into Mexico. Some of Bill's columns have related exciting adventures that he and Graff have had south of the border.

Although Frank and Bill continued to write a "Grain" several times a week and Greenberg made no major changes in syndicated columns on the editorial page, one of the major differences between the old and the new *Facts* has been the editorial page. Greenberg has moved readers' letters from the local pages to the editorial page. Whether for that reason or another, the number of letters increased substantially. The Moores apparently chose news pages for letters because they were unpredictable in number and length and would have interfered with the standard editorial page makeup that featured editorials in a traditional upper left corner, the "Grain of Salt" in its regular location next to the editorials, and a set number of columnists in their respective places. Greenberg removed the daily "Almanac" provided by United Press International, but he kept "Redlands Yesterday," tidbits from five, ten, and fifteen years ago, and "A Little Prayer," a one-sentence prayer for the day. He said he had no intention of removing the prayer. It had been left out by mistake a time or two, and he had heard instantly from irate readers.

Two years after the change of ownership, editorial columnists remained unchanged: Andy Rooney, Dave Broder, Tom Braden, Patrick Buchanan, Richard Cohen, William Raspberry, Joseph Sobran, Bob Wagman, and Robert Walters. But Greenberg has introduced some harder-hitting cartoonists. One cartoon that never would have appeared on Frank's editorial page, drawn by Scrawls of the *Atlanta Journal* and syndicated by the Newspaper Enterprise Association, depicted the changing attitude of a male desk worker after he had spotted an ERA pin on the "knockout" at the next desk. After first thinking of flirting with her, then facing the prospect that she might be making as much money as he, and finally foreseeing that she might be promoted, he concludes, "She's probably dating the boss . . . yes . . . that's it." In the last panel, he yells at her, "Slut!!!" Another cartoon, by Bennett of the *St. Petersburg Times,* distributed by Copley News Service, depicted a map of the United States on which pigs (male, no doubt) were drawn in the shapes of the fifteen states that had not ratified the Equal Rights Amendment.

But, while Greenberg has brought readers' voices onto the page, he has not fully brought his own voice. He readily acknowledged that editorial writing took a distant second to the newsroom in his first months as editor. Editorials about local topics, except for an occasional praise of a local endeavor, have been almost nonexistent. Usually one editorial appears each day. Greenberg estimated he had written about half of the editorials in the first months. The other half came from canned editorial services. After trying one service, Greenberg settled on what he regarded as a superior package provided by the Copley News Service in San Diego. The package has the additional advantage of containing state editorials from time to time. He said he has received quite a few compliments on the Copley editorials. Asked why he did not credit the original sources of the canned editorials, Greenberg said, "Readers would not think we were doing our job if we did not have unsigned editorials." One could not help but recall Frank's admission that he had "shamelessly" run canned editorials forty years before for the same reason—not enough time to do everything an editor would like to do.

It takes years of experience to develop the capability to turn out a couple of editorials every day, which Frank eventually achieved, and to write them with the light touch that he mastered. Greenberg, to many of those who knew him from his first assignments with the *Facts,* was a sports writer. Several of the best-remembered by-lines he had received in the *Sun* were on his experiences as a serious jogger.

Graff said he saw the *Facts*'s editorial policy as pretty much middle-of-the-road. Greenberg said some of the editorials he had written could be considered liberal, such as those supporting gun controls, more money for education, and the environment. Others, such as support for Reaganomics and the death penalty, he saw as conservative.

After several months as an editorial writer, Greenberg was still displaying a pretty heavy hand. To his credit, he was starting to address local issues. One of his early editorials on drunk driving won a state prize.

When a local architect, Leon Armantrout, singlehandedly stopped the city from tearing out several troublesome trees in the city's historic district, Greenberg wrote: "We'd like to see the carob trees on Eureka Street stay right where they've been for years. We salute Armantrout's efforts, the concern and flexibility our city officials showed in delaying removal of the trees and eagerly await Armantrout's promised alternate solution."

Actually city officials were not all that pleased with Armantrout's last-ditch stand, nor the *Facts*'s prominent page-one feature on his efforts.

Greenberg's most controversial editorial in the first few months also related to city government. "Relax a little bit" was the title—advice aimed at the city manager. The editorial noted that the city council had approved salary increases for the police chief and city manager. The first half of an eight-paragraph editorial expressed approval of these increases and confidence in the city's financial condition, although stating "our heads spin every time we try to decipher the city budget." Then abruptly the editorial changed tone. "In his job, it's easy for our city manager to get into a number of adversary situations. But we get this feeling he seems to like it and that's not good." The editorial noted that, several weeks before, police and firefighters had voted "no confidence" in the city manager during contract negotiations and that:

> In dealing with the media, the city manager has shown his defensive colors many times. We are not out to 'get' our city manager. We don't think the police and firemen were either.
> Chris Christiansen has a tough job. We are not asking him to tell us everything. Many times he can't legally. Nor are we asking him to give employees everything they request. Good managers can't do that all the time.

But the public—whether they are negotiating employees, or a newspaper's readers—have a right to know what government is doing with their money.

All we wish is that our city manager would learn to relax a little in some of these situations.

Frank Moore probably would not have used that approach to encourage the city manager to "relax a little bit." Nor would he have played so prominently the ticklish contract negotiations between the city and police and firefighters. Of course, during most of Frank and Bill's era, editors did not have to concern themselves with open confrontation between public employers and public employees. Only recently in such communities as Redlands have teacher and other public employee negotiations reached impasses. Greenberg repeatedly made the city negotiations his number one front-page story. "Police, firemen making offers the city can refuse" read one seventy-two-point banner headline; "Police, fire reject city's offer" read a slightly shorter seventy-two-point head another day. Some on the city's management side thought the *Facts* was displaying sympathy for police and firefighters. Perhaps that impression resulted because of what one of those officials described as being "spoiled by the Moores."

Police Chief Robert Brickley said he had seen a difference in coverage of his department. Reporters were displaying a more aggressive attitude in getting the news. "It's getting to be more like the *Sun,*" he said, referring to earlier head-to-head confrontations with reporters from that paper. Brickley was particularly displeased when the *Facts* reprinted vague charges against Brickley and the police department, distributed in an anonymous letter at a time when an officer was being considered for disciplining.

Some other locally written stories would have seemed out of place on the front page of the old *Facts*. Such stories reported that charges had been filed against a California Highway Patrol officer in an alleged murder-rape case, that the county assessor had been charged with misappropriating public money, and that the death penalty had been imposed in a murder involving two little girls. Regarding the last instance, the story of the murder and of the defendant's arrest had appeared on page three a year before.

One story that ran across the top of page one, above the newspaper's name, recounted court testimony in a supposed local land fraud. Another such story told of a visit by Alex Haley, author of *Roots,* to the University of Redlands.

Also run across the top of the front page was a series, which Greenberg cited as one of the best things he and his staff had done in the first several months. The three articles in the series attempted to spell out, as specifically as possible, what might happen in the event of a major earthquake. The series was based partly on research done by the Policy Research Center of the University of Redlands; partly on an article in *Atlantic* ("Living on the Fault Line") by Redlands native James Fallows; and partly on a variety of other sources, including local officials. In the previous three years of the Moore ownership, the *Facts* had not produced anything approaching this reportorial effort. But this type of dramatization of an issue presents the possibility of distortion, especially when an editor wants to create a strong image. In this case, City Manager Christiansen was rankled by the handling of one of his quotations. The *Facts* story quoted him as saying, "If we get hit with an 'eight' [on the Richter scale], we'll have to depend on outside help. Every major disaster area worldwide depends on outside help." Christiansen said he was thinking of the San Francisco earthquake. Even after the San Fernando Valley quake outside help was required, he said. When the article appeared in print, in eighteen-point type in a box with a gray background, these words were included: "You're kidding yourself if you think you can gear up for a major disaster."—Chris Christiansen, City Manager. Immediately following it, in the same box, was: "The first six to ten hours are crucial, once you're in gear, you'll have all kinds of help."—Ray Sharp, Southern California Gas. Christiansen thought that made him appear to be much more defeatist than he actually meant to be.

Another top-of-page-one story, about teen-age runaways, was written by Greenberg. Teen-age runaways? Why would anyone want to run away from Redlands? One more page one story that the Moores never would have run should be noted. "Frank Moore, Kay Mason named Man, Woman of Year" proclaimed a three-column, forty-two-point headline on January 15, 1982. The two honored persons appeared in a three-column picture in the upper lefthand corner of page one. Frank's smile suggested that he might even have been pleased to have received such an honor—but on page one?

Greenberg waited about three months before starting to make visible changes in the *Facts*. Then in a series of five personal columns, he announced the changes that were going to be made. Each day he reran all the previous explanations, so that by the end of the five days the series filled the left half of page three all the way to the bottom.

He kept Bodoni headlines, but boosted the size and went to more horizontal makeup. He widened column measures, but he has been stuck with narrow columns on some pages because the *Facts* retains an eight-column ad format. To make stories easier to read, body type was enlarged from 8½ to 9 points. The "difference of half a point isn't a whole bunch," Greenberg wrote in his second column. He did not mention, however, that the next day the page width would shrink from fifteen to fourteen inches, and so would the column widths. Page one is six columns wide; but because ads are displayed on an eight-column format, inside pages are a mixture of four columns and eight columns.

One of Greenberg's favorite make-up devices is what he calls gray bars, half-tone backgrounds for standing heads. Once launched, use of the device seemed to have no logical stopping point. Bars for section heads, with two or three words at the extreme left of the page, ran the width of the page about a half inch deep. As many as eight bars ran on the editorial page. One subscriber thought the bars made the *Facts* look like the *National Enquirer,* especially the colored background behind the "Inside Facts" box on page one. After several months of the bars, Graff expressed doubts that they were worth the newsprint they required.

The *Facts* had boxed stories under Frank and Bill, but Greenberg has out-boxed them. One type of box, intended to serve readers in a hurry, is used to summarize quickly actions of board and council meetings. The boxes run alongside the full stories.

One of Greenberg's goals was to move stories and features around so that similar items would be grouped. Readers would know exactly where to find them. In one explanatory column, he described this as "moving the furniture." He wrote, sounding somewhat defensive: "But before I pick up the easy chair, put away your baseball bat and just listen. First, there will be no more 'Family page'; and the front and 'Area News' pages, three and four, will be completely different. Trust me."

He moved "Peanuts" from the bottom of page one to the comics page. He added United Press International's gossip column, "Peopletalk," to page two, to be joined by the "Almanac" and expanded weather coverage. He created "Up Front," a boxed summary of a half dozen wire stories. After some experimenting, it wound up covering the bottom quarter of page one, with a jump to page two. He grouped meeting, entertainment, and crime stories; and he moved weddings, engagements, and anniversaries to the vital records page. As mentioned earlier, he brought local news stories to the front page, and he stressed local features. One of his early innovations was a business column that includes both features and news tidbits about local businesses and business persons.

In the last of the explanatory columns, he wrote:

> Why are we doing all of this? What's the matter with leaving it the way it is?
>
> Before we explain, we'd like to clarify an important point. Many people have assumed these changes are orders from the Donrey Media Group, which recently bought the *Facts.* They were not. The ideas are

mine and those of General Manager Graff Moore and the entire staff. . . .

So why are we changing?

Simply we feel these are the best ways to improve your newspaper and in the process give you more for your money. We feel we are enhancing the *Daily Facts,* not taking things away.

We hope you enjoy the additions.

About six weeks after the changes were made, Greenberg delivered a progress report to readers. The tone of the article was conciliatory, perhaps apologetic in a few instances, but basically confident. He acknowledged that he had made a mistake in dropping the stock market. (A few months later, when the Saturday edition was switched to morning, the *Facts* added two pages for a complete review of the week's stock market activities.) He acknowledged he had second thoughts about eliminating the "Family" page. A page called "Around the Town" was created for community, social, and wedding news, with a special "Here and There" heading for meetings. The new page was not much different from the old "Family" page.

One reader liked the larger type, more local news, and continuation of "Grain of Salt." Another wrote: "The *Facts* has moved unacceptably in the direction of parochialism. Having done extensive research in the *Facts* published during the 1930s, I am acutely aware of the international interest of the paper during that period."

Some critics said they spent less time reading the *Facts* because they could not find what they were looking for. Others said they spent less time because they could find what they were looking for and did not have to bother reading the rest. A comment heard several times was that readers appreciated more hometown news but did not like the consigning of international news to whatever space was left over in the back of the paper.

A tabulation of stories published during a week in January 1981 and a comparable week in January 1982 illustrates some of the changes. During six days in 1981 the *Facts* published twenty-seven international, sixty-two national, and forty-five state wire stories. A year later the figures were nineteen international, fifty-four national, and forty-seven state. The number of local stories increased from 119 to 132. Major local stories increased from twenty-three to thirty-two; local features jumped from one to five. Minor local stories remained at exactly ninety-five. Local pictures also remained the same—fifteen.

The figures also show how page one had changed. International stories dropped from thirteen to seven and national from twenty-four to seventeen. But state stories increased from eleven to twenty-four, local stories from zero to twelve, and local pictures from zero to three. The total number of page one stories increased from forty-eight to sixty, about half published in the "Up Front" summary. One of Greenberg's initial goals was a major page one feature each day. That proved to be too heavy an assignment for his thinly stretched staff. The week in 1982 had five features, only one of which made page one. During the week of the previous year, the *Facts* carried one feature, not on page one.

Greenberg inherited what must have been the most complete coverage of church announcements that any paper in any town ever carried. Church publicists were allowed to provide almost any information they wished about forthcoming services and meetings. The *Facts* allocated space on three or more pages on Saturday. Announcements went even so far as to say who would greet people at the door, who would read the scripture, and who would sing a solo. The paper not only provided space, but its editors also wrote specific and different-sized headlines for each of twenty-five to thirty stories. Greenberg's only change, at least in the first months, was to cut out the headlines and to affix each church's name at the top of the story. He had raised enough suspicions among Redlanders by publicizing the evil ways of the community without appearing to take on the churches.

The proportion of news and advertising in the *Facts* has remained virtually unchanged. A tabulation of two weeks in June, October, and January in the years before and after the sale showed that in each instance advertising accounted for slightly less than 40 percent; and news, features, and promotion slightly more than 60 percent. The paper carried exactly the same number of pages in the June weeks; the percentages also were almost identical (38.4 percent advertising in 1980; 38.9 in 1981). A drop in the number of pages from 196 to 190 in the October weeks accompanied a 20 percent decline in classified advertising (mostly cars and housing); the percentage of advertising varied only from 37.9 to 37.8 percent. With classified ahead of the previous year in January, total pages increased from 182 to 184 and nonadvertising columns from 889 to 893. The paper had a slight increase in advertising percentage, from 38.9 to 39.3. Number of pages ranges from twelve on most Tuesdays to twenty-four on most Wednesdays, for an average of between sixteen and seventeen Monday through Saturday.

Graff said the *Facts* has no overall news-advertising goal for the year or any lesser period. Whatever space is needed for news and features, within limits, is set aside. He said he hopes to build a larger advertising base. Redlands has not been a strong shopping community because of proximity to San Bernardino and Riverside. But another in a series of modest-sized shopping centers opened near Redlands in 1981. Graff also hopes that Bill Webb, the advertising manager whom he brought in six months before the sale, will be able to build that base through more professional advertising

Kenneth Rystrom

techniques. Webb said he had no magic formulas to offer, but he thought much could be accomplished through training what had been a largely untrained staff.

Eight months after the change in ownership, Jim Mundy, Webb's predecessor, who had left the *Facts* to join a local real estate firm, said that now as a buyer of advertising he could see no significant changes in advertising policy, except possibly for a greater number of paid promotions. He said he doubted whether these would boost advertising appreciably, since most businesses have only so many dollars for advertising.

Webb said one of his problems was trying to convince area merchants that local subscribers read the *Facts* more thoroughly than they do a regional paper such as the *Sun,* and that therefore they should advertise in the *Facts* as well as in the regional paper. Another problem, he said, was convincing advertisers that every change that is made is not the result of the change in ownership. The *Facts* increased advertising rates 11 percent on the same day the sale took effect, but Webb said that July 1 had been a customary date for raising rates and that the increase had been planned before the sale was known. Another rate increase, of 7 percent, the following February also had nothing to do with Donrey, he said; the July 1 date was just being moved ahead because of rising costs. Later in 1982, Webb left, and ad salesman Bob Romero was promoted to advertising manager. Ad rates were raised again in October 1982 and once more in October 1983.

Mundy, who said the Moores had held religiously to the first of July for increases, speculated that the *Facts* might be working its way back to a January 1 date, a more customary time for rate changes. He said he always thought that the off-season July 1 notice called special attention to itself. Mundy said that the rate increases were similar in amount to those of the past. Subscription rates as of March 1982 were still $4.25 a month, but in early 1983 they went to $5.00.

If the new ownership was not the immediate reason for changes in news or advertising, a direct effect was evident on the business side of the paper. Even though circulation had grown from 7,662 in 1976 to 8,310 in 1980, it stood only at 8,343 on October 1, 1981. Donrey almost immediately began pushing for a more aggressive sales effort. But the first efforts resulted in a drop of more than two hundred in circulation. Circulation Manager Ted Dixon attributed the decline partly to a stricter accounting of unpaid subscribers. Some subscribers also were lost, at least temporarily, he said, when the paper switched from delivery by carriers who had been employed directly by the *Facts* to contract carriers. He said very few cancellations resulted from dissatisfaction with changes made in the paper.

By the end of February, circulation had risen back to 8,382. Dixon said he hoped to reach nine thousand by the end of the year. A year and a half later, in

171

October 1983, circulation stood at 8,696. Only about 50 percent of Redlands's sixteen thousand or so homes (population forty-three thousand) subscribe to the *Facts;* but the percentage of penetration varies from 75 to 80 percent in the upper- and upper-middle-class sections of the community to 15 to 20 percent in middle- and lower-class sections. It drops off to 5 percent in the adjacent communities of Yucaipa and Loma Linda.

The *Facts's* principal competition, the *San Bernardino Sun,* owned by Gannett, distributes approximately fourteen thousand papers in the Redlands, Loma Linda, and Yucaipa area, for a penetration of about 45 percent. *Sun* Editor Wayne Sargent speculated that his paper's circulation probably would have been higher except for Gannett's traditional aggressive pricing policy. The *Sun* costs eight dollars a month for daily and Sunday.

When advertising revenues declined in the fall of 1981, Donrey moved promptly to cut costs. Laid off were one person in advertising, one in composing, and one part-time person in the newsroom. That left Greenberg with ten news-editorial persons: himself; a news editor; a city editor; two persons in sports; one person who wrote about arts, community happenings, and weddings; three reporters; and one photographer. Then in 1982, in another economy move, Greenberg lost another position and moved a sports person to the newsroom. The rival *Sun* has a four-person bureau in Redlands that concentrates on major stories in Redlands, Yucaipa, and Loma Linda.

When ownership of the *Facts* changed, staff members in all departments began talking about "the bottom line." The word was that Donrey did not much care what local management decided to do with its product so long as the bottom line was met. There was talk that, while Frank and Bill might have been content netting something like 18 percent on gross revenue before taxes, Donrey was asking for 25 percent. Graff said he had been given no such firm figure, but he said that Donrey's Western properties had averaged 28 percent the previous year.

One reason Frank and Bill may not have set profit goals was that they never had a budget, Graff said. They made out a list of things they might want to do during the months ahead. If they had the money when the time came, they bought what they had in mind, he said; if they did not have the money, they put it off. In those days Graff said he could take out the checkbook and just buy something. Now everything goes through Donrey. The budget for the year ending June 30, 1982, anticipated $1.975 million in gross revenues. Eight months into the budget year, Graff said that the figure looked just about on target.

One thing that Graff saw as not being a step forward with Donrey was the handling of accounts receivable. The *Facts* had installed a computer system to give instantaneous printouts of these accounts. But Donrey insisted that the system be abandoned, that the accounts be done by hand, and that records be mailed in batches to corporate headquarters in Arkansas for input into the central computer. Printouts then are mailed back. Thus, instead of knowing instantly, Graff may have to wait up to ten days to get the figures.

Graff acknowledged that the *Facts* should have had budgeting procedures long before and that many of the new procedures are just good business practice. Donrey has provided budgeting and accounting models, and it has provided models for evaluating personnel. Greenberg expressed enthusiasm for the new evaluation procedures he was using with new staff members. He also was pleased with results of a Donrey editors' seminar that he had attended for several days at the corporation's facilities at Lake Tahoe. Information provided during the panel discussions (one dealt with stress management) was helpful, he said. He said he picked up a lot of ideas by associating with other editors (including advice on how to get more money for news budgets).

Donrey business practices paid off immediately in one area. Because of the clout wielded by the group, Donrey was able to negotiate a substantial reduction in rates charged by United Press International and the feature syndicates.

Bill and Frank had paid people whatever they thought they deserved. Greenberg said that, when he returned to the *Facts,* he realized that the paper was paying news people pretty well because it was having to compete with San Bernardino and Riverside papers. Greenberg said that a person who had joined the *Facts* at about the same time as he did was getting more money than he had worked up to on the *Sun.* Newsroom salaries in 1982 on the *Sun* started at $248 and went to $404.50 after six years, but Sargent said many staff members were being paid above scale.

The *Facts,* having no unionized departments, never has had a set pay scale. But Graff said that a salary study had been started to try to bring more uniformity into pay patterns. The *Facts* also had never had a retirement program, and its medical program was expensive. Employees were immediately included in the Donrey retirement program, and they were paying about fifty dollars a month less for medical benefits.

One area in which Donrey has held tough is in authorizing financial contributions to the community. Graff said the group has a policy of not giving to united charitable agencies because of what it considers to be high administrative costs. The company prefers that its foundation give to individual agencies, he said.

In the fall of 1981, Redlands Chamber of Commerce, in looking for new quarters, was attempting to raise money to buy and remodel a new building. When Donrey Foundation was asked to contribute, chamber officials were given a set of forms that one person said might have required a stack of documents six inches high and might have taken two weeks to complete. The chamber did submit a half dozen pages of explanation of the project, but it had received no response more than three months after submission.

One change brought by the new management has been a greater interest in competing for recognition among newspapers. Apparently, 1981 was the first year that the *Facts* had submitted entries in contests sponsored by the California Newspaper Publishers Association. It received an honorable mention for overall advertising excellence. Greenberg was disappointed that the series on earthquakes had not won a prize.

Facts executives have never been particularly active in state or national newspaper organizations, though Webb served as president of the California Advertising Executives Association. The paper on occasion had sent staff members to seminars.

Graff said that Donrey encourages local participation by its newspapers and their employees. In early 1982 the paper was making plans to sponsor a Little League team in the spring, something the *Facts* had not done before. Greenberg had joined the Kiwanis Club and was giving speeches at other organizations in the community. Beyond membership in the Rotary Club, Graff had not previously been deeply involved in community activities. He did not anticipate that moving into his father's old office would make any difference in that regard. His out-of-the-office interests were likely to remain flying airplanes and driving across the desert.

Graff had agreed to stay with the *Facts* for one year. In February he seemed inclined to stick with Donrey. Between Thanksgiving and the end of January, he had heard from a company vice-president only three times, and then only by memo. "He must be pleased," Graff said. "We're doing some good things, things we should have been doing before."

Greenberg said he had the feeling he had fewer bosses between him and the top of the organization than he did when he was working for Gannett in San Bernardino. He said he knows Donrey has knowledgeable people in Pomona and Ontario who can give him advice if he needs it, but they have given advice only when asked. If it were not for the little matter of "the bottom line," he said, he would be perfectly happy working for Donrey. What he would really like is enough money to bring back the part-time news clerk laid off in the fall and add a reporter and a part-time photographer—plus a little extra for salary increases.

Most readers, of course, knew little about the newspaper's internal activities. They knew only what appeared in print. They seemed to be growing accustomed to the bolder look and the more aggressive news style of the *Facts,* but they still were waiting for the paper to find its editorial voice.

On May 7, 1982, Donrey Media suddenly announced that Mel Wagner, age forty-five, had been appointed general manager of the *Facts* to succeed Graff Moore, who had resigned to pursue other business interests. Wagner's background had been primarily in circulation. He most recently had been circulation consultant for Donrey's Western Newspaper Division. Wagner said he was given the *Facts* assignment not because of his work in circulation but because of his managerial skills, including experience in personnel, budgeting, and profit and loss statements. He said his goal was to make the *Facts* the dominant paper in the area in advertising and circulation. He said Greenberg would continue to be fully responsible for the news and editorial product. Wagner said he looked forward to participating extensively in the community.

In January 1983, the *Facts* launched a Sunday edition which has ranged from sixteen to twenty pages, plus comics and a television guide. The news staff, which then consisted of the former sportswriter and two recent University of Redlands graduates, was reassigned to cover seven days in order to produce the new edition. The result, Greenberg acknowledged, was that he was not producing as good a newspaper as he had been. Immediate prospects for additional help did not look bright.

Loren Ghiglione

I n December 1979, when Ralph Ingersoll II bought the *Transcript* of North Adams, Massachusetts, for $5 million cash, newspaper executives throughout New England gulped in disbelief.

The price staggered them. North Adams was losing jobs and population (the school rolls had fallen nearly 25 percent in a decade). The thirteen-thousand-circulation *Transcript* also appeared to be headed nowhere. Annual sales were $2 million, the net never better than $83,000. How could Ingersoll justify the price?

But equally staggering: Who was selling to whom?

The seller, Affiliated Publications, reeked of New England respectability and journalistic prestige. Its main property, the *Boston Globe,* could claim more than one hundred years of Taylor family ownership, four Pulitzer Prizes, the rank of one of *Time* magazine's "best ten newspapers," and the title, as one *Globe* editor immodestly but accurately described it, of "the most influential newspaper in New England."

The buyer was Ingersoll Publications, owner of twenty-two other papers, including four dailies in New England. More than one of the region's news executives felt Ingersoll sacrificed outstanding journalism to gain outstanding profits. Peter DeRose, copublisher of the *Daily Hampshire Gazette,* Northampton, Massachusetts, said of Ingersoll, "You don't hear that name mentioned when they're handing out the laurels."

James Ottaway, Jr., president of Ottaway Newspapers, a division of Dow Jones & Company, predicted Ingersoll would "squeeze the *Transcript* tight, probably not run a very good newspaper, and . . . get his money back in time."

With three years' hindsight, what did happen to the *Transcript* under Ingersoll ownership?

Ingersoll and the *Transcript*'s management acknowledge the paper's previous strong journalistic tradition. They say the tradition continues. And they contend that the paper under its previous owners—Affiliated from 1976 to 1979 and the family of James and Robert Hardman prior to that—operated as a wasteful and paternalistic nonbusiness. No one had to care about profits.

So no one did. The *Transcript,* Ingersoll argues, now is run as an efficient, economical, and—it almost goes without saying—highly profitable business.

Jim Hardman responds that he and his brother never ignored profits—a profit-sharing program provided up to four weeks pay annually for each *Transcript* employee—but that they attached equal importance to improving the paper and serving the community.

Many readers, asked their views a year after the paper's sale to Ingersoll, argued the *Transcript* was more of a *news*paper under forty-six-year veteran Jim Hardman, its editor until Ingersoll's purchase.

"It was a more personal paper. It has lost its local identity," said Edward B. Nassif, from behind the counter of Nassif's Professional Pharmacy on Ashland Street. "The day I lose my local identity in this drugstore is the day I start going downhill."

"It's laboring with an enormous shortage of space for news," said Michael Munley, managing editor for two years, 1976 to 1978. "I see compromises when you have a sixteen-page paper." (More recently, the *Transcript,* on very slow advertising days, has published twelve-pagers.)

Advertising, some argued, had assumed more importance, news less. Readers talked about the small news staff—now down to three full-time reporters, less than one-third its earlier size. A few readers mentioned the placement of news. "I was almost shocked to find pages two and three were full-page ads one day," said Michael Haines, advisor to the student paper and journalism professor at North Adams State College. "Now that's the kind of thing I can't imagine Jim Hardman letting happen."

Invariably readers make a comparison to the editorship of Jim Hardman, who represents to North Adams people quality journalism and a glorious newspaper tradition that is measured not in years or even decades, but in generations.

In 1827, Caleb Turner, Hardman's great-great-grandfather, helped found the first newspaper for western Massachusetts' Berkshire County. After two years, the weekly *Berkshire American,* according to a local historian, "sunk beneath the waves of adversity, with all its freightage of ambition, hope and capital."

James Angell, Hardman's great-grandfather, revived another local weekly, the *Hoosac Valley News,* in 1870. And Aaron W. Hardman and Susan Bryant Hardman, Jim Hardman's grandparents, bought the *North Adams Transcript* in 1898. (Susan had journalistic juice in her veins from her mother's side too; she was a cousin of poet-editor William Cullen Bryant, who ran the *New York Evening Post* for fifty years.)

Four generations of Hardmans built the *Transcript* into what was, in virtually every way, smalltown daily journalism at its best. Begun on a shoestring, the paper was located for a while in rooms over G. W. Alford's harness shop. The Hardmans accepted stove wood from cash-poor subscribers to be delivered to the paper "at the first sleighing." The competition that came at first from another daily, the *Evening Herald*, was so devastating that James A. Hardman, Jim's father, left Williams College in his sophomore year to keep the *Transcript* going—as reporter, ad-taker, editorial writer, and when payday approached, bill collector.

The *Herald* died in 1926 and the *Transcript* gained breathing room. Circulation increased from five thousand to almost fourteen thousand. Earnings were put into making the paper a technological and journalistic leader. In 1948 James A. Hardman began operating radio station WMFM (now WMNB), the first FM in the county, with the thought that someday printed news might be transmitted facsimile by FM radio. In 1950 the *Transcript* became the first paper in the state to install an electronic engraver, permitting expanded photo coverage. In 1969 the *Transcript* built an open-space, seventeen-thousand-square-foot plant, designed by the prestigious Charles Main Associates. The paper installed a Rolls Royce–quality press, a five-unit Goss Urbanite, capable of printing four-color photos and completing the entire daily run in less than thirty minutes.

The *Transcript*'s news operation kept pace with its equipment. By 1974, the *Transcript*'s reporting, strongly local, caused the New England Daily Newspaper Survey, an evaluation of the region's 106 dailies, to conclude, "The paper . . . must rank among the best in the state." The next year, as if to confirm that opinion, the New England Press Association judged the *Transcript* the best small daily in the six-state region.

A large news staff, the equivalent of twenty-four full-timers—twice what one might expect at a paper the *Transcript*'s size—produced an exceptional editorial product, including such special sections as "Hoosac River Cleanup," an eight-page ad-free tabloid on the local effect of amendments to the federal Water Pollution Control Act.

The *Transcript* also devoted an extraordinary amount of space to news. Of the region's ten dailies with ten thousand to fifteen thousand circulation, the *Transcript* gave over the largest portion of space—64.5 percent—to news. The other nine dailies averaged 48 percent.

The editorial page was as strong as the news pages. Jim Hardman's "Memo from the Editor" and his informal Saturday column, "The Short of It" (which he described as "a compendium of wit and witlessness"), gave the page the flavor of one man's mind. Editorials by Hardman and Lewis Cuyler, executive editor, portrayed Richard Nixon (beginning with his famous "Checkers" speech) as a dishonest phony, supported George McGovern's 1972 presidential bid, and opposed the Vietnam War. The *Transcript*'s opposition to United States involvement in Vietnam started early, Hardman recalls, "with the sending to that unhappy land of the first American military 'advisors.' "

Editorials on local subjects were equally forceful. A 1973 editorial dismissed a ballyhooed project as having "all the earmarks of the classic story of a developer buying land in a small town, taking advantage of its minimum requirements for roads, sewage, and water, selling the land to city people wanting vacation homes, making a profit, and clearing out."

Even the *Transcript*'s business manager put the news product first and profits second. Of course, the business manager was Robert Hardman, Jim's younger brother, who had been trained as a reporter on papers in Maine, New Hampshire, and Worcester, Massachusetts, and who, in the words of a *Transcript* reporter, "never separated the news responsibilities from his work."

The *Transcript*, founded in 1843 as a Whig weekly "devoted to the dissemination of Political Intelligence, Moral and Entertaining Literature, Temperance, the News of the Day," had evolved into a public trust. Jim Hardman said, "My father, grandfather, and my brother felt we had an obligation to the community to try to put out the best damn paper that we could."

In 1976, the Hardman brothers, in their sixties with nine children between their two families, faced the question of what to do with the paper. "We were worried," Jim Hardman recalls. "If one of us popped off, where would we have gotten the money to pay the estate taxes." (Robert Hardman would die in 1978, the victim of two heart attacks within three weeks.)

William D. ("Davis") Taylor and John I. Taylor, the chairman of the board and the president of Affiliated Publications, the parent company of the *Boston Globe,* had been talking for several years to the Hardmans about what Jim Hardman still calls "a great idea": a joining together under Affiliated's umbrella of New England's family-owned newspapers. Affiliated Publications would be a "nongroup group" to protect the region's independent papers from being gobbled up by national media conglomerates with little concern for quality or local autonomy.

"The elder Taylors—John principally, with some assistance from Davis—really sold us on the idea," Hardman says. "They painted a beautiful picture. They were going to save good small newspapers forever. They were going to leave them under local control. The headquarters was going to be here," in North Adams, Hardman says. "We were to be the flagship."

On October 1, 1976, the Hardmans sold the *Transcript* to Affiliated for two hundred thousand shares of Affiliated stock worth $1.8 million.

The Taylors' vision—the *Transcript* as the successful cornerstone for a group of independent dailies—crumbled quickly. Affiliated was used to publishing a five-hundred-thousand-circulation daily with revenues of $100 million, not a paper fifty times smaller. Affiliated was out of its element. Its management had, Ingersoll later said, "no intuitive feeling for what was wrong."

"We were their first paper," says Claire Piaggi, the *Transcript*'s publisher who served as business manager during Affiliated's ownership. "They didn't give us the proper guidance. They didn't know how to get it across to us." Two or three times a year, Piaggi says, Affiliated would send from Boston a young, by-the-book controller. Other times, advice came by telephone. Piaggi's evaluation of the advice: "a lot of criticism—nothing constructive—not, 'This is the way it should be done.'"

Larry O'Keefe, hired as a copy editor in June 1978, applauded Affiliated's hands-off management of the *Transcript* as a news operation but wanted more hands-on management for the *Transcript* as a business. Affiliated's people, he said, "allowed themselves to be absentee landlords. I was surprised that they didn't try harder to run the *Transcript* better financially. It looked as if they were allowing extravagance." (Don Sprague, the *Transcript*'s publisher, questions O'Keefe's expertise—"He obviously was not in a position to evaluate"—and his opinion. During the 1970s, under both the Hardmans and Affiliated, "we held production costs through technology and didn't have to fire one person," Sprague says.)

Second, even if Affiliated had known how to run a small daily more efficiently, it would have refused to undertake major economies in the news operation. "We were not willing, and that was our option, to cut the way some of these other guys are . . . to really make the thing look good," William O. Taylor, then executive vice-president and treasurer of Affiliated, recalled. Affiliated was not going to embrace what Taylor later would describe as "the Ingersoll approach." That approach, said Taylor: "Chop it to the bone and make a buck out of it."

Third, Affiliated's efforts to boost profits in ways it judged acceptable failed. The Hardmans had developed a commercial printing business, Sprague said, "to afford more quality in the newsroom." Affiliated planned to increase the *Transcript*'s commercial printing. Instead, the paper lost its major printing customer, Sears, and printing sales dropped 36 percent. In 1978 Affiliated approved the purchase of two weeklies—the *Shoppers' Chance* of Pittsfield and the *Shoppers' Companion* of Adams—and converted them into a two-edition, forty-thousand-circulation shopper called the *Berkshire Advertiser*. In its first quarter, the *Advertiser* lost $24,684; the losses continued, and within months, the shopper was killed.

Fourth, the changing of the guard in Affiliated's leadership brought control to a younger management more interested in diversifying and less interested in preserving the independence of New England's family-owned dailies. John I. Taylor and Davis Taylor were giving way to Davis's son, William ("Bill") O. Taylor.

Though he never went to business school, Bill Taylor is described by some newspaper acquaintances as more of an M.B.A. type than the previous generation of Taylor management. He followed four years at Harvard with service as the *Boston Globe*'s treasurer, business manager, and general manager, and with a stint as president of Kaiser Broadcasting's UHF television station, WKBG, Channel 56, in Boston.

Affiliated, the *Globe*'s parent company, had gone public in 1973. Stock analysts were interested in profitable new ventures. By 1979 Affiliated had bought eight radio stations, and Bill Taylor was telling analysts, "We are pursuing the purchase of additional radio stations . . . as you know, we can go to fourteen stations. . . . We have not ruled out television. . . . We've looked at CATV, too."

(Today Affiliated owns twelve radio stations, a cable television company, a microwave common carrier, and 45 percent of a cable television and radio common carrier.)

Fifth, stockholders and financial analysts kept asking tough questions about the *Transcript*'s profitability. Yes, it was nice that the *Transcript* ranked as an excellent small daily. But its prospects for growth were not excellent. And its net was not excellent.

In 1976, the year that Affiliated bought the *Transcript*, its profits after taxes had been $82,594 on sales of about $2 million. Sales remained even for the next two years. Profits also fell asleep (1977: $70,825; 1978: $124,610, but that apparent increase benefited from $60,000 in proceeds from an insurance policy on the life of Robert Hardman).

On April 27, 1979, at a meeting in New York of analysts interested in newspaper stocks, Bill Taylor was questioned about the *Transcript*'s financial progress. "I wish I could say it has dramatically improved," he replied. "It's flat. . . . It's essentially a flat picture."

Affiliated decided to sell the *Transcript*. "They wanted the cash and the *Transcript* wasn't a terribly profitable property," Jim Hardman says. Bill Taylor planned to use the cash to retire some short-term debt (on which Affiliated was paying 15¾ percent interest) and to purchase more radio stations—the company was in the process of buying WHYN in Springfield, Massachusetts—but he offered assurance, Hardman says, that the *Transcript* "wasn't going to the highest bidder." Hardman recalls, "My son said, 'Just you wait and see.'"

Affiliated apparently began its search with the intention of selling to a respected newspaper firm or to the *Transcript*'s management. It talked with some of the better companies in New England, including Ottaway Newspapers (a subsidiary of Dow Jones & Company, publisher of the *Wall*

Street Journal), which put out seven papers in the region, and Newspapers of New England, owner of the *Concord* (New Hampshire) *Monitor* and the *Holyoke* (Massachusetts) *Transcript-Telegram* and co-owner of the *Greenfield* (Massachusetts) *Recorder*.

Affiliated also invited a bid from Donald Sprague, Jr., the publisher of the *Transcript* who had worked for the Hardmans for seven years, four as advertising director and assistant business manager and three as assistant to the publisher. In June 1979 Sprague had asked for the chance to become part of the *Transcript*'s ownership if Affiliated ever decided to sell. In late August Sprague was given one month to put together a North Adams group and make an all-cash offer.

Affiliated's search for a good newspaper operator may have been motivated by more than what the Taylors thought best for the *Transcript* and North Adams. "If Affiliated ever hoped to be in the bidding again on the basis of its reputation," one New England publisher explained, "it had to be very careful about the sale of the paper." If Affiliated sold the *Transcript* to a company notorious for milking its newspapers—of putting profit ahead of the product—the Taylors would find it exceedingly difficult to persuade the owners of other good papers to sell to Affiliated.

John Taylor, a member of the older generation of Taylors, says he was willing to sell the *Transcript* for a price not significantly greater, given inflation, than the $1.8 million Affiliated had paid for the paper in 1976. He recalls advising, "If we can get $2.5 million, grab it." Several New England publishers valued the *Transcript* at $2 to 2.5 million.

But Affiliated's younger generation of management appraised the paper differently. The two hundred thousand shares of Affiliated stock the Hardmans received for the *Transcript* (1976 value: $1.8 million) were worth, three years later, more than $4 million. One interested publisher remembers being told by Bill Taylor, "In order to come out even, we have to get $3 to 4 million."

Sprague found it virtually impossible to put together a syndicate of North Adams investors. Sprague offered Affiliated $1 million cash. Affiliated showed no interest. Sprague went to Jim Hardman. Together they offered $2 million.

Bill Taylor, says Hardman, seemed uninterested; $3 million was his minimum price. "We would have gone to $2.5 million," Hardman recalls. "But I felt I was talking to empty space when I talked to Bill. We weren't on the same wave length. He has a streak of toughness that John and Dave don't have. He doesn't understand what you're talking about—responsibility to the [North Adams] community—but as far as the *Globe* [and its responsibility to Boston] is concerned, he does."

Finally, one publisher recalls, Bill Taylor "lost patience."

He asked the First Boston Corporation to prepare a formal prospectus on the *Transcript* and mail it to several possible buyers respected by the Taylors (the cover letter from First Boston Vice-President Nicholas Paumgarten described them as "people who we feel are the most appropriate prospective purchasers"). They were asked to submit a written offer to Bill Taylor by noon, November 14.

But that deadline did not bring an acceptable offer. Taylor then gave First Boston permission to talk to a wider circle of publishers. Something of a bidding war developed. "All these offers came in," recalls John Taylor. "It was insane."

Bill Taylor could be excused if he considered opting for the highest bid. At least one important stockholder reportedly argued that the Taylors had—in the patois of the boardroom—a fiduciary responsibility to the trustees to maximize return and enhance the company's assets. An executive at an interested newspaper company says Affiliated received a high bid of $7 million from Thomson Newspapers, which has the reputation of starving its news operation to reap exceptional profits. (Canada's 1980 Royal Commission on Newspapers described the Thomson chain as "a lackluster aggregation of cashboxes.")

Affiliated will not confirm or deny a $7 million Thomson offer. Regardless, the winning bid came from Ralph Ingersoll who had learned at the eleventh hour the *Transcript* was on the block. A call to the Taylors brought a prospectus. Without even visiting the *Transcript,* Ingersoll shrewdly offered $5 million, roughly equivalent to the value of two hundred thousand Affiliated shares, the number of shares Affiliated had traded in 1976 to the Hardmans for the *Transcript*. (On November 30, 1979, Affiliated was selling for $25¼ a share.) The value of the two hundred thousand shares had special significance to Affiliated. Sprague recalls asking John P. Giuggio, now Affiliated's president, what it would take to buy the *Transcript*. Giuggio replied, "All the Hardmans' Affiliated stock back."

The Taylors felt kindly toward Ingersoll. That summer, as Affiliated had tried to learn what it could do to improve the *Transcript*'s financial position, Ingersoll had bothered to explain his operating methods and had shown John Taylor the books for several of his papers in markets of comparable size.

Ingersoll does not deceive himself about the Taylors' view of his management techniques—"they equate what we did with being the sons of bitches that they can't be"—but he suspects, rightly, that he gained their respect for his business acumen.

The announcement that Affiliated was selling to Ingersoll brought something less than applause from New England's publishers. Peter DeRose of the *Daily Hampshire Gazette,* Northampton, Massachusetts, believed that Affiliated and First Boston "could have made it possible for the *Transcript* to be bought by people who would do an excellent job with the paper." Carter White, publisher and member of the ownership family of the *Meriden Record-Journal* in Connecticut, said, "I don't want to see anyone from the *Globe* ever again."

The *Transcript*'s December 5 announcement to readers of its purchase by Ingersoll emphasized three points. First, despite Ingersoll's ownership of twenty-three newspapers, each was independent, "owned by a separate corporation." The article concluded, "The papers are not operated as a chain, and each is under local management. Mr. Ingersoll said the independence of local operations is a hallmark of Ingersoll newspapers."

Second, readers were assured that their *Transcript* would remain very much the same. Ingersoll, the article reported, "said he plans no operational changes at this time." Sprague, the publisher, was quoted, "I don't anticipate changes in the operation."

Third, Ingersoll expressed great confidence in Sprague's management of the *Transcript*. Ingersoll said he was made aware of Sprague's worth by the publisher of another Ingersoll paper in New England. "Our principal incentive [to buy the *Transcript*] is that we have known of and admired Don Sprague for several years. He will be continuing as publisher, with our active and enthusiastic support."

But other New England publishers, personally familiar with Ingersoll newspapers, doubted Sprague should take Ingersoll's statements at face value. Two former Ingersoll publishers, who asked not to be identified, said Ingersoll prodded his new publishers to earn large profits—25 to 30 percent before taxes—almost from the start. "He seemed obsessed," one said.

Both publishers disputed Ingersoll's claims about the independence of his papers from corporate supervision. Jim Plugh acted as a regional manager, carefully monitoring operations. A company manual—"Financial Control Standards"—set goals for every aspect of the papers. "They say 'one man, one paper,' " one former publisher recalled. "That's a crock." Ingersoll may have left editorial policy to the local management, the publisher concluded, but Ingersoll definitely set profit policy.

Ingersoll's "impatience to see fast progress in terms of profits," says an official at a New England press association, means that, "Unless there is fast progress, the publisher loses his job." The *Eagle-Times* of Springfield, Vermont and Claremont, New Hampshire may prove the point. In a 1980 study published by a statewide weekly, the *New Hampshire Times,* Tom Ferriter referred to Ingersoll ownership when he reported, "By one official estimate, the *Eagle* has been managed—and often mismanaged—by ten different publishers during the past ten years."

So Sprague could take little comfort in Ingersoll's public declarations of support for him, former Ingersoll publishers felt. They believed, despite

Ingersoll's talk about "no operational changes," that Sprague would be expected to make many changes quickly. Ingersoll did order, Sprague says, a "tightened-up" *Transcript*—a leaner, more local paper. Ingersoll was sure such a *Transcript* would result in "more money falling out the bottom—it always does."

For the Hardmans and Affiliated, Sprague had been asked to be community leader as much as cost cutter. He had served as a director of the Community Development Corporation, the Chamber of Commerce, the Economic Development Corporation, the Northern Berkshire United Way, and the Berkshire Housing Development Corporation.

For Ingersoll, Sprague became profit booster.

The cover price of the *Transcript* was raised from twenty to twenty-five cents, prior to an increase by the *Berkshire Eagle*. "Traditionally," said the *Transcript*'s Rod Doherty, "we had gone up nine months after the *Eagle* went up."

What Ingersoll described as "old-boy" advertising rates—low rates possible when owners "don't have any debt and any needs"—were raised twice, a total of 12 percent in six months. A ten percent discount for cash prepayment by advertisers was eliminated. The *Transcript*'s percentage of advertising, which under the Hardmans had been allowed to hit 35.5 percent, the lowest of comparably sized papers in New England, was pushed higher, toward 50 percent.

The paper's number of pages and its newshole shrank.

The number of holidays on which the *Transcript* would not publish was cut to Christmas and New Year's; the additional holiday issues ("put out with a skeleton force," Sprague said) increased advertising and circulation income.

The Christmas bonus was eliminated.

Newsroom expense, 17 percent of the paper's total budget under the Hardmans, was to be chopped to 10 or 11 percent, Ingersoll said, "not in a year but we are going to take a bite and another bite and another bite." Sprague says he already had reduced news costs to 15 percent during Affiliated's ownership. The prospect of further reductions, more difficult to make without hurting the *Transcript,* depressed the staff and Sprague.

They felt, one laid-off member explained, as if Ingersoll only "looked at a newsroom as a machine with cogs that are more or less replaceable. He can make a newsroom operate at 11 percent so why operate it at 17 percent." (Sprague would later say that "the Ingersoll management's idea of success is the Glens Falls, New York paper where the newsroom expense is only 8 percent.")

Under the Hardmans, the newsroom budget had been a set of numbers to be ignored. Executive Editor Lew Cuyler recalled, "I was never particularly concerned with the budget. I never knew how much there was in the budget. I certainly didn't know the percentage." But under Ingersoll, the budget became gospel.

Ingersoll's budget did not allow for a full-time editorial writer. He believed the *Transcript* should have locally written editorials, but he felt editorial writing on a thirteen-thousand-circulation daily should be apportioned among the managing editor, the copy editors, and others in the news operation. So two weeks after Ingersoll took over, Sprague fired Executive Editor Lewis C. Cuyler, who had begun reporting for the *Transcript* twenty-two years before.

Ingersoll saw Cuyler as an expensive frill, "a $27,000 salary for one editorial a day." (Ingersoll, Cuyler says, underestimated his workload and overestimated his pay, which was actually $23,192.)

The community saw Cuyler differently than Ingersoll saw him. Cuyler had led the effort to beautify Main Street. He had chaired the Bicentennial Commission, which raised five thousand dollars and obtained a state matching grant to build a Main Street mini-park with benches, flowers, and a fountain. He almost single-handedly had established the local Hoosac Tunnel Museum. And he had launched other community programs—from Project Tree, which financed the planting of trees along the area's main highway, to the annual ascent of 3,491-foot Mount Greylock on cross-country skis. Five months before he was fired, Cuyler had been selected by the Fall Foliage Festival parade committee to be the parade's grand marshal. He later received a write-in vote for mayor of North Adams. The community loved him.

But Cuyler, who now operates a company he started in 1981 to produce audio-visual slide photography programs, did not blame Ingersoll for having him fired. In a valedictory column, he wrote that he "probably would not have stayed . . . because I have cared too much for the editorial page as it has been managed under my tenure, and before me, Jim Hardman's." Cuyler also acknowledged privately that, despite the accolades for his work, he was getting stale as a journalist. "I was ready. Ingersoll did me a favor." But that did not make it any easier for Sprague to fire Cuyler.

Cuyler's layoff was followed by others. Some, in fairness to Ingersoll, were the result of equipment changes that had been initiated by the Hardmans. In September 1979 an electronic front-end editing system, tied to a central computer, had been introduced. After Ingersoll's purchase of the *Transcript* in December, the *Berkshire Eagle* reported a dozen full-time production positions would be eliminated. Sprague found himself having to print in the *Transcript* a "publisher's statement." It read in part: "As production procedures are improved, there exists a possibility three full-time positions in production will be eliminated, not the dozen or so reported."

But people in all departments, fairly or not, began to think of Ingersoll in terms of layoffs. To Larry O'Keefe, the layoffs were a form of psychological warfare on those who remained. The staff was expected to work longer hours and handle more tasks. O'Keefe not only performed the duties of copy editor, but wire editor, twice-a-week editorial writer, and reporter.

Furthermore, as second- or third-highest-paid member of the news staff, he feared he would be fired next. "They did hit the higher paid, longer term people."

Michael Burke, who worked at the *Transcript* as a reporter and then copy editor from July 1977 to April 1982, agrees. "They began canning the most expensive employees. It was systematic. It was a fact." Who was going to be fired next, says Burke, was on everyone's mind. "You played Russian roulette each day going into work."

Sprague, to the surprise of Ingersoll, resigned in May. Sprague was the only publisher or general manager, says Ingersoll, ever to quit his company.

On his last day, Sprague packed his office furnishings, including the two-foot-long alligator that Jim Hardman had given him. The alligator went with the expression, "When you're up to your ass in alligators, it's difficult to remember the main objective is to drain the swamp." Hardman, Sprague joked, "didn't want me to ever be out of alligators."

Seated in front of a print of a Rubens portrait, "Man In Armor" ("I like the title," Sprague said), he explained his departure after more than a decade. "I've gotten rid of one, two, three, four, five people in the news and editorial department. Our editorial page is very weak. I don't think we're doing some of the news things we used to do. We can all tighten up our operations—I'd be the last one to cast stones at that—but I don't think there are any formulas."

Ingersoll's formulas are laid out in a large loose-leaf—"Financial Control Standards"—that set cost and income goals. A page should be composed in no more than one and a half hours. The cost of soliciting advertising should be no more than 12 percent of total advertising volume.

"I'm not saying that every company doesn't need operating procedures," Sprague continued. But pointing to "Financial Control Standards," he added, "It's like a military manual. There is absolutely no room for innovative thinking. You're not a publisher or a general manager because you're really not supposed to have any of your own ideas. The bottom line is the deciding factor. If you have to cut newshole, reporters—anything to control that bottom line."

Other staff cuts bothered Sprague for a different reason. The five-unit Goss Urbanite press was to be operated with three people on each of two shifts. But, with one person on vacation, that left two to run the press, Sprague said. "It's unsafe. But I have a tendency not to knock that because they're successful. But it's not for Don Sprague."

(Later, after Sprague left, Ingersoll decided to send the *Transcript*'s five-unit Goss Urbanite press to one of his California papers and replace it in North Adams with a smaller eight-unit Goss Community press. While the move probably made good business sense, the message to the staff, Larry O'Keefe says, was clear. "We were a declining product to Ingersoll. It was like taking the heart and soul of the newspaper right out of the plant. It was a devastating blow.")

As to Ingersoll's influence on news content, Sprague said, "They don't influence your editorial decisions, but they just constrict you." He gave two small examples. To dress up the photos on the front pages of the first and second sections, the *Transcript* had the policy of stripping in halftones and bordering them. But Sprague was told that the production goal of composing a page in no more than one and a half hours would be threatened if the *Transcript* kept stripping in and bordering photos. "They said, 'You can't do it.'"

The second example: the elimination of some news features. "There again," said Sprague, "it's that, 'This is what you should be spending for features. We don't care what you select just as long as you don't spend above a certain amount.'" The financial pressure was not only important because of the shortcuts it encouraged and the quality it eliminated, Sprague argued. It also created a one-dimensional value system. "There is nothing people can be dedicated to," Sprague said, "except the bottom line."

Sprague, now vice-president of operations at the *Middletown Press* in Connecticut, acknowledged that the cost cutting had not been as detrimental to the news operation as he had thought it would be. He attributed that to Rod Doherty, executive editor. "He is the type of taskmaster who doesn't allow a story to be missed."

In another year, however, it was Doherty who would be missed. He had joined the *Transcript* in October 1977 as assignments editor. In August 1978, he had been promoted to managing editor; in January 1980 (when Lew Cuyler was fired), to executive editor; and in October 1980, to executive editor and assistant general manager. He joked about his promotions. "I came here three years ago as assignments editor. Every time they've promoted me, they haven't hired someone to take the position I left. I guess I'm still assignments editor."

Doherty credited Ingersoll management—Murray Schwartz, partner, Tom Geier, editorial consultant, and Jim Plugh, partner—with thoroughly understanding the business of the business. And he recalled a meeting in Philadelphia of the publishers and general managers from Ingersoll papers. "Everybody I met I was impressed with. They really know their job. That made me feel good, or better," about nagging worries over Ingersoll and its reputation.

188

In July 1980, after Sprague's departure, Schwartz, a New York lawyer who had been made a partner in Ingersoll Publications, moved to North Adams for three months to run the *Transcript*. Doherty admired Schwartz's ability to straighten out quickly long-existing messes. Fifty-five percent of circulation receivables, for instance, were over thirty days old. One carrier's route of forty customers had gone uncollected for a year.

Doherty also appreciated the way Ingersoll management took a hard look at every aspect of the business. The question arose whether to keep a rural route of seventy subscribers that took four hours to deliver. (The paper's circulation for the first quarter of 1982 was 11,623, down from a Hardman high less than a decade earlier of almost 14,000.) Previously, admitted Doherty, he could have just said, "Let's keep the route," because he didn't want to lose seventy subscribers. But Ingersoll's Geier studied whether the subscription income could be justified in terms of the route's costs. Fortunately, from Doherty's perspective, "It came out that it paid," he said.

Also, people were expected to perform. Someone on the staff for twenty-five years "who does nothing" might have survived under the Hardmans, Doherty said. "That luxury isn't there anymore. You don't protect anyone just because that's what you want to do." Before long, the *Transcript* not only had a new editor but a new circulation manager, a new advertising manager, and a new commercial printing head.

Schwartz's efforts, Doherty said, "smoothed out a lot of aggravation." When Schwartz left in September 1980, he recommended the promotion to general manager of Claire Piaggi, who had joined the paper as assistant office manager in 1961. Piaggi had no news-side experience, but the North Adams native was the logical choice. "Claire's an outstanding woman, involved in the community. She knows more about the newspaper than anyone they could have found," Doherty said admiringly. Schwartz agreed, "There's not a cranny that doesn't feel Claire's influence." On September 23, 1980, Ingersoll named Piaggi general manager, and exactly a year later, publisher.

Doherty, the assistant general manager and executive editor, was not as satisfactory to Schwartz and Ingersoll. Doherty thought he was "doing a good job, holding the thing together." Schwartz acknowledged that Doherty was a fine newsman, though "abrasive, too quick." But Doherty had four strikes against him.

First, Ingersoll saw him as being too independent, too resistant, someone who had to be "gotten in tow"—a Hardman-tainted fifth columnist who, Schwartz said, "came in with a real chip on his shoulder for Ingersoll." When Lew Cuyler was fired, Doherty learned that no one was to be hired as an editorial writer. Doherty could write the editorials or the space could be filled by letters to the editor. "He took umbrage," Ingersoll says. "After all, he had studied under the Hardmans." (Doherty responds: "What was perceived as umbrage was a two-fold fear. I had never written editorials before, and with the reduced staff and increased personnel and fiscal management, I was really scared about how the tradition of writing daily local editorials would be accomplished.")

Second, perhaps unknowingly, Doherty antagonized Ingersoll by developing as an experiment a *Transcript* local-news summary service for broadcast on the North Adams cable system, Cox Cable Berkshire. The service, begun in 1980, continues today. "I couldn't take it off," says John Kashynski, general manager of Cox Cable Berkshire. "The advertisers would complain."

The service gained publicity in the trade press, including a full-page article in *Editor & Publisher*. But Ingersoll, no great fan of cable, questioned the value to the *Transcript* of Doherty's efforts. "He was receiving delegations. He was traveling around the country visiting other delegations." (Doherty says he entertained only one delegation—"we had coffee"—and visited none.) Ingersoll preferred the quiet, nose-to-the-typewriter style of Elizabeth Brewer, the *Transcript*'s assistant managing editor and an eighteen-year veteran of the paper, whom he described as "a terrific gal, the closet character who did the work."

Third, the existing management structure was two-headed—Piaggi as general manager, Doherty as assistant general manager and executive editor—and even Doherty acknowledged that "the paper would be divided as long as I was there." The financial as well as psychological climate may have been wrong too. When Piaggi became general manager, she was paid less than Doherty, her subordinate, an Affiliated/Hardman carryover.

Fourth, Doherty wanted to spend more than Ingersoll on the news operation. Doherty was concerned about the increasing competition from the *Berkshire Eagle*. In April 1979, three months after Ingersoll's purchase of the *Transcript,* the *Eagle* had gone to morning publication. Later that year it had opened a North County office in Adams. In February 1981 it had started a North County zoned edition.

Doherty was aware of the message from those circulation experts of the street, the newsstand vendors. John Andrews, an owner of the Corner Market in North Adams, said the *Eagle* went from 7 to 70 copies while the *Transcript,* which had been selling 150 copies, was delivering 135 copies to his store "with returns galore." He volunteered an explanation: The *Eagle,* in addition to benefiting from morning publication, "does decently enough with North Adams news. . . . The only thing the *Transcript* has going for it is the obituaries; the size of the paper, once twenty-six to thirty pages, now drops to sixteen pages."

Augustine "Gus" Jammalo, an owner of the Eagle Variety Store, said his sales of the *Eagle* went from between one and three to twenty-five, while the

Transcript's daily sales fell from fifty to twenty-five. "In fact I'm ordering more *Eagles;* the people are buying them like crazy." He complained about the "overpriced" *Transcript*—sometimes only sixteen pages for twenty-five cents—and pointed to that day's Berkshire edition of the Springfield paper, the *Morning Union,* forty-four pages for fifteen cents. "The *Transcript* is going this way," Jammalo said, pointing his thumb toward the floor. "My sales are down."

While Doherty did not believe the *Eagle* was having an impact on the *Transcript*'s circulation—the drop in circulation, he said, only reflected the decline in population—he felt that the news department, because of the competition, had to be kept as strong as possible.

He resisted a proposed cut in news expense from 14 to 12 percent of the *Transcript*'s total budget. Each percent represented a loss of about twenty thousand dollars for the newsroom. Doherty argued—successfully, he thought at the time—for 13 percent, "a major victory." Ingersoll saw Doherty's move as "holding me back."

On June 9, 1981, Piaggi fired Doherty, who now edits the twenty-three-thousand-circulation *Foster*'s *Daily Democrat,* Dover, New Hampshire. Piaggi told him that Ingersoll, Doherty recalls, "didn't think I would be one of his boys." She replaced him with Brewer, elevated from assistant managing editor to managing editor. Michael Burke says "there weren't too many sighs" on the news staff when Doherty was fired. Some of the staff felt his toughness bordered on belligerence. But Brewer's selection was more controversial.

The staff universally applauded Brewer's journalistic skills, her knowledge of the area (she had begun at the *Transcript* as an urban affairs reporter sixteen years earlier), and her willingness to work. But they questioned then—as they do now—whether she should be the newsroom's leader. As one former newsperson, who asked not be named, said, "She's a very good mechanic—she gets the paper out—but there's not much creativity in coverage, in thinking up stories."

Brewer believes she earned her promotion. "I'm no bra burner. But I get what I want. I got what I want." While she acknowledges the Hardmans' desire for a quality newspaper, she also believes they discriminated against women in management. "I was their token nigger," she says. A woman was allowed on the copy desk, no higher. The credit for her elevation to managing editor, she says, "goes to Ingersoll Publications and Ralph Ingersoll. If it were not for Ralph Ingersoll, neither Claire [Piaggi] nor I would be sitting where we are now. Period.

"In many other Ingersoll papers, women have been promoted to management positions. [Piaggi is one of five women running Ingersoll dailies.] Quite obviously I approve of Mr. Ingersoll."

At least one former staffer, who requested anonymity, disputes Brewer's charge that the Hardmans were sexist, arguing that Brewer "had opportunities to lead the newsroom but did not have the ability either as a manager or news director to really pull it off." Some Ingersoll-watchers take a more cynical view than Brewer of the company's policy toward female managers, contending women are paid less to do the same job or given a lesser title—general manager instead of publisher, managing editor instead of editor—to justify a lower salary.

Regardless, Brewer seems prepared to live with whatever management judges necessary. So far that has meant cutting the full-time reporting staff, reducing the news budget, closing the Adams office (once staffed by two full-time reporters and one part-time stringer), and replacing it with a part-time stringer assigned from North Adams. "Cooperation, communication, and adjustment are vital," Brewer explains. "You have to work together. . . . You have to be flexible."

Piaggi and Ingersoll, for their part, believe in Brewer. So it's likely that the musical-chairs management of the *Transcript* newsroom has come to an end. And that tomorrow's *Transcript* probably won't be too different from Brewer's *Transcript* today.

How good is the *Transcript?*

It's hard to generalize. The editorial page may be as good as the Hardmans' and getting better. The news report—handicapped by a significantly smaller newshole and a tiny full-time reporting staff—appears to offer a solid diet of local news. But that report no longer earns the *Transcript* recognition as New England's finest smalltown daily.

Tom Morton, managing editor of the *Berkshire Eagle,* watches the *Transcript* closely not only for competitive reasons. He was raised in Adams. "The *Transcript*'s my hometown paper," he says.

He describes the Hardmans' *Transcript* as "a damned fine newspaper." Today's *Transcript* provides bulletin-board local coverage—"sports news and the chicken-and-peas stuff"—but, says Morton, "beyond that they don't have the manpower to do all the things they used to do—the niceties." He believes that is one reason the *Eagle* has cut into the *Transcript*'s circulation. Ingersoll says the *Eagle* has not. "Our net loss of circulation is attributable to population loss."

The *Eagle* also opened a bureau in Adams. (The *Transcript* later closed its Adams office.) The *Eagle*'s bureau, staffed for both advertising and circulation sales, also provides two full-time reporters and a thirty-hour-a-week part-time reporter. The Pittsfield paper's circulation, which stood at thirty thousand when the paper changed to morning delivery in April 1979, now pushes thirty-three thousand. "Most of that increase—99 and 44/100 percent—comes from northern Berkshire," Morton says. But, he adds, "I have no illusions about moving the *Transcript* out of North Adams. You can put out the world's god-awfullest paper and make nice money and still hold the major part of your circulation."

Brewer and the rest of the *Transcript*'s news staff are certainly aware of the threat from the *Eagle*. She says, "We're an island in a Miller sea," referring to not only the *Eagle,* but the four other Miller-owned papers in the region, the *Bennington* (Vermont) *Banner,* the *Brattleboro* (Vermont) *Reformer,* the *Winsted* (Connecticut) *Citizen,* and the *Register* in Torrington, Connecticut. Joseph Day, who writes editorials, reports, and copy-edits for the *Transcript,* says, "It really is a war. At least it's a war in the south—Adams and Cheshire."

Brewer acknowledges the *Eagle* may provide a broader regional news package than the *Transcript.* She adds, however, "They cover Berkshire County and we cover northern Berkshire. Obviously, we can cover it better."

She also admits that "some frills"—for example, photo pages and locally produced news in many special supplements—are no longer available to *Transcript* readers. But she says her staff, by condensing wire news and local news into tightly edited stories, provides as much as ever.

"People get used to a two-section paper with a 20 percent ad hole," she says, characterizing the Hardmans' *Transcript.* "Then all of a sudden reality is here. People who are businesspeople take over and do all those things that should have been done before, that are necessary to the business."

The readers, Brewer continues, "think they are getting less. I say they're not. They may not be getting stories about a rainmaker in Louisiana and an Associated Press photo or a long feature about a grape picker in California, which they got before. But this is a local paper and they're getting the same local news they got."

Brewer defends the quality as well as quantity of the news report. One observer, after discounting the significance of journalism prizes, noted, nevertheless, that the number of awards for the *Transcript* in the New England Press Association's annual competition had declined steadily since Ingersoll's purchase: 1979, seven awards; 1980, six awards; 1981, four awards; 1982, three awards. Brewer insists, however, that the quality has remained the same. "Year after year, it has been consistent."

But former staff members contend that Brewer overemphasizes daily output from reporters at the expense of quality. With only three full-time reporters—"I've lost five people in the last calendar year"—Brewer, not unexpectedly, applauds reporters' "time management." She says every small daily, not just the *Transcript,* needs high-volume workaholics. "Anybody who can't produce both quality and volume will not stay. Anybody should be able to produce a minimum of two columns [of copy] a day," she says. "I certainly did it."

Some staffers contend, however, that the emphasis on productivity has led to a quota system of stories the paper expects each reporter to write daily. They say the quota, in turn, encourages the abandonment by reporters of more demanding, more complex—and more important—stories requiring extra time to research and report.

Michael Burke, now a copy editor on the *Hollywood Sun-Tattler* in Florida, says the quota system began in Ingersoll's first year, during Doherty's editorship. "There were exceptions to the rule," Burke recalls, "but there definitely was a pretty well-established quota system—five substantial stories, five good stories."

Timothy Heider, a reporter who left in April 1982 after three months to take a higher paying position at another Massachusetts paper, the *Fitchburg-Leominster Sentinel and Enterprise,* talks about a requirement under Brewer "to do, I think, eight stories a day—there wasn't an emphasis on how good they were but just to file. I was told this is what Ingersoll wanted, that Ingersoll had a story count. They were pretty much sticklers on it." Brewer denies that reporters have been instructed to file a set number of stories or columns of copy daily. "I don't tell anyone here that they have to produce this or I'm going to fire them."

Heider also contends that, to save money, the *Transcript* continued to turn on its head the notion of last hired, first fired. The more experienced reporter—the reporter with the higher salary—was replaced with the less experienced, less expensive cub. Heider, a recent Worcester State College graduate, was hired for $165 a week. About the same time, David Vallette, a four-and-a-half-year veteran who was paid $312 a week, was laid off. "For my salary they could get two people," Vallette says. Piaggi and Brewer, he recalls, "said they did not make the decision. They went to a budget meeting with Ingersoll and they came back with the decision."

Experienced or not, the reporters who remained were placed, Burke says, in a "Catch-22" position. As the staff shrunk, each reporter needed more time to complete his portion of the work. But, says Burke, the paper enforced an unwritten policy: "You did not put in for your overtime if you wanted to stay." The situation led a reporter to complain to the wage and hour division of the United States Department of Labor. The *Transcript* was required to make a twenty-two-thousand-dollar payment for two years of overtime. If the *Transcript* had appealed, Piaggi says, the complaint would have been extended to three years and the amount in contention would have been thirty-one thousand dollars.

The substitution of inexperienced for experienced full-timers has given way to the substitution of inexperienced part-timers for inexperienced full-timers. Twelve part-time reporters—"some have had a little experience, some have had none," says Brewer—now do (for fifty cents a column inch) the work that used to be done primarily by better-paid full-timers. By June 1983 the most senior member of the full-time reporting staff—down to three people—was Dianne Cutillo, with only two months professional experience.

The reporters are not the only ones affected. For forty-four years (until 1979), the *Transcript*'s chief—and, for most of that time, only—photographer was the gifted P. Randolph (Randy) Trabold. Two photographers, Richard Lodge and Nick Noyes, replaced him. Weeks after Ingersoll bought the *Transcript,* Lodge became, the paper reported, "the victim of a necessary budget cutback."

Noyes, the chief photographer, was fired January 1, 1983. A consistent prize winner, Noyes's most recent award—a first place in spot news from the New England Press Association—was announced, ironically, days after he was fired.

Noyes was succeeded by half a dozen photo stringers led by Peter MacGillivray, eighteen, a freshman at North Adams State College. Reporters, editors—even copy editors—are also expected to take photos. The results, as might be expected, are uneven. On January 10, 1983, for instance, *Transcript* readers were given two line-'em-up-against-the-wall cliches from the annual Old Timers reunion and a retirement party. But other times, MacGillivray and company excel.

Noyes now freelances for Associated Press and the *Berkshire Eagle.* An *Eagle* staffer recounts, with a competitor's delight, the day in March 1983 when Noyes and a *Transcript* photographer covered a plane crash at Mount Greylock in which two were killed. The *Transcript* photographer did not get a picture. The experienced Noyes, who knew local officials, did. The *Transcript,* which three months earlier had fired Noyes, wound up publishing his photo, with a credit to the *Eagle.*

While the *Transcript*'s reporting and photography may underwhelm, the editorial page has developed into the strongest part of the paper. In the early days of Ingersoll ownership, without Hardman or Cuyler to guide it, the page atrophied. In stolid prose, the *Transcript* frequently practiced an especially somnolent brand of editorial Afghanistanism.

The readers noticed. Frank Matrango, former state representative from the First Berkshire District, said at the time, "I don't bother to read the editorials anymore. Today they're more about national things, rather than local or statewide things. They used to be more controversial."

But the page was revived by Joseph C. Day who, in Ingersoll fashion, serves as editorial page editor, copy desk chief, city editor, reporter, and says a former staffer, "essentially the managing editor."

Day writes three strongly local editorials a week (others are written by Ron Mills, an editor, and Maynard Leahey, a retired editor). Day also writes a column (a 1981 effort on the demolition of St. Joseph's School won him first place in the annual New England Press Association competition), devises questions for "f/STOP," a weekly person-in-the-street feature (photos by MacGillivray), and supervises "Backward Glance" (a local history column), "Berkshire Beat," and a reporters' and correspondents' notebook.

One of the most popular new features is the "Etc." column, brief personal comments by Day, written in the tradition of Jim Hardman's "The Short of It." The column ranges widely—from a questioning look at local mudwrestling, to an examination, on the fiftieth anniversary of Hitler's appointment as Germany's chancellor, of the *Transcript*'s editorials in 1933. Did the paper, Day asked, fail to recognize the danger Hitler represented?

Day conducted a readers' survey about the editorial page in January 1983. Following the survey, he stopped publishing three syndicated columnists— Richard Reeves, Neil Pierce, and Michael McManus—but kept Ellen Goodman, David Broder, Philip Geyelin, Joseph Sobran, and A. A. Michelson, a statehouse columnist who writes for the *Berkshire Eagle*. The money saved was spent on upgrading the page's local content.

Ingersoll does not dictate the *Transcript*'s editorial viewpoint. Even with editorials endorsing candidates, says Day, "I've never been told what to write." The editors try to reach agreement. When there is no consensus, the editorial may walk a thin tightrope. "I'm opposed to abortion," Day says. "Liz is pro-choice. I pick away at the edges."

On its news pages as well as its editorial page, the *Transcript* tries to do a responsible job. The shrinking staff, Day says, "has made inordinate efforts to maintain good coverage and to be thorough." When mistakes are made, they are openly corrected, even in the September 1981 case of Emma Lively Kemp, reported dead, who was still very much alive. The paper's management participates in the life of the community, apparently without creating troublesome conflict-of-interest problems or falling prey to knee-jerk boosterism.

But still, there is the question of the Ingersoll vision.

Ingersoll clearly wants his papers, including the *Transcript,* to march to a different drummer than the one to which the Hardmans marched. In North Adams, Ingersoll's goal does not appear to be greater circulation (he judges expensive outlying circulation to be expendable), or journalism awards, or an exceptional news product.

On the last point, Ingersoll says, "I emphatically disagree that we do not strive for an excellent newspaper in North Adams." Nevertheless, he seems satisfied to produce an extremely local brand of bulletin-board journalism, one that does not prevent him from achieving his profit goals. Under the effective management of Piaggi, the paper annually nets at least five times what the Hardmans netted.

Ingersoll undoubtedly faces economic pressures that were not faced by the Hardmans. His company paid $5 million ($3.5 million of that borrowed) for the *Transcript;* annual interest charges alone are more than what the Hardmans netted in their best year. The North Adams economy continues its descent. Three of the paper's top twenty advertisers no longer exist. The town's population, like its advertising base, shrinks. The recession refuses to end. Ingersoll responds to those pressures by asking from Piaggi—and receiving—tight, bottom-line management.

Piaggi follows Ingersoll's system of financial controls. She keeps a close eye on personnel (employment has gone from seventy full-time and thirty part-time to forty-seven full-time and twenty-eight part-time). Each noon, she visits the composing room, watching the makeup of the last pages. At one o'clock she inspects the first copies off the press. The people in Ingersoll management "get involved," Piaggi says. "I stick my nose in where it's never been stuck before. Especially editorial." She records daily the number of local versus wire-service stories (she wants a two-to-one ratio in favor of local). She monitors how long it takes for the local press releases she receives to make their way into print.

Whatever can be said for the management, however, the *Transcript* pushes too hard for greater profitability, and in the process, sacrifices journalistic quality. "Eighty percent of all that Ingersoll does is usually good for the papers," Doherty says, "but that last 20 percent is just enough to drop the papers routinely below a quality product. I always felt frustrated knowing that it was possible to have a good newspaper and successful fiscal management, if they just didn't need such a high profit margin."

Schwartz, a partner in Ingersoll's company, defends the quality of the *Transcript.* He says Ingersoll's profit goal is not set too high. "We have a different pressure from most, and I think it's harder for Ralph. We know how to make more money and we make a conscious effort not to." But many *Transcript* readers feel Ingersoll fails to make enough of a conscious effort not to. They compare Ingersoll's *Transcript* to the Hardmans' *Transcript.* To them, the *Transcript* is definitely not the paper it once was.

Contributors

Ben A. Franklin, the Middle Atlantic regional correspondent of the *New York Times,* is an avid reader of newspapers in the seven-state area stretching from Pennsylvania to Kentucky. He began his reporting career on the *Annapolis Evening Capital* in Maryland in 1948, immediately after his graduation from the University of Pennsylvania. Following a stint at Columbia University's Graduate School of Journalism, he worked at the *Washington Evening Star* and at ABC News with "Edward P. Morgan and the News." He joined the *Times* in 1960. In 1971 he won the first W. D. Weatherford Award, presented by Berea College in Kentucky for reporting on the Appalachian South. With four other *Times* reporters, he won the Sigma Delta Chi Distinguished Service Award in 1973 for coverage of the decline and resignation of Vice-President Spiro T. Agnew.

Loren Ghiglione, forty-two, is editor and publisher of the *News,* Southbridge, Massachusetts, and president of Worcester County Newspapers, a company that owns twelve newspapers and one radio station. He has edited four journalism books, including *Evaluating the Press: The New England Daily Newspaper Survey,* for which he won a national Sigma Delta Chi Award for Distinguished Service in Journalism. He has served as editorial board chairman and publisher of *The Bulletin* of the American Society of Newspaper Editors. He is a graduate of Haverford College (B.A., 1963), Yale University Graduate School of City Planning (M.U.S., 1966), Yale Law School (J.D., 1966), and George Washington University (Ph.D., American Civilization, 1976).

Lloyd Gray, twenty-nine, is managing editor of the *Sun* and the *Daily Herald* newspapers in Biloxi, Mississippi. He was state Capitol Bureau chief in Jackson, Mississippi, for the two newspapers from 1978 to 1982. Before joining the *Sun* as a staff writer in 1977, he was a summer intern and later a staff writer for the *Delta Democrat-Times* in Greenville, Mississippi. A native Mississippian, Gray received a B.A. degree in history from Millsaps College in Jackson in 1976. He is a past president of the Mississippi professional chapter, Society of Professional Journalists, Sigma Delta Chi.

Peter Katel was born in New York in 1949. A New Mexico resident since 1970, he graduated from the University of New Mexico in Albuquerque. He worked for the *New Mexican* under both its owners and subsequently covered the state capital for the *Albuquerque Tribune.* As a free-lance writer, he contributed to the *Santa Fe Reporter* and several national publications. Katel is now a staff writer for the *Albuquerque Journal.* He has won first-place awards in investigative and interpretive reporting from the New Mexico Press Association.

Suzan Nightingale is a 1974 graduate of California State University at Fullerton, a former Pulliam Fellow, and past president of the Alaska Press Club. After working for the *Register* (Orange County, California) and the *Indianapolis News,* she worked for the *Anchorage Times* from 1975 to 1976, and the *Anchorage Daily News* from 1976 to 1980. She joined the staff of the *Los Angeles Herald Examiner* as a columnist in 1980, and was a senior lecturer at the University of Southern California School of Journalism until she returned to Alaska in late 1982. She is now a columnist for the *Anchorage Daily News.*

John N. Rippey, a graduate of Bates College and the Columbia University School of Journalism, was a reporter for the *Providence Journal and Bulletin* for nine years. He covered local government, the state legislature, and naval and military affairs. He subsequently worked in public relations posts at the University of Rhode Island for eight years. Since 1975 he has taught reporting courses at Penn State and has done applied research on business reporting, local government reporters, and the use of polls as reporting tools by newspapers.

Kenneth Rystrom had twenty years of newspaper experience in the states of Washington and Iowa before becoming professor of communications at the University of Redlands in Redlands, California, in 1978. He was an editorial writer on the *Des Moines Register and Tribune* in Iowa from 1960 to 1965, and editorial page editor and later managing editor of the *Columbian* in Vancouver, Washington. He has been a visiting professor at the University of Montana and Washington State University. He served as president of the National Conference of Editorial Writers in 1974. He earned a B.A. in journalism from the University of Nebraska at Lincoln in 1954, an M.A. in political science from the University of California at Berkeley in 1955, and an M.A. in journalism from the University of Southern California in 1981. He is pursuing a Ph.D. in political science from the University of Southern California. His dissertation examines the apparent effects of newspaper endorsement editorials.

Griff Singer, senior lecturer in journalism at the University of Texas in Austin, has spent almost equal time as a journalist and as a teacher of journalists over the past twenty-seven years. After graduation from the University of Texas in 1955, Singer got his start at the *Arlington* (Texas)

Citizen-Journal. He then worked for the *Dallas Morning News* as a reporter and assistant city editor. In 1967 he returned to his alma mater to teach full time and to complete a master's degree in communication; he also served as acting chairman of the journalism department and head of the newspaper sequence. He returned to the newspaper business in 1978 as city editor and assistant managing editor of the *San Antonio Light.* He rejoined the University of Texas journalism faculty in 1981. In addition to teaching duties, Singer also does newspaper critiques and conducts workshops on writing and editing.

Tony Tharp, thirty-eight, is a staff writer stationed in Greenville, Mississippi for the *Clarion-Ledger* of Jackson. He previously attended Delta State University, Cleveland, Mississippi, and reported for the *Delta Democrat-Times* of Greenville from 1978 to 1982.

Bill Williams graduated from Villanova University in Villanova, Pennsylvania, in 1963 with a B.S. in political science. He has worked for United Press International in the Richmond, Virginia bureau; *Broadcasting* magazine in Washington, D.C.; the *Hartford Times,* the Hartford Insurance Group, and the *Hartford Courant* in Hartford, Connecticut; and the *News-Times* in Danbury, Connecticut. He has worked as a reporter and editor for thirteen years, and has been a journalism instructor for nine years at Central Connecticut State College. A first-place winner in the 1980 Connecticut Business Journalism Awards competition for an article in *Connecticut* magazine on the trend to group ownership of daily newspapers, he has also won two honorable mention awards from the state chapter of Sigma Delta Chi for news writing. He has been a member of Sigma Delta Chi for eight years.

G. Mark Zieman is a reporter for the *Wall Street Journal.* He formerly reported for the *Kansas City Star* and served as editor of the *University Daily Kansan,* while completing a bachelor of science degree in journalism and a bachelor of arts degree in English at the University of Kansas. He has written several articles on the history of Kansas newspapers, including one on William Allen White and the *Emporia Gazette.*